T0294764

JULIETTE M. ENGEL, MD

SPARKY
surviving sex magick

MEMOIR

Published by:
Trine Day LLC
PO Box 577
Walterville, OR 97489
1-800-556-2012
www.TrineDay.com
trineday@icloud.com

Library of Congress Control Number: 2020931391

Engel, Juliette M.
SPARKY—1st ed.
p. cm.
Epub (ISBN-13) 978-1-63424-296-7
Kindle (ISBN-13) 978-1-63424-297-4
Print (ISBN-13) 978-1-63424-295-0
1. Engel, Julette M., -- 1949- 2. Sexually abused children -- United States -- Biography. 3. Family & Relationships -- Abuse -- Child Abuse. 4. Behavior modification. 5. Brainwashing. I. Title

FIRST EDITION
10 9 8 7 6 5 4 3

Printed in the USA
Distribution to the Trade by:
Independent Publishers Group (IPG)
814 North Franklin Street
Chicago, Illinois 60610
312.337.0747
www.ipgbook.com

I dedicate this book to the lost girls--my angels, sputniks and stars.

TABLE OF CONTENTS

FOREWORD

In the early 1950s, Secretary of State John Foster Dulles officially sanctioned an illegal program of mind control and drug experimentation to be conducted on unwitting American citizens.[1,2] The program, called MK Ultra, was based on the work of Nazi scientists brought to the United States from Germany under the auspices of Project Paperclip following the Nuremberg Trials.[3] The program was headed by Sidney Gottlieb and initiated upon the order of CIA director Allen Welsh Dulles on April 13, 1953.[4]

In 1975, the Select Committee to Study Governmental Operations with Respect to Intelligence Activities, Foreign and Military Intelligence was chaired by Senator Frank Church. Initial investigations led to revelations that at least 80 American universities, colleges, hospitals, plus 185 private contractors had engaged in 149 separate CIA funded subprojects involving mind control experimentation including forced administration of mind-altering drugs (particularly LSD), hypnosis, sensory deprivation, isolation, sexual abuse, and torture.[5] Unfortunately for the investigation, the CIA Director Richard Helms ordered all MKUltra documents to be destroyed prior to their being subpoenaed by the Church Committee and the Gerald Ford Commission to investigate CIA activities within the United States.[6]

In 1977, a small cache of 20,000 documents was discovered and senate hearings were resumed later that year.[7] Subsequent testimonies from

1   "The Select Committee to Study Governmental Operations with Respect to Intelligence Activities, Foreign and Military Intelligence." Church Committee Report, no. 94-755, 94th Cong., 2d Sess. Washington, DC: United States Congress. 1976.
2   "Chapter 3, Part 4: Supreme Court Dissents Invoke the Nuremberg Code: CIA and DOD Human Subjects Research Scandals." Advisory Committee on Human Radiation Experiments Final Report. US Government Printing Office. 1995.
3   *Project Paperclip: Dark Side of the Moon*: www.bbc.co.uk/l/hi/magazine/4443934.stm - 2005-11-21.
4   Church Committee; p. 390: "MKUltra was approved by the DCI [Director of Central Intelligence] on April 13, 1953."
5   US Senate Report on CIA MKULTRA Behavioral Modification Program 1977 | Public Intelligence.
6   "An Interview with Richard Helms.". Central Intelligence Agency. 2007-05-08.
7   "Project MKUltra, the Central Intelligence Agency's Program of Research into Behavioral Modification. Joint Hearing before the Select Committee on Intelligence and the Subcommittee

victims, researchers, and officials revealed that unsupervised experiments were carried out on an unprecedented scale involving thousands of victims in the United States and Canada, including children.[8] Each of those victims has a story. *Sparky* is my story.

It begins in Seattle in 1955. I was six years old.

on Health and Scientific Research of the Committee on Human Resources, United State Senate, Ninety-Fifth Congress, First Session." US Government Printing Office. August 8, 1977.
8   "Private Institutions Used in CIA Effort to Control Behavior. 25-Year, $25 Million Program. New Information About Funding and Operations Disclosed by Documents and Interviews Private Institutions Used in CIA Plan." *New York Times*. August 2, 1977.

CHAPTER ONE

SEATTLE, 1955

I lost Daddy.

I left him in Seward Park reading *Life Magazine*. Fog coated Lake Washington. Mist wrapped around the trees. I galloped and whinnied. My breath steamed. When I circled back, everything was grey. "Daddy? Where are you?"

I heard him strike a match. His cigarette glowed. "Scared of a little fog, Fatso?" Relieved, I breathed in his smoke. Silly me. "Be a good sailor. Go find the lake," he said.

I raced blindly downhill until my feet splashed water. I ran along the shoreline to the breakwater and back until I had to stop for breath. Then I shivered. Something was wrong. Footsteps approached – a figure shrouded in mist. "Daddy?" I sniffed the air. My father wore Old Spice. This man smelled different, but familiar. My stomach hurt. I wanted to run, but my feet were stuck. This was all wrong. Vito couldn't be here. I'd kept my promise. I forgot him when we left Illinois. I'd started first grade in Seattle as a new kid from nowhere.

"Where's my pal Jimmy?" Vito stalked past me. I held my breath until he disappeared.

"Bosun!" Daddy exclaimed.

"Hey, Skipper," Vito laughed. He shook Daddy's hand.

I gasped. Daddy could not know this terrible man. It wasn't possible. I followed their voices into the fog. They were talking about some destroyer called the *Dortch*. They knew each other from the Navy. Daddy spotted me. "C'mere." He wiggled a Coca Cola bottle. "Bosun brought you a treat." I'd never had a Coke. I edged close to Daddy while keeping an eye on Vito. I grabbed the bottle and gulped it. My vision blurred. I felt light-headed. Daddy patted his lap. "Come on aboard, sleepyhead."

I woke up face down on a bed. I tried to lift my head, but the room spun. I was naked. My arms and legs were tied to the bedposts. A pillow under my belly pushed my bottom up. I heard voices. Two men came into focus. I smelled Old Spice. I was saved. "Daddy, Daddy, Daddy..." I screamed.

He had his back to me. He wouldn't look, but Vito did. Vito was counting money into my father's hand. He winked at me. "Gotta pay the piper."

I thrashed in panic. "Daddy, help me!"

"Shut up, Fatso." Daddy slurred his words. "This is what I raised you for."

I did shut up, strangled by hopelessness, gagging on my heart.

Vito stuck a needle in my thigh. The room sparked and exploded. I was propelled through a swarm of buzzing ladybugs, landing hard on a black horse with my legs spread wide. I galloped bareback across the Great Plains. Pain shot up my spine with each pounding blow. I begged the horse to stop, but he ran wild. Vito's fingers grasped my throat. I couldn't breathe. He beat against me faster and faster. He screamed. I passed out.

I woke up on the back seat of the Plymouth. My bottom hurt. I tried to move. Everything hurt, but mostly my heart. It was a hot ball in my throat. I wanted to cry, but I was all dried up. My father was driving. I stared up at his dark hair, longing to touch it, aching for the comfort of his arms and the safety I'd been sure of in the warm curve of his neck. I was doomed.

I pushed myself up on the backseat and pressed my face to the window. The cold glass cleared my head. My brain clicked on. We were speeding across the floating bridge. One of those lights above Lake Washington was my house. I had to figure this all out before we got home. My father had sold me. I could never call him Daddy again. "Father," I croaked, testing the new name. He didn't answer. A thousand-foot-thick glass wall had slammed down between us.

Ahead, yellow lights flashed. I knew what they meant: *Warning! Slow down. This bridge has a big bulge in the middle.* The car lurched and sped faster. Tires squealed. I was pressed against the door. It wasn't locked. It wasn't even closed properly. I tried to push myself back onto the seat but couldn't. What if I pulled the latch? People died at the bulge every day. Would I feel better dead?

I grasped the handle and yanked. The door flew open, launching me in slow motion. I changed my mind before bouncing once, twice, three times on the pavement. Then nothing hurt. I skimmed over warm, cotton clouds, brushing them with an arm, a leg, my face. My clothes shredded and ripped away. Cartoon birds chirped under a yellow sun. I was pelted by ladybugs that felt like rain.

I came to on my back with arms flung wide. Father squatted over me. I struggled to breathe. He pinched my ribs. I sucked air, then coughed and spat blood. A match flared. Father lit a cigarette. He squinted through the smoke. "You're okay. Let's go home."

Another car stopped. People ran toward us. Father waved his Lucky Strike. "It's okay, folks. It's just my kid." He wrapped me in his jacket. Back in the car, I let loose a gusher of hot snot and tears. My teeth had cut through my lips. Bloody drool soaked his fur collar and covered the upholstery.

Father carried me upstairs. I sat on my bed shivering. Mother wiped me with a cold washcloth. "You're drunk, you idiot," she shouted at Father. "What'll the school say now?"

"It's her fault," Father whined. "The kid jumped. She did all this when she hit the road."

I blew bloody bubbles and sang under my breath, "Bye, bye, Baby... time to hit the road to dream land."

Mother shook out my nightie and lifted it over my head. "You forgot to lock the door, didn't you? How could you be so stupid? Now some busybody will call the police again. You ready for more social workers?"

Father inspected my back. "At least Vito didn't leave a mark on her."

"Vito? Vito's in Seattle?" Mother gasped. "You promised we were through with that creep."

"What do you care who handles the kid?" He gave Mother the wad of bills. "Vito pays."

Mother burst into tears. Father put his arm around her. "Come on, Weezie. Fatso's tough. Lots of girls do this. She's okay."

Father was wrong. I wasn't okay. Besides, Mother wasn't crying about me. Vito had done to her what he'd just done to me. He'd made me watch. I'd tried not to but couldn't stop staring at his strange red sac bouncing against Mother's bottom. Mother was crying when Vito pulled up his pants. My baby brother stood in his crib wailing. I was three years old – too big to cry. Vito grabbed my arm and shook. "Forget I was here or that brat dies." He pushed my baby brother onto his butt. He screamed louder, his face turning bright red. Mother grabbed my hair, slapping me until I cried, too. "Not a word to your father or you'll be sorry you were born."

She didn't have to worry. I was an expert forgetter. Before the front door slammed behind Vito, I'd sent my little vacuum cleaners to suck the memories from my brain. I shattered his memory into a million billion pieces and blew them away. I scrubbed the smell of him out of my nostrils. I had kept my part of the bargain, but he was back.

Mother pulled the covers to my chin. Father turned out the light. I waited until they left, then flipped it back on. I swore I'd never sleep again.

CHAPTER TWO

GOD'S ANTENNA

In my nightmare, iron spikes pierced the mattress and skewered me from behind. I screamed, "Daddy, help me!" Father stood with Vito, counting his money. "This is what I raised you for," he laughed. A spike went into my bottom. The room was on fire. Blood ran out of my mouth. The bed caught fire. I woke up when Mother stuck a thermometer under my tongue. "She's burning up."

"Bleeding like a stuck pig," Father examined my sheets. "I better get the car."

At the hospital there were the usual needles, x-rays, and doctors. They probed me in bad places, mumbling, "Does this hurt?"

"Dunno," I said, fighting back tears.

"Who did this to you?"

"Dunno." I had stitches in my lip now, so it sounded like "Dummo." I'd tried to tell them about Vito but gave up.

"No need for cops," said Father. "Stupid kid's always falling on her head. What was it last time, Weezie?"

"Fell off a ladder in Wheaton, Illinois," said Mother.

"Who's this Vito she keeps talking about?" asked the doctor.

"We don't know any Vito," said Mother.

"He's her uncle," said Father.

The doctor eyed them, shaking his head. "We're required to report this to Child Services. The police will interview you and the child. You say Vito is her uncle? Which one of you is he related to?"

"He's not her real uncle, per se," said Father. "He's an old buddy from the Navy. Now he works for the government. Top secret. You know how it is."

"Not really, no. Here's the social worker."

She looked like a nice lady, but I knew from experience that there wasn't much the police or Child Services would do to help me. Besides, I needed my parents because I was too little to live on my own. I'd tried it a few times without success.

Once when I was four, I ran away as far as the Wheaton Diner. They gave me a cheese sandwich and I sat on the steps and ate it until a policeman came to drive me home. Then Mother gave me "something to cry about." That's what she said before she clobbered me. Now she sat beside me at the hospital, squeezing my hand until it hurt. I knew what she wanted – so I lied. I told the social worker that I'd snuck out of bed, stole a bicycle, flipped it, and landed on my head. I was always doing stupid stuff like that – haha. Dumb kid. Lies spewed from my swollen mouth in a pink froth. I couldn't even ride a bicycle yet.

In a few weeks, I was back at school. The class plodded through math while I fidgeted in my seat. I couldn't wait for recess, but not to play. I had plans. I was going to transmit a message to God. I wanted Him to take me to Heaven. I wanted Him to be my new daddy.

I finished my addition quiz and stared through the window. The flagpole soared skyward from the playground. It was my antenna to God. I knew all about antennas. When Mother threw out her father, Mepa's, old tube radio, I pulled it from the trash, cleaned it off, and hid it under my bed. I'd go to bed at night and pretend to sleep. When I heard my parents turn on the television downstairs, I'd plug in the radio and turn it on. It had an extendable antenna that was finicky. I had to adjust it and experiment with the squealing dials, twisting them back and forth until I heard organ music. Then a voice boomed, "Hear my cry, O God. Attend unto my prayer. From the end of the Earth will I cry unto thee when my heart is overwhelmed. Lead me to the rock that is higher than I." The *Rosicrucian Bible Hour* was the only program I could get on Mepa's radio. I fell asleep every night listening to scary stories of serpents in the Garden of Eden or of men being sucked into dry husks by giant spiders because they had angered God.

Sometimes I'd talk to the radio, imagining that God was inside. He didn't answer. Then I realized that He must be in Heaven, which was very far away. He couldn't possibly hear me from Seattle. I needed a more powerful antenna.

I spent days stringing coat hangers together and rummaging in the basement. I found an old ski pole that looked pretty good. I wound it with more hangers and attached it to the radio. God still didn't answer me. Then I realized that I didn't need the radio to call Him. I had the biggest antenna in the world right there at John Muir Elementary School – the flagpole. I could settle things with God on the playground. I'd ask him to take me to Heaven.

At recess, I ignored my friends, who wanted to play cowboys. Instead, I pressed my head against the flagpole. As fast as I could, I recited, "Hear my cry, O God ... From the end of the Earth ... lead me to the rock that is higher than I." The wind picked up. The big antenna hummed. It sucked my thoughts out and shot them to Heaven. My teeth rattled. I clenched my jaw and rolled my eyes skyward, waiting for an answer – nothing.

Did God hear me? I wasn't sure. I couldn't see Him. That didn't mean He wasn't there. Kids stood around the flagpole, watching me. I was glad when the rain started because it hid my tears. I heard breathing. Mark and Tommy had stuck their heads against the flagpole, too. I ignored the copycats. Recess was nearly over, and I hadn't made my bargain with God. Clearly, if He were going to take me away, I'd have disappeared by now. I needed another strategy – a compromise. I gazed to Heaven and revised my proposition. "If you let me live, God ... If you let me grow up ... I'll never try to kill myself again ... and I'll never ask you for anything. I'll be perfect. I promise." The bell startled me, and I jumped, my heart racing. Was that my answer?

Mrs. Thompson, my teacher, shooed the boys away. Her face came level with mine. "You're soaking," she said, pulling me under her umbrella. We walked back to class. I sat at my desk and shivered, my face burning with a fever. I coughed and wiped snot on my sweater. Would God let me die of double pneumonia just when I'd decided to live?

"See Spot run. Run, Spot, run," recited the class.

I was silent, watching the clouds part through the window. A bolt of lightning struck the flagpole. I gasped and looked around – nobody saw it but me.

CHAPTER THREE

RORSCHACH

"It's an airplane," I said.

"That's very good," said Mrs. Thompson.

"Um hmmm," Mr. Calloway took notes. He'd come to John Muir specially to give me this test. The three of us sat in the principal's office. I thought he'd ask about my stitches or my talks with God. Instead, he held up ink blots.

"That's Paulie's airplane," I added.

"Um hmmm."

His disinterest egged me on. "He's a Viking. He's not scared of anything. He flew in the war. Now he's a crop duster." I remembered Paulie's car rattling up our drive in Wheaton, Illinois. It didn't have fenders, backdoors, or floorboards. Mother called him "that berserker." When he took me for rides, he'd smash beer bottles on the road and howl like a wolf. I let loose with a wolf howl for Mr. Calloway.

"Goodness," said Mrs. Thompson.

I clammed up. Was I saying too much? My parents had warned me not to say anything to anyone at school. I assumed they meant that I shouldn't talk about them. What harm was there in remembering Father's cousin Paulie? He'd been on my mind a lot since Mother said he'd crashed on the Great Plains. I gave Mr. Calloway the evil eye and decided to take control. He held up another ink blot. "What do you see here?"

"Pretty flowers," I smirked. He held up another. "That's a kitten." This was too easy. I yawned, willing Mr. Calloway to go away. He didn't. He had a big pile of ink blots. They progressed from black and white to color. Up came a vivid smear of primary colors. "Plane crash!" I screamed. The red smear looked like blood. The jagged slices of yellow were crumpled wings. I burst into tears. I'd heard my parents whispering about the fiery wreck, the closed coffin, and "burned beyond recognition." But no one had said that Paulie was *dead.* In my dreams, I flew the yellow biplane over the Great Plains, looking for him.

"How about this one?"

"A stupid chicken," I snapped, recovering from my appalling lapse. "A stupid cow…Cow poo …Horse poo…Pig manure…" Up flashed another splash of blood. I saw a cat in the middle. "PooPoo," I screamed.

"That's enough poo, young lady," said Mrs. Thompson.

"PooPoo my cat's dead," I wailed. The cross on my forehead was on fire. Surely, they could see it burning. Blood ran into my eyes. I put my arms over my head, rocking and groaning, but the blood kept flowing. "Mepa cut him open. Mepa cut me too." I struck my forehead on the desk to make it stop. Mrs. Thompson put her arm around me, and I collapsed into her scent of baby powder. "See?" I pointed to the scar that Mother's father had sliced into my forehead.

Mepa had cut me deep and the bleeding wouldn't stop. I'd run away and tripped over poor PooPoo. The yellow tabby was as big as me. His throat was bubbling red, but he was purring. I gathered him in my arms. He tried to lick my face. The floor was slippery with blood. I pulled him into the street, screaming for help.

Mrs. Anderson came running from next door. The police came with sirens, then an ambulance. They couldn't tell who was bleeding worse – PooPoo or me. His eyes rolled up and he wasn't purring any more. I wouldn't let him go until Mrs. Anderson put him into a box on top of his blanket. "It's for the special cat ambulance," she said. "You have to go in the people ambulance." The police had Mepa in handcuffs. They took him to an insane asylum. I never saw him or PooPoo again.

"Mepa got cremated," I said from the safety of Mrs. Thompson's arms. "They flushed him down a giant toilet. He comes out of my walls at night…" The bell rang. I blinked. The blood was gone.

"You can go play," said Mrs. Thompson. I ran from the room and flew the yellow biplane down the hall like a kamikaze, plunging into a screaming dive and strafing the boys on the playground. Rat-a-tat-tat – I gunned them down with my machine gun. They fought back. We had a good dog-fight until the teachers told us to settle down and made us sit on a bench.

I kept an eye on the flagpole. It looked disappointed. It even drooped a little. I hoped it wasn't going to report those bad memories to God. I'd have to vacuum out my head before I used the antenna again. There were things I didn't want Him to know about – like that cross over my left eye. Mepa said it marked me for the devil. I didn't want God to think it was true.

Chapter Four

Devil Cats

"Three eunuchs threw her down ... her blood spattered on the wall ... he trampled her underfoot... They found no more of her than the skull and the feet and the palms of her hands." I lay on the floor, eyes wide, listening to the final flourish of organ music at the end of the *Rosicrucian Bible Hour*. But how could I sleep? What was a eunuch? Why did dogs eat Jezebel?

I shivered but couldn't get into bed. There was no room for me. I'd taken every toy and book I could find and piled them under my covers. I even added discards from the basement. My plan was to fool the devil-cats by sleeping under the bed.

Father had started wearing Mepa's robe and sneaking into my room at night. He'd lay on top of me threatening that devil-cats would come out of the walls and eat me if I didn't keep my mouth shut. It scared me every time. I hated that shiny purple robe that smelled like dust. Mepa had been wearing it with his Shriner fez when he cut me. It still had my blood on it.

I'd forgotten about him, until he died. My parents took me to his funeral at the asylum. They seemed to think that showing me the body of a bearded old man in a box would make the scar on my forehead stop hurting. I'd had twelve stitches. They made me watch Mepa's coffin move into the wall while Mother cried and said that they were creaming her father.

I could defend myself from Father as long as I stayed awake. But it didn't matter how hard I tried – lights, radio, a mountain of toys – I'd fall asleep and wake up face down with his weight crushing me. He'd squeeze my neck until I couldn't breathe and whisper things like, "If you don't want the devil-cats to eat you, you'll forget everything."

How could I forget when he kept reminding me? Every morning I had to vacuum my head all over again. I still desperately loved the smell of his breath, the warmth of his hands. I wanted to cry out, "Daddy, I'll do whatever you want." I wanted to kiss him.

"You are damaged goods," he'd say. "You're a mental case. Everybody says so."

One morning I was eating the middles out of my toast when Mother said the same thing: "You're a mental case. Everybody says so."

My parents must have been talking to Mr. Calloway. My latest session with the ink blots had been a disaster. I'd been so good about answering things like Bambi and Peter Pan and Jiminy Cricket that I l got bored and let my guard down. Then he got me. He flipped up a card that looked like dogs ripping the insides out of a woman. There was blood everywhere. "Rosicrucians!" I screamed.

"What?" Mr. Calloway stared at me. "What did you say?"

"Good lord," exclaimed Mrs. Thompson.

Trouble! I tried to backpedal, but my mouth ran ahead of my brain. "They threw Jezebel out of her castle and the dogs ate her head...no, everything but her head...I heard it on the radio."

"The radio?" Was he deaf? "What are you listening to?"

I couldn't stop talking. "The Rosicrucians keep away devil-cats. They live in the walls with Mepa. I saw him get flushed down the toilet after he was creamed. They promised me he was dead. Now he comes out at night disguised as Father and chokes me. That's why I keep the light on..." I hadn't mentioned Vito or the piles of toys. That was good.

Mr. Calloway put away the ink blots. "It's time we talk to the parents," he said.

"I'll call them," Mrs. Thompson nodded.

They must have called Mother and Father right away with this mental case thing.

"Eat your crusts," Mother said. "We're going to the university today."

"On the bus?" I was fascinated by the rumbling giant that stopped across the street from our house on Hunter Boulevard. Every morning it picked up all the fathers, taking them to work and bringing them home again at night. Where did they go all day?

When the bus squealed to a stop and the doors hissed open, I ran ahead of Mother to stake out a window seat.

CHAPTER FIVE

THE ANNEX

"A-N-N-E-X," I sounded out the letters. "What does that mean?" Mother rang the buzzer and ignored my question. "Shut up and behave." A man with black-framed glasses opened the door and directed us down a long corridor with white walls and black-and-white tiles on the floor. At the end, another man in a white coat waited. His nametag said, "Dr. Green."

"Weezie," he smiled, kissing Mother's cheek. He didn't look at me when he said, "So this is your daughter." He guided us to chairs in front of his desk and sat down. "If this girl has half your brother's brains, she'll be a star asset."

I climbed onto a seat next to Mother's, straining to understand how these two knew each other. Mother had one brother – Uncle Wally. He lived in a big house in England. What could he possibly have to do with me?

"I doubt she'll be a star anything," said Mother. "She's too pig-headed by half." I fidgeted, craning my neck to examine Dr. Green's desk. I was looking for his stack of ink blots. I'd been practicing my responses on the bus, rehearsing words like bicycle…truck…stoplight. I had to get this right or Mother would slap me. Mother read my mind: "Sit still or I'll slap you."

"She's very young." Dr. Green smiled at me. I gave him the evil eye. "Defiant, isn't she? Dr. White says that she's physically strong enough for the program. Mentally? Well, time will tell, won't it? Now the sixty-four-thousand-dollar question: Did she jump out of the car on the floating bridge or was it an accident?"

"I don't know. Jimmy was drunk. He's always forgetting to lock the car doors." Mother bent close enough to pinch me. "Did you jump?"

"I dunno," I mumbled, leaning away from her. "Can't remember."

Mother frowned. "The school's been nosing around."

"So, we hear. It's that new psychologist, Calloway. He's seen some of our other Bluebird girls. We're trying to get his files from the Department of Education, but they aren't on board with the program yet. What has she told him?"

"She's been blabbering about Rosicrucians," said Mother.

"What?"

"The kid dug my father's old Rosicrucian radio out of the trash. It only has the one station. She's been listening to that dreadful *Bible Hour*."

"Oh my."

"Now she's making a spectacle out of herself, trying to call God on the school flagpole."

I stared at Mother. Visions danced in the space between us: plane crashes, Mepa with his knife, devil-cats, PooPoo dying in my arms, and me with my head pressed to the flagpole sending my thoughts to God. I wondered if she saw them, too.

"Imagination is a good thing in a six-year-old," said Dr. Green. "With enough trauma, her personality will split into multiples that we can use." He leaned forward on his desk and smiled at me. "Rosicrucians is a big word for a little girl like you. Do you know what it means?"

"Dunno," I shrugged, staring at my shoes. I'd put on one pink sock and one yellow. It was kind of pretty.

Dr. Green plunked a little white box in front of me. "Would you like to join our special club, young lady? Would you like to be a secret Bluebird?"

"Sure." I wanted to be a Camp Fire Girl someday, but I was way too young. Some of the older girls at school were already wearing uniforms. Maybe this was some kind of shortcut for special kids. I opened the box and stared at silver wings. There had to be some mistake. "This is a butterfly."

"Other people will say that it's a butterfly. You'll know that it's a secret Bluebird. But if you tell anyone, we'll take it away. Understand?"

"And I'll make you sorry you were born," Mother threatened.

I'd be whatever they wanted me to be. The pin had one sparkly diamond eye and I wanted it.

Dr. Green smiled. "You're a very special girl."

I felt the warm glow of pride. I liked being special. I fingered the pin, pretending not to care. It looked like real silver.

Mother said, "There's a social worker coming to the house next week. I don't like it that the police are involved so soon."

"We don't have the Seattle Police on board. We've got a few judges, but that's not enough. It might be time to relocate you." Dr. Green pushed a button on his desk. "Get me Dr. White."

"I'd like to go back to Laguna Beach," said Mother.

"Your aunt lives there, doesn't she? Let's see what can be arranged. You'd have to take the child to the Annex in San Luis Obispo. We've started the Monarch program there for Southern California."

A lump swelled in my throat. I didn't want to leave Seattle. I had friends. I liked my school. I knew my way around the neighborhood. I had a savings account at Washington Mutual and a library card. Was this all because of the ink blots? Had I broken my promise to God and caused more trouble?

"Ah," said Dr. Green. "Here's Dr. White."

The door opened. Vito walked in and I lost it. I screamed and threw my arms around Mother's neck. She tried to push me away, but I wouldn't let go. "Take me home … take me home. …" I sobbed. I was face down in her lap, clinging to her skirt when a needle stuck me in the butt.

CHAPTER SIX

NANNY BLACK

I woke up in my bed, wedged under my pile of toys. I didn't remember coming home. The light was on. My head pounded. My throat burned. I struggled to sit up. I was in my nightie. My pants and sweater were folded on the dresser. I pulled them on over my nightgown, then buckled my shoes.

This looked like my room, but something was wrong. My wallpaper had yellow roses – these were pink. I threw off the covers to look at my toys. My teddy bear was there, my Golden Books and my milkman doll. I picked up my doll bed and chair. Mine were pink. These were blue.

I tried the door. It was locked. I ran to the window and pulled up the blind. The window was fake, there was no glass. Nothing made sense. Maybe I was a mental case because this had to be my bedroom. What other explanation was there? Or maybe I was about to be sucked dry by giant spiders, like the Rosicrucians said happened to bad people. I paused to imagine myself as a human husk and remembered my radio.

I fell to my knees and peered under the bed. No radio. There was something else, I could see a handle. I reached in as far as I could and pulled out a beat-up suitcase. It looked familiar – like something I'd left behind in Illinois. I snapped the latches. One look inside and I jumped to my feet. It was Mepa's record player. I'd played it many times back in Wheaton, even though I wasn't supposed to. Was this my punishment for scratching the "Nutcracker"?

I started to sweat. The walls moved in on me. The spiders would be here soon. I heard them rustling. "She needs to learn duality." The voice sounded like Dr. Green. "When we apply enough stress, she'll split. They all do."

"Can we wrap this up? I'd like to be on the 4:10 bus." It was Mother's voice coming from a mirror that spanned one wall. I walked over and stared at my terrified face. I looked like a crazy kid. I pressed my ear against my reflection.

"Can she see us?" said Mother. "She looked like she could see me."

"She can hear us. We need thicker glass," said Vito. "Send in Nanny Black."

Keys rattled. A huge woman in a black dress carried a tray with milk and a plate of chocolate chip cookies. I was ravenous and they smelled delicious. I didn't care that Nanny Black had hairy arms and a moustache. The cookies were warm from the oven. I wolfed them all.

I woke up in my bed again. The light was on. I was wedged under my pile of toys. Was I really at home this time? I searched for my doll bed and chair. This time they were pink. I ran to the door. It opened onto the dark hallway of our house. I could see the nightlight in the bathroom. I ran to the window and opened the blind. It had real glass. Streetlights shone through leafless trees on Hunter Boulevard.

Relieved, I sat on the bed. There was no mirror on the wall now – just wallpaper. But something still wasn't right. My roses were supposed to be yellow. These were pink. I climbed over the bed to look for pictures I'd drawn on the wall with crayons. I could see them, but they were faint, covered over by fresh paper. I touched the wall. It was wet. I smelled my fingers – paste? Had Father changed my wallpaper? Why? I liked the yellow roses. I didn't want pink.

How could I prove that I wasn't dreaming? My radio. I dropped to the floor and searched under the bed. No radio. Instead, I pulled out Mepa's record player. I froze, confused. There was something else on top – a big album with records inside. They'd been Mepa's favorites. I stared at the colorful cover of men on horseback waving swords. I sounded out the name, The Don Cossacks and lifted the cover. I'd never been allowed to touch these special records that Mepa had brought back from Russia, but here they were under my bed in their brown paper sleeves.

I pulled one out and put it on the turntable. I put the needle on the record and pushed the only button I could find. Nothing happened. Then I remembered to plug it in. I found the cord coiled at the back and stretched it to the wall. The turntable whirred. Wild Russian Cossack music blasted out. Hoof beats thundered and cannons boomed while I pushed and twisted every button and knob, trying to turn down the volume. Nothing worked. I ran around the room in panic until I thought to pull the plug. I slammed the lid and dove under my toys. Too late – my parents were at my door.

Father said, "There's only so much of this that I can take." I squeezed my eyes shut, pretending to snore. Father opened the record player and fiddled with the knobs. "That's better."

"I know you're awake, you goddamn pest," said Mother. "One more peep out of you tonight and I'll slap you stupid."

CHAPTER SEVEN

48 CRAYOLAS

Mrs. Thompson fingered my collar. "That's a lovely little broach." Caught! I wasn't supposed to wear my secret Bluebird pin to school. Mr. Calloway was squinting at the pin.

"Where did you get that?" he asked. "Have you heard of the Bluebirds?"

"No, never!" I said, vacuuming the word Bluebird out of my brain so he couldn't read my thoughts. "It's just a silly butterfly," I lied.

He didn't seem interested any more, but I knew he was. He opened a box of forty-eight Crayolas with all the colors I'd always wanted. "Can you draw a picture of yourself?" he asked.

"Yup," I said. Of course, I could draw myself. I was the best drawer in class. I upended the box and took my time arranging the crayons by color, savoring the waxy smell as they warmed in my hands.

A big sheet of white paper covered the desk. I picked up a peach crayon and set to work. This was too easy. I drew a girl in a pretty blue dress with lots of black curls. Mother had gotten tired of my braids, so she'd bobbed my hair and given me a permanent wave for my seventh birthday. I was supposed to wear pin curls at night. I refused.

Mr. Calloway asked, "Do you have pets?" I drew Tina the turtle.

"I have a brother too," I added a small stick figure with sandy hair.

He spread a fresh sheet of paper. "Let's draw your whole family." I drew our house on Hunter Boulevard with its hedge of red fire-bush berries. I drew my brother's head in the window and Mother on the porch wearing a hat. I drew myself about the same size as the trees in the parkway. I never imagined that Mr. Calloway would show this to Mother, or I would have made her bigger and prettier. That night, she complained at dinner that I'd drawn myself as a giant and her as a midget.

"What about me?" Father asked.

"You're not even in the picture."

"He's on the bus," I said in a quick save. "He went to work with the other fathers."

On Saturday morning, Mother and I rode on the bus to the Annex. Mother huffed and fidgeted the whole way, working herself up into a red-faced volcano by the time we got there. My stomach burned. Nothing good would come of this.

"She's a goddamn mental case," she fumed to Dr. Green. "She thinks everything is all about her."

My drawing of myself was on his desk. I'd been betrayed. "The child has a healthy ego, that's all," he reassured her. "That's what we like to see in any subject of this age."

"Did you see how little she drew me?" Mother fixed her crazy gray eyes on me.

"Yes, well, that's something to look at," Dr. Green had his hand on the buzzer button.

"And she's a thief." Mother slapped my face, knocking me out of the chair. I cowered on the floor, hands over my head. "You stole my earrings, you goddamn little tramp. Don't lie about it – I found them under your pillow."

I knew better than to argue, or even open my mouth when she was this angry. I'd seen her burying a paper bag in the backyard and dug it up. There were earrings and a pin inside. I couldn't believe she'd thrown away her special yin/yang earrings – a gift from Uncle Wally, her brother. I thought she'd want them back some day. I'd hidden the earrings in my pillowcase, but she'd found them. The pin was still in my pocket. I didn't want her finding that, too.

"Get over here, you little bitch," screamed Mother, coming at me. Nanny Black arrived and I crawled behind his black skirt, away from Mother's grasp: Nanny handed a syringe to Dr. Green. Two men in white pants and jackets held Mother down while Dr. Green gave her a shot in the neck. Nanny Black hurried me out the door.

I had a different Nanny Black every week – some were men, some might have been women, I couldn't tell. This one had a bald head under the white lace cap. They had all been nice to me. I wasn't afraid to go for a nap in the pink room, now that I could tell where I was when I woke up.

I ate two of Nanny's cookies and lay down on the bed, wondering what was under the pink roses in this room – more mirrors most likely. Nanny pulled off my shoes while I picked at the paper. I started to float. Hot melted chocolate oozed through my body, making me light as air. I flew away with the bluebirds.

I woke up squinting into a spotlight. I was naked, unable to move. I squirmed but couldn't break free. My eyes adjusted and I saw my reflection in a mirrored ceiling. I looked around at mirrored walls. I had been strapped to a round table that looked like Mother's yin/yang earrings – two big fish wrapped around each other, one was black, one white.

Old men in purple robes who looked like Mepa came into the room and circled around me. Some wore yellow turbans, and some wore red fezzes. The table started to turn. I struggled, but my hands and feet were stretched apart and held with cuffs. It spun faster and faster. The old men chanted, "Yin is yang… Black is white… white is black… there is no good… there is no evil… there is no life… there is no death… there is no God… there is only green…" Faster and faster – until green was all that I saw.

I closed my eyes and surrendered.

CHAPTER EIGHT

YIN/YANG

"End of the line." I was startled awake when the driver touched my shoulder. "Hunter Boulevard, young lady. You've got to get off." It took me a moment to realize that I was on the bus. I sat up and stared at all the empty seats. He looked concerned. "Are you lost?"

I wasn't lost. I'd never taken the bus by myself before, but I could see my house across the street. I rubbed my eyes, trying to remember how I got on the bus in the first place. "I'm okay," I said, heading out the door.

I walked across the grassy parkway, marveling at the green leaves. When I'd left, the branches were bare, the ground muddy. Wasn't it just that morning that I'd gone to the Annex with Mother? Now it was spring. How long had I been away?

I looked for the kids who played in the park. Where were they? Was it dinnertime – had they gone home? I pulled off my coat, sweating in the heat, overcome with dizziness. I leaned against a tree to take my bearings. Lights were coming on in peoples' windows, but not at my house. I crossed the street and climbed the front steps.

I pushed open the door and called out, "Mother?" My voice echoed. The furniture was gone. The house was empty, stripped to bare walls. I checked the kitchen – nothing in the refrigerator or pantry. I tried to get a drink of water, but the tap was off. I climbed the stairs to my room, calling, "Mother? Father?" No one answered. I stepped into my room. Where were my furniture, clothes, and toys?

I sank to the floor fighting back panic, my brain in a muddle. I chewed my fingers. I must still be at the Annex. My stomach growled. Surely Nanny Black would come through the door with cookies and milk or a plate of spaghetti. The room tilted. I lay down to stop the spinning. I had to rest a few minutes and then I'd go to my neighbors for help. My best friend Annie lived across the street. Her mother would give me some dinner. I just had to close my eyes.

I woke up in the dark and felt my way to the light switch – no response. The only light came from streetlights shining through the bare windows. Had my family gone away and left me? What was I going to do? How would I live? I was feeling my way along the landing when I heard the front door.

"Goddamn it." Father swore, tripping on the stairs. "Fatso? Are you up there? Let's go."

Mother was waiting in the Plymouth. My brother was stretched out asleep on the back seat, so I climbed onto the ledge of the rear window. Father started the car and Hunter Boulevard disappeared behind us. The lump in my throat exploded in a sobbing howl, "Noooo…" I screamed. "I don't want to go."

"We're going to California so shut up," Mother swung her hands blindly behind her. She hit my brother. He woke up and started to cry. "Look what you've done now. It's always all about you isn't it?"

I gagged and sobbed. I tried to stop but couldn't. All the tears that I'd held back flooded the car. Deep from my belly, I grieved for Paulie and PooPoo. I mourned for Mepa with a mixture of love and terror. I grieved for the loss of Daddy and all my friends in Illinois and now Seattle. I cried until I gagged and vomited on my brother. Then he vomited on Mother. She swung her fists at me shouting, "You're going to pay for this." I lay curled out of her reach on the window ledge.

"My flagpole," I wailed as we drove past John Muir Elementary on the road to Highway 99.

CHAPTER NINE

GONE GIRL

"...there is no me...there is no you...there is no God...only the Dark Sun...the Great Creator..." The yin/yang wheel spun me around in one Annex after another – and I went missing. I vanished from school after school in California, attending just enough days to pass to the next grade. It didn't seem to matter because I was always one of the smartest kids. The schools thought that I was home sick a lot, but I wasn't.

I was gone away from home so much that my picture was no longer on our family Christmas card. There was an empty place where I should have stood with Mother, Father, and my brother. When I asked Mother why I wasn't there, she said, "You have a weak heart. You're not expected to live past high school."

She said the same thing to principals, teachers, and nurses. I was examined by school doctors who declared me anemic, but pretty healthy. They asked about the needle marks on my arms. They asked about where I stayed and what I ate. They wanted to know who took care of me.

I'd stare at the purple bruises on my white skin and mumble, "Dunno...don't remember." At the Annex, they gave me drugs to make me forget. They spun me on the wheel while voices droned "...there is no truth...there is no lie...there is no good...there is no evil..."

In the world of the secret Bluebird, survival meant forgetting to the point where the lie became the truth. I didn't show the school doctors the burns on my chest. I wasn't sure how I got them, and the doctors couldn't make me take off my undershirt when I refused. They did send me to do ink blots with psychologists and social workers came to the house. I was expert at giving the right answers. It didn't matter anyway. We would soon move to a new place and begin the whole thing over again.

Was it "all about me" like Mother said? Was I the one causing so much trouble? Then God must be disappointed. When I started third grade at Aliso Elementary in Laguna Beach, I gave the flagpole wide berth. I didn't want God seeing into my mind until I could clean away the terrible things that were in there.

My new Annex was in the basement of a Spanish mission church in San Juan Capistrano. Father drove Mother and me down the Coast Highway and waited while Mother took me inside. Although the sign on the office door said Dr. Green, same as in Seattle, I'd never seen the man behind the desk before. Every Annex had a different Dr. Green. He certainly knew Mother. He greeted her warmly: "Weezie. It's been too long." I sat next to her while he opened a manila folder and shuffled papers. Finally, he looked me over. "She has haunting eyes, doesn't she? She'll be a beauty like her mother." I rolled my eyes. I did not want to look like Mother, but I did. Everyone said so. At least my eye color was unique. Mother's eyes were pale gray and Father's pale blue. Mine were hazel green with flecks of brown. I hoped it meant that I was adopted.

"I don't know," said Mother. "She's kind of big. Look at those feet." My toes were busting through the ends of my loafers. "I can't keep buying new shoes. She's going to have to wear sandals until she stops growing."

Dr. Green leaned toward me. "We have a special program for pretty girls like you." I watched him turn into a cartoon wolf with bulging eyes and slobbering tongue. He smacked his red lips and punched his intercom. This time Nanny Black was a woman with a syringe instead of a plate of cookies.

Mother grabbed my arms and held me away so Nanny could get me in the butt with the needle. The room spun. I staggered and fell. I woke up with my arms and legs tied to the familiar yin/yang wheel. It started to turn while voices chanted "there is no day...there is no night...there is no right...there is no wrong...there is only the Prince of Air..."

We moved three times that year. I started fourth grade in Chula Vista. The next Annex I frequented was on Lookout Mountain where there was a movie studio and lots of little girls with haunting eyes. The next Dr. Green was much younger. He had a black moustache and buck teeth that looked fake. He gave me the name Arabella the Movie Star. The studio was a busy place. It bustled with lights and microphones and sets they trucked in from Hollywood movies like *Godzilla* and *Ben Hur*.

I wore wigs, white powder, and nothing else. Nanny Black gave me a pill that made my ears buzz and I danced for the cameras with other naked kids while cameras moved around us on trolleys. "Make it sexy," Dr. Green would shout, and a grownup movie star would drop his bathrobe and ride me from behind, poking my bottom with his big red thing until he screamed, and Dr. Green yelled, "Cut! That's perfect."

For some movies, we had to shoot guns at each other. One gun was loaded. The rest had blanks. We'd keep shooting until one of the kids died for real. It was always one of the Mexican kids. I only shot in the air, but even so I'd become a terrible person. Everything I was doing was bad. God would probably blow my head off with a lightning bolt if I even touched a flagpole.

At night we were kept in a long white room with black-and-white tiles on the floor. It was called The Ward. We slept in beds with bars over the top like cages that they locked with keys every night. We weren't allowed to speak. We could only stare at one another, locking eyes and sharing our thoughts. I learned to read minds and project ideas. Dr. Green called it remote viewing and said I was coming along nicely.

My family moved twice that year, too. I became a better forgetter with each relocation. By the end of fourth grade, I could hardly remember that I existed. My parents had taken to complaining about "that kid" in front of me as if I wasn't there. The only place I felt alive anymore was in the school classroom where I drew pictures, wrote stories, and learned arithmetic. I made friends at school and played sports. I giggled with the girls and played kickball with the boys. I signed up for student savings accounts and library cards. I sang with the choir.

And then I was gone.

CHAPTER TEN

CHICAGO, 1959

When I was ten, I spent the sweltering summer with Father's parents, my Grandma and Grandpa, in their Chicago apartment. Father and Mother were on vacation in Indiana or somewhere. For a few months I enjoyed the luxury of doting grandparents. I tried to tell them about Dr. Green and the Annexes, but they just smiled and nodded, not believing me.

I gave up, letting my vacuum cleaners suck out the bad memories out of my brain while I sank into boredom. Time slowed to a hot, lazy trickle. The air scarcely breathed in the old brick building. Heat wafted in waves from the street. I sucked an ice cube on the third-floor fire escape.

I'd climbed out the window to dangle my legs over the metal railing and wait for Mema, my other grandmother. Mother's mother lived in Lansing, Michigan, which wasn't far. She was coming for a visit, bringing her hatbox of old photographs on the Greyhound Bus. Her taxi was due any minute.

Behind me, curtains hung limp. I heard Grandpa cough a long, wheezing hack and flick through the channels on their Zenith TV with his remote. I hadn't been back to this apartment since I was four years old. Grandpa was coughing and smoking then, too – grinding cigarette butts into his Smokey the Bear ashtrays. I heard the click of his lighter and smelled smoke. I loved the scent of the ashes. They covered the coffee table and darkened the carpet.

Grandma was chopping something in the kitchen. The smell of onions frying made my stomach growl. She was making Swedish meatballs with mashed potatoes and gravy – my favorite. Grandma had decided to cure my anemia with lots of good Norwegian cooking and shark's liver oil. Grandpa brought home boxes of fresh fruit and pastries to fatten me up. Unfortunately, he was also determined to make me eat sardines. He took great pride in them because they were his family's business in Norway. Grandpa had every kind of King Oscar Sardines lined up in the refrigerator like library books.

"Give this a try," he'd say, passing me a peanut butter sandwich with a fish tail sticking out of it or a head and fins mashed into a banana on Wonder Bread. I'd shake my head and give him the evil eye, but just a tiny one. I didn't want anything to happen to Grandpa. It worried me the way his lips turned blue when he coughed. I just didn't like sardines.

At night, they made me a bed on the big, soft sofa. I'd kneel and say The Lord's Prayer with Grandma and sleep soundly, wrapped in the safe smell of their bodies that clung to the upholstery. My little brother was there, too. He slept on two chairs pushed together – the way I used to when I was small. Here, I wasn't afraid to sleep with the lights out.

A Yellow Cab pulled up to the curb. "Mema!" I shouted. I was through the window and downstairs before the driver popped open the trunk. He pulled out a black and yellow hatbox from Peck & Peck, New York. I knew it as the magical box, full of family photographs from Mother's side.

Mema'd had it with her when she came to visit us in Seattle two years before, but I was too little to handle the pictures. Now that I was ten years old, I intended to inspect every one of them. I was determined to find myself. I needed these photos to prove that I existed. I was breaking apart inside, vacuuming myself into pieces.

The Dr. Greens called it splitting identities and considered it a good thing. I'd been Arabella, Rose Red, Wendy, Chun Lin, and Highland Beauty, to name the few that I still remembered. Even worse, I had to lead one life at home and a separate one at the Annex. They called it "duality."

I was afraid that I'd soon be nothing but hollow, shattered pieces floating in air that popped like soap bubbles. I knew that's what the Dr. Greens wanted. I heard it when I was tied to the yin/yang wheel and spun into green: "…there is no light…there is no dark…there is no flesh…there is no blood…only the Prince of Air…"

I'd gone through Grandma's scrapbooks of Father's family many times. I'd seen pictures of Father and his cousin Paulie growing up together. There were pictures of me as a toddler with ice cream smeared on my face or examining mushrooms with a magnifying glass, looking for fairies. Beyond the age of four, when we moved from Wheaton to Seattle and away from my grandparents, there was nothing. Was that when I caught my heart disease?

Mema's hatbox was my last chance to find myself before I disappeared on the wheel, "…there is no life…there is no death…there is nothing."

"I'm not nothing," I said, emptying the hatbox onto the guest room bed.

"I'll have to organize these pictures someday." Mema picked up a brownish photo. It looked old. "This is me with your mother as a baby. It's the last time I headlined in *Carmen*." Mema sang at the Metropolitan Opera in New York until Mother was born, then they moved to California to become rich Christian Scientists. Mema liked to show me photos of their mansion in Beverly Hills and her movie-star friends.

I pulled out a postcard of Charost, the family's chateau in France. There were a lot of postcards from St. Etienne where they spent summers away from their apartments in Paris. Mema's father had been a surgeon and Communist revolutionary. He was shot during the Paris Commune, barely escaping to America with a bullet still in his arm. There were photos of him with his uncle Barat who ran an atheist newspaper in Paris, and later with his new American family at Musky Inn in Wisconsin. I pulled out a photograph of pyramids in a desert with camels and men with shovels. "What's this?"

"My grandfather's construction company dug the Suez Canal," said Mema. "Then he lost his shirt in Panama because of yellow fever." I knew it all already but loved those stories.

I kept digging until I found a picture of Mother holding a baby. "Is that me?"

Mema turned it over and shrugged. "Sorry honey, that's your brother." I dug further and found school photos of my brother from several years, including the latest one. There wasn't a single picture of me – not even as a toddler. This was terrible. Who would remember me when I died young from my dodgy heart?

"Where are my pictures?" I shook the box upside-down, hoping I'd missed something.

"I guess your mother never sent me any."

"There have to be some." I felt around inside. Something was wedged at the bottom. "What's this?" I pulled out part of an old book. The cover was missing. The title page was dated 1860.

Mema adjusted her glasses. "I'd forgotten all about this. It's one of those vanity books the family liked to publish. We used to have quite a few of them. This one is about your Scottish ancestors."

"I'm Scottish?"

"You're a MacGregor. That's an old Highland clan on Mepa's side."

I struggled to read the old-fashioned script of the title. The letters looked strange. Mema read aloud, "*The Miracle Sword of the Clan MacGregor*."

I opened it and lifted a piece of tissue to reveal a color frontispiece. A slender woman with flowing brown hair hovered above a sparkling pool. She lifted a sword by its jeweled hilt. I gasped, jolted by an electric charge. She looked like me. "Who's that?"

Mema read the caption. "That's the Lady of Loch Tay."

"What's she holding?" I stared at the sword, riveted, stunned by the magnitude of this discovery. I could feel the cool metal pressing my fingers.

"That's the sword of the MacGregor chief Robin Abroch. He's your ancestor." The room darkened. The curtains stirred. Mema shivered and said, "Thank goodness I beat that storm." Thunder rolled in the distance. I stared as the illustration came to life. With a flick of shimmering hair, the Lady of Loch Tay locked onto my eyes and smiled at me. I shrieked and threw down the book before she could speak.

"Meatballs," called Grandma from the kitchen. "Dinner's ready."

"I'm going to wash up," said Mema. "You tidy up here."

I put everything back in the hatbox – except the book. I knew I shouldn't take it, but I had to. My life depended on it. I hid it under the sofa. Later, while everyone else slept, I pulled it out, marveling at its heavy, yellowed paper and frayed edges.

There were two hundred and six pages. I had no way of knowing how many were missing. I looked at each of the black-and-white illustrations, willing the text to paint them in vibrant colors. But the printed words just lay there, looking as useless as I felt. Even though I was always the best reader in school, I couldn't read the tight, old-fashioned script. It covered the pages in a tangle so dense it looked like mouse footprints and spider webs.

I wanted to ask God for help, but I'd made a promise not to need Him. I tucked *The Miracle Sword of the Clan MacGregor* back under the sofa. I would keep working at it until I unlocked the secrets of the book. I fell asleep – grateful to have something that proved I existed.

In the morning, I put a 5 x 7 school portrait of myself from Ella B. Allen Elementary in Chula Vista, California into the hatbox as a fair trade. It was the only picture of me that I had.

CHAPTER ELEVEN

THE ATCHISON, TOPEKA & SANTA FE

I left Grandpa and Grandma waving from their bay window. Before I'd kissed them good-bye, Grandpa made us wait while he loaded color film into his camera. He took my picture with Grandma, Mema, and Father. It wouldn't be my best. My eyes were red. I'd spent the night crying because I didn't want to go. I was out of tears by the time Father drove my brother and me to the train. We were going to California.

"Stop sniveling, Fatso. You'll like Imperial Beach." Father lit a cigarette before starting the car. "You'll swim in the ocean, get a suntan, and wear a teeny-weeny bikini." I rolled my eyes.

Mother met us at Union Station. Father paid a porter to load the bags. He kissed Mother a big one on the lips and said good-bye. He'd be flying ahead to find a place for us to live.

Soon the Atchison, Topeka & Santa Fe rattled westward. We settled into our cabin and pulled the bed down. There was one for Mother and a pull-down, upper berth for my brother and me to share. I dangled my feet over the edge, watching Mother. I hadn't seen her all summer. She looked like a movie star with her new hairdo and tan. She was slumped in her seat, smoking and staring into space. She always looked sad like that when she was away from Father.

I wanted to ask her about the pictures in Mema's hatbox. I wanted to know why she'd sent pictures of my brother, but not of me. I decided not to risk it. She could go from sad to violent in a flash. Besides, I was sad myself. I felt hot and motion sick. My brother played with his box of army men, trying to shoot me off the bed. I took the hint and slipped into the corridor and the safety of strangers. I had *The Miracle Sword of the Clan MacGregor* hidden under my shirt.

I made my way to the passenger car, stopping to stare at French sailors with red pompoms on their hats. "C'est la vie," I said, quoting my *Babar the Elephant* book. They smiled and saluted, then said things I didn't understand. I jostled my way past black ladies with funny hats and little black babies. I was searching for a safe place to read.

The train was full. Men stood in the aisles, reading newspapers and smoking. Porters shuffled bags. Blue smoke drifted above my head, mixing with the oily smell of fish. The motion and heat made me dizzy. I needed to find a seat and sit down.

A fat woman took up a seat and a half. She was so big that I couldn't see her head, but there was just enough room for me to squeeze in next to the window. I climbed over her legs and sat down. I tried to see her face above the jiggling chins, but couldn't, so I imagined her head to be the size of a marble and perfectly round.

One of the French sailors shrugged and winked at me. I winked back. I was a good winker. The chug-chug rhythm of the wheels made me drowsy. My head dropped forward but snapped up again when someone cleared her throat in my face. The fat lady's neck had stretched so far that her pea-sized head was level with mine. I stared into her tiny cartoon eyes.

"Who are you, little girl?" she squeaked.

"Nobody." I snorted, wishing she'd go away.

"Nonsense. Who are you?"

"I'm damaged goods. I don't exist."

"Sure, you do. You just need a new friend."

I looked around. "Where is she?"

The train whistled into a dark tunnel. I came fully awake when it burst into sunshine on the far side. The fat lady was sitting up straight, just as she'd been when I fell asleep. I couldn't see her head at all.

I wiped train sweat from the window and pressed my face against the glass. We rolled through farmland with gentle hills of brown and green. Crows in rows on the telephone wires listened in on the party lines. I heard the conductor tell the sailors, "These are the Great Plains."

Planes? I perked up – Paulie must be nearby. I scanned the sky for his crop-duster. The horizon was clouding, threatening thunder. "Wild as the wind," Grandpa had called him. Paulie had burned down a barn, run away to Cincinnati, and crashed the family car before he was my age – ten. When he was sixteen, he ran away to Canada and joined the RAF. He won medals flying in the war over Africa. I liked having Paulie's blood in my veins.

I searched the flat farmland for a sign that he wasn't dead. Lightning flashed, rain swamped the window and I couldn't see anything but a veil of water. Loss burned my chest. I ached for Grandma and Grandpa, certain that I'd never see them again. I swallowed a sob, morphing it into a cough. The last thing that I wanted to do was to break down and cry in front of the French sailors.

The rain stopped and a rainbow arched across the sky – a slice of color shining through gray clouds. I wiped my eyes and nose with my shirt. *The Miracle Sword* plopped onto my lap. I flattened it and opened it to page one. I'd been working to decipher the small, dense print, but it was very slow reading with its old-fashioned words and Scottish phrases. I worked at it until I spotted Mother towing my brother down the aisle. She signaled that it was time to eat.

We ate hamburgers surrounded by the racket of the dining car. I climbed into the bunk next to my brother. The train sped into the twilight, but I willed it to slow down. I didn't want to go to Imperial Beach. I wanted to fly away with Paulie in his biplane. We'd howl like wolves all the way to Scotland.

CHAPTER TWELVE

SPARKY MACGREGOR

After breakfast the train stopped in Peoria. A lot of people got off and a few boarded. I wandered the aisle with *Miracle Sword*, remembering what the fat lady had said about finding a friend. I'd taken a pencil and paper napkins from the dining car. My head was bursting with pictures that I wanted to draw. Maybe if I drew enough pictures, I'd discover my new friend in one of them. Then again, maybe she was in *Miracle Sword* and I just hadn't tried hard enough to read it. Either way, I had work to do before we arrived in San Diego.

I decided to find the fat lady to ask if she knew where my new friend was. I slipped into the passenger car, but the fat lady was gone. In her place sat a little girl who seemed familiar, though I couldn't quite place her. She must have boarded in Peoria. She looked to be about ten – same as me. My heart skipped a few beats. Could she be my new friend?

She saw me and smiled a big crooked grin, patting the empty seat beside her. I sat down and gawked at her. She had shiny black hair like Prince Valiant and bright blue eyes like Paulie. I couldn't stop staring. It was rude, but I didn't know what to say. She was perfect – the opposite of me in every way. I was a drab, skinny child with anemia.

She was bright, colorful, and strong. I had a weak heart. She had rosy cheeks and glowing skin. My pants were too short, and my toes stuck out over the ends of my old-lady sandals. She wore a neat red and green Scottish kilt with a matching cap and socks. She had shiny black penny loafers with new copper pennies. I tried to be cool in spite of my pounding heart.

I opened *Miracle Sword* to my favorite illustration. The MacGregor clan was gathered around a campfire on the shores of Loch Tay. Men in tartans held up burning candles that looked like the sparklers from the Fourth of July. A hand with a sword was rising from the water.

"That's my sword," the girl pointed. "The Lady of Loch Tay is making me the next chief of Clan MacGregor. My name is Sparkler MacGregor. Everybody calls me Sparky. Have you read *Miracle Sword*?"

"I can't. It's too hard."

"It's that old-style print. It's hard to read, isn't it?" She laughed. "Let's read it together. I can tell you what the Scottish words mean. If you want, I'll teach you magic spells and curses – in Gaelic."

We leaned together and read page one. It did not disappoint. Fierce Scottish Highlanders fought a great battle. By page five, we'd had sword fights, ambushes, battlefields, evil spells, and bodies riddled with arrows. The pages were bursting with warriors, villains, witches, fairies, and fair maidens. I fell in love with my ancestor, the handsome, black-haired Robin Abroch MacGregor – the legendary outlaw and military genius who was destined to be the last chief of our line. "He belongs to me," said Sparky.

I told her all about Paulie, who belonged to me. When we got tired of reading, we spread paper on a table in the dining car and drew pictures of the sword. "It's got mysterious writing on it and the hilt has diamonds and rubies," said Sparky. We were shooed out of the diner in Kansas City when it was time to set the tables. We had drawn pictures on all of the napkins.

The train was crowded again, so we sat on floor of our cabin covering the pages of Mother's address book with drawings of battles. In bed that night, Sparky squeezed in between me and my brother, finger to her lips. "Shhh, I'm invisible," she said. She taught me foul curses in Gaelic until my brother woke up and threatened to tell Mother that I was talking to myself.

The next day, we passed through Dodge City, drawing up plans for armor and weapons. Mother smoked and flipped through magazines while my brother flushed his army men down the toilet one-by-one onto the tracks. I ignored them both. Sparky and I had to get ready for Imperial Beach. I knew what it meant to be the new kid in a new school. We needed armor to protect ourselves from whatever threats awaited us. I showed her my latest designs.

"Excellent," she said. "I'll make a Scottish warrior out of you yet."

Chapter Thirteen

San Diego, 1959

Sparky and I were at the door when the train rolled to a stop in San Diego. A porter came for our bags and we followed him through the station, his cart stacked high with suitcases. In the arrival hall a mariachi band sang " …bailar bamba…bailar bamba…" Guitars and maracas echoed off the marble walls. Crowds poured from the trains. I couldn't see the musicians until I nearly tripped over a big hat on the floor.

"That's a sombrero," said Mother. "You can throw in a penny."

I dug in my pockets. "I don't have any."

The musicians wore black velvet suits covered with spangly little mirrors and white sombreros on their heads. They smiled, flashing white teeth under their black mustachios. I spotted a penny on the floor and tossed it into the hat. I wanted to stay and listen, but Mother hurried us outside.

The air was hot and wet with a briny tang. "You can smell the ocean," said Mother, lighting a cigarette. I spotted Father and waved. He was leaning on the hood of a huge, mustard yellow convertible that I'd never seen before. The top was down.

"Jimmy!" Mother ran to his open arms and hugged him.

"What d'ya think of our new Mercury, Weezie?" He loaded our bags into the trunk while we piled into the longboat of a car – Mother in the front seat, my brother and me in the back with Sparky in the middle. Father drove with his arm around Mother. She lit him a cigarette using hers. "I rented a place that's a block from the beach," he said.

I looked at Sparky. She smiled and winked. Life seemed perfect. Maybe this really was the new beginning that Father always promised. I was tempted to ask if there was an Annex and another Dr. Green here but decided to stay quiet. If my parents had forgotten, best not to remind them. Also, if Sparky learned that I was damaged goods, she might leave.

"The Battle of New Orleans" blared on the radio. We passed a Hunts tomato plant that smelled like ketchup and another factory that stank like rotten fish. Near the harbor, the massive hull of an aircraft carrier loomed above the road. "That's the Navy Yard. I'll go there for Navy night," Father said. He was an officer in the Reserves. We stopped at a fruit stand piled with lemons, oranges, grapefruits, and limes. "I heard from Dad that Fatso likes fruit now." Father hopped out and bought a paper bag of oranges.

"Those Mexican wetbacks stole this fruit." Mother scowled, handing out the oranges. "They sneak across the border from Tijuana and take it at night." She was the expert on California. She grew up rich in Beverly Hills. Our relatives were still rich even if we weren't. Her brother, Uncle Wally, worked for the government and lived in an English mansion.

Our family had to live on my father's salary as an architect, which was never enough as far as Mother was concerned. She was always complaining that she didn't live in a big house with servants and that my brother and I weren't being raised by au pairs like my cousins. I was too busy peeling the orange and dripping juice down my shirt to notice much more about San Diego.

I was a sticky mess when we drove into the carport of the Imperial Beach Garden Apartments and Father announced, "We're home." Apartment C was in a newish complex of wooden buildings with a grassy courtyard. Carports extended back in long, covered rows to a street called Caspian Way. Our assigned parking space was a few feet from the kitchen door of our new home. Father unlocked it and we ran around the tiny two-story townhouse, banging doors and looking into closets until Mother chased us upstairs to our new rooms. They were empty except for cots. Our furniture would arrive the next day.

My bedroom was over the front door, looking down on a courtyard with a swimming pool. Sparky and I ran outside, across the grass and pressed our faces to the chain-link fence. I'd never been in a pool. I couldn't wait to jump in – as soon as I found my bathing suit. We tried the gate. It was locked. On the other side, children laughed and splashed, watched by a glamorous woman with blond hair in rollers. She was stretched out in a bikini, painting her nails red to match her lipstick. A charm bracelet flashed on her wrist. "Are you the new girl?" she called to me. "Don't you want to go swimming?"

I pretended not to hear her. I whispered to Sparky, "I want one of those bracelets."

"Come on," Sparky whispered back. "We have more exploring to do."

We found another courtyard with a second pool, and a playground with swings. There were palm trees and flowering bushes. A cloying odor of decay hung in the air. I thought it must be the ocean.

"Let's go to the beach," said Sparky. We ran down Imperial Beach Boulevard. In less than a block, we were stopped by a wooden barricade with yellow warning signs rimmed in red: "Quarantined. Raw Human Sewage." We could hear the crash of surf and the hiss of waves racing over pebbly sand. We were a few yards from the Pacific Ocean but couldn't see it. Instead, a foul mist advanced toward us.

"What do you think that means – raw human sewage?" I asked.

"Nothing good." Sparky shrugged. "I guess we can't go swimming in the ocean."

We were shuffling back, disheartened, when I heard Mother screaming. She had been subdued for five days on the train. That was a long time for her to be quiet. She was due for an eruption. "Tidelands, my ass." she shrieked. "This is the goddamn Tijuana Sewer. What the fuck were you thinking?"

I perked up and said, "Come on! We've gotta see this." We ran back through the complex to the carport. Mother stood on the far side of Caspian Way, arms akimbo, staring down at a sandy marsh that stretched into the distance. About a mile away was a fence with a huge sign – "Welcome to Tijuana." Father had chosen an apartment less than fifty yards from acres of colorful ponds that stank like poo.

"Can we ride our bikes down there?" I asked her.

"Don't be stupid. It's a goddamn sewer," said Mother.

"The beach has raw human sewage," I added. "It's quarantined." That did it. Mother exploded like an atomic bomb and took off after Father, swearing and punching him.

He held her by the shoulders. "Gimme a break, Weezie. You know I've got a job to do here. This'll give me the best view of the border so I can stay home at night with you." We watched while he calmed her down and led her into the apartment. My brother followed close behind, demanding to know what raw human sewage was.

Sparky and I were left alone outside to wonder at the intriguing possibilities that stretched from the IB Apartments to Tijuana. My sixth sense tingled. Other kids were watching from the shadow of the carport. I pretended not to notice. Sparky and I were the new kids. School started in just two days. We'd have to be the super-cool kids. I shivered. The mist rolling in from the ocean was cold. We ran up the steps to Apartment C and slammed the door.

That night, after I'd said my prayers, I listened to Father snoring down the hall. I couldn't read *The Miracle Sword* because there was no electricity. I slid the window open to let in cool air. A full moon lit the landscape and I could see all the way to the Tijuana.

The flat tidal marsh had come alive. Lines of people wended their way in single file across pools of sewage that reflected the moon. Many carried children in their arms and bundles on their backs. Sometimes, there were groups of children herded along by men. Parallel to the walkers, motorcycles roared past and big-wheeled trucks raced to and fro. Military jeeps flashed their lights. Men in sombreros boiled corn-on-the-cob in big vats and sold bottles of beer from a truck marked "TAMALES 5¢." Music blared. Across the border, a big, round stadium was lit like a beacon. Shouts of "Ole! Ole!" thundered into my room.

Someone started to play honkytonk on a piano next door. A pink light came on above our neighbors' porch. Motorcycles pulled onto the curb. Young men with greasy ducktails and black leather jackets dismounted. They laughed and spoke rapidly as they entered our neighbors' apartment.

Red lights were coming on in windows around the courtyard. Blond ladies in low-cut dresses pulled up their blinds and sat in open windows. They jangled charm bracelets, calling to men in sailor suits and Army uniforms, telling them they were handsome and sexy. Gunshots went off nearby and a woman screamed. I looked at Sparky. She shrugged. If she wasn't afraid, then I wasn't either. Pretty soon, thumping and bumping, huffing and shouting started on the other side of my wall. It grew louder and faster, accompanied by moans.

Sparky didn't seem to notice. We pulled the rough blanket over us on the cot and I tried to get comfortable. She went right to sleep, but my eyes stayed open until the honkytonk stopped and the room next to mine grew silent. I had just dozed off when a gust of warm air brought the stench of hot, silent fart wafting through my window.

Down the hall, Mother erupted. She ran through the apartment slamming windows, slamming doors, screaming at my father, screaming at me as if I'd made the awful smell. She'd slept through all the bumping, banging, laughing, shouting, and honkytonk, but the Stink from the Tijuana sewer defeated her.

CHAPTER FOURTEEN

ARDCHOILLE … ARDCHOILLE!

A Bekins moving truck arrived after breakfast. Furniture was stacked on the sidewalk. Mother looked frazzled. "Go out and play," she said. "Don't come back until the truck leaves."

That was fine with me. I spotted my J.C. Higgins bike named Blue Balloon being rolled off the truck. She was old, rusty, and dented. I jumped on the seat and she flew under my feet. Sparky appeared on the handlebars in her kilt and loafers. I pedaled to the end of the carport. "Where should we explore first?" I asked her.

Sparky pointed to the wetlands. "Down there, of course."

"Mother said we can't. It's a Mexican sewer."

"Nonsense. That's the Scottish Highlands. I oughta know."

I pedaled hard and Blue Balloon took flight across Caspian Way. We paused at the top of a long steep incline and gazed at the wetland marsh.

There was no one in sight. Sunlight cast the ponds in a pinkish tint with foaming streaks of orange, yellow, and blue. The walkers, motorcycles, and trucks from the night before were gone now. Bare patches of sand between clusters of reeds were cluttered with trash. Corncobs and beer bottles were piled where the TAMALE truck had been. A flock of seagulls squabbled over the garbage. "Looks a lot different in daylight," I said.

"Things usually do. Look down there." She pointed to a narrow dirt dike between ponds of sewage. "That's how the walkers cross the sewer. Let's go."

"You want me to ride over that?" I pedaled cautiously down the hill, stopping short of the ponds. "It's only two feet wide." I stared at the bubbling brew on each side. It smelled worse up close. "That's poo. If we fall in, we're dead."

She gave me a scathing look. Still, I hesitated. She leaned close to my ear and whispered, "Don't look now but we aren't alone."

I looked up the hill. A line of bicycles had appeared along the rim of Caspian Way. I'd never seen so many. I wasn't ready for this. We were trapped out in the open. "Let's go home," I hissed through my teeth, my pulse racing.

"No." Sparky leaned into my face until we were nose-to-nose across the handlebars. "We're MacGregors, you and me. We don't run away." I saw the wild courage so much like Paulie's in her. Did I have it in me too? Our eyes locked. "Let's go find out what you're made of," she said. "Let's show them how we do this in Scotland."

I took a deep breath, turned my bike around and pedaled uphill toward the kids until I could see their eyes. They towered over us, looking big and mean. Sparky asked, "Do you remember our war cry?"

"Sure, I do." We'd practiced it every day on the train. Turning the bike downhill, I stood on my pedals and flew like a biplane with my arms in the air. "Ardchoille! Ardchoille! Ardchoille!" I screamed.

Grit stung my eyes, but I kept them open, centering Blue Balloon on the dike with my knees. It was a risky maneuver, but we zoomed across and down the next embankment onto flat, wet sand. Wow! That felt so good that I threw back my head and let out a wolf howl.

I forgot all about the other kids until I reached the shallow, stinking trickle of the Tijuana River. I heard them coming so fast that some must have crossed the dike right behind me. I glanced over my shoulder – most were riding down a road that I hadn't seen before. They were howling, too. Either my daring had intrigued them, or they intended to kill me. It was hard to tell.

I pedaled into the river, pushing hard to keep from tipping into the filthy water. Some kids followed me, but most stopped short. Catching my breath, I turned to face the three boys who had crossed. The closest one was bigger than me with blue eyes and a red crew cut. We scowled at each other, panting for breath. He looked mean. What should I do?

"Let me handle this," said Sparky. She jumped off Blue Balloon and walked toward the boy. I became invisible and let her do the talking. "I'm Sparky MacGregor. I'm from Scotland."

"Where's Scotland?" The tall boy crinkled his nose. The other boys came closer.

"It's an island in the North Sea. I'll be going back soon."

"I'm Patrick MacDonald. This is Gary and Rock. We're from right here."

"Hey, Patrick," a girl with blond braids shouted from across the river. "Come back over. You'll get into trouble."

"That's my sister Theresa. She has leukemia and she isn't supposed to be down here, but she follows me everywhere. I have to be nice to her because she could bleed to death."

"Patriiick …" she whined. "I'll tell on you."

Patrick rolled his eyes. "She always gets her way. I've gotta go back."

Sparky jumped back onto Blue Balloon's handlebars. I pedaled across the river behind Patrick and the boys. Once on the bank, the rest of the children crowded around. Up close, they looked like nice kids – around my age or younger. We'd probably all be at Imperial Beach Elementary tomorrow for the start of school.

"This is Sparky MacGregor. She's a new kid," said Patrick.

"Sparky's from Scotland," announced Gary.

"Do you want to come and see our clubhouse?" asked Theresa.

"Sure," said Sparky. "Do you know where I can find some aluminum, like old pie tins and TV dinner trays? I need to make some armor. If we're going to fight battles in the Highlands, you'll need armor too."

"There's always stuff in the dumpsters," said a boy with dark, curly hair. "We find all kinds of cool things in there. We can make everything in the clubhouse. I'm Albert. This is my sister Linda."

"Come on," said Patrick, leading the way uphill to Caspian.

This time we took the access road, which was still a long, hard climb. The clubhouse turned out to be a space behind the dumpsters in the carport where our Mercury was parked. The kids hid their bicycles there and passed the hot summer days on a cool, shady patch of concrete. Treasures they'd dug from dumpsters were piled in a corner.

Albert pulled out an old radio that had tubes in the back like Mepa's Rosecrucian radio. He plugged it in, cracked his knuckles, and turned it on. The radio squealed and squawked as he tuned the dials with skillful fingers. It burst into "Yakety yak, don't talk back … Take out the papers and the trash … Or you won't get no spending cash …"

"Works pretty good," said Albert proudly.

"That's Radio KGB," said Rock. "It's our favorite."

"When the cars are out, this whole place is ours," Gary swept an arm over the carport. It was Sunday and the cars were in. The Bekins truck was still parked outside our kitchen. A sofa and chairs blocked the sidewalk.

"When Los Lobos come around, we hide behind the dumpsters. Mostly, they leave us alone."

"What are Los Lobos?" I asked.

"Mexican greasers on motorcycles," said Linda. "We stay away from them."

I nodded, remembering the men with leather jackets and ducktails who'd visited my neighbor last night.

"Tell us about Scotland," said Theresa. She nursed a nosebleed. Patrick had run home and brought her ice cubes in a washcloth.

"Yeah, Sparky. Tell us about Scotland." Eager faces crowded around while I sweated. I'd been stuck like a bug in the web of my own lie. I'd never been to Scotland. All I knew about the Highlands was what I'd read in the first ten pages of *Miracle Sword*. The rest I had imagined. How I could possibly translate what I saw in my mind into a world that other kids could see?

"Ummm…ummm," I stuttered, panic rising.

"Out of my way," said Sparky, pushing me aside, "I'll handle this."

She climbed onto the hood of a baby blue '53 Chevy. With sweeping gestures, she launched into a story from *Miracle Clan* of how the great and brave MacGregors had their lands stolen by wicked Clan Campbell. She told of the cruel way the MacGregors were declared outlaws. Anyone caught using the name was sentenced to death on the spot. "The MacGregors fought many famous battles."

So far so good, but now what? That's all that I'd been able to read. I wanted to run to my room and slam the door, but brave Sparky wasn't finished. She conjured up a mental paintbrush that danced across the carport, transforming concrete, dumpsters, and cars into the high green woods and an enchanted stone village.

"One night a MacGregor raiding party was ambushed on the shores of Loch Tay. The MacGregors were cornered. The Campbells were going to chop them into little pieces and feed them to their pigs. Suddenly, a hand came out of the water. It held a magic sword. It was the Lady of Loch Tay. She said, 'Where is Robin Abroch?'

"'I am here, my lady,' said Robin.

"'I declare you the next chief of Clan MacGregor. This is your sword. Take it, and you will slay your enemies without spilling a single drop of MacGregor blood.'

"Just then, the Campbells attacked. Robin raised the sword up over his head and most of them dropped dead. The rest ran away." Sparky paused. The kids were so wrapped up in the story that nobody was fidgeting or talking. "That's my sword now. I'm going back to Scotland to get it." She jumped down from the hood of the car, triumphant.

We were all sweating. The day had grown much hotter. Patrick said, "Let's go to the pool."

I stowed Blue Balloon behind the dumpster and dodged around Bekins men in our apartment. I found a box of clothes in my room and pulled out my bathing suit. Patrick and Theresa's mother came to watch us play in the water. Mrs. MacDonald was the glamorous blonde that Sparky and I had seen earlier.

We splashed and shrieked, doing cannonballs and belly flops, then we played Marco Polo and a new game that Sparky made up called "huzz-bees" about sea monsters from Scotland that slithered through the water making a sound like "huzz ... huzz" and pulled victims down by their ankles.

CHAPTER FIFTEEN

FUSING

I dreaded the thought of starting another new school. Sparky and I were up early to get ready. I was wearing the same, too-short dress that I'd worn the year before and new, too-big Dr. Scholl's sandals that Mother bought at a drugstore. I hid *Miracle Sword* in the back of my closet under a bag of old comic books, ate a bowl of cornflakes and waited for Patrick and Theresa by the pool. We were joined by other kids who toted lunch boxes and wore shiny, new shoes.

The school was two blocks from the apartments. We crossed Imperial Beach Boulevard and cut through the fields of Mar Vista High School, joining others on the way. Sparky strode alongside me looking prim and smart in her pressed white blouse and kilt. Her black hair was brushed to a shine. She wore the penny loafers that I wanted. Soon we could see the classrooms of IB Elementary. "There it is," said Patrick. He and I would be in fifth grade, along with Albert, Gary, Rock, and Donna. I had just met Kenny Smith, the boy who lived next door in the apartment with the pink porch light and honkytonk piano. He was a fifth grader, too.

The gang sped up when they spotted kids from the Navy base getting off a school bus. They shouted greetings and kicked up a dust cloud in their hurry to meet old friends. I fell behind, staring down at my filthy white socks, hating my stupid sandals. My emotions were a jumble.

I didn't want to like these new kids because I'd be leaving soon, same as always. I already cared about Sparky and that was stupid. I'd never get to keep her. She'd desert me once we got to school. Why would a girl like that stay with a loser like me when she could play with those cute Navy girls in their flouncy poodle skirts and white blouses?

I had to will my feet to keep walking. My head hung low. I didn't want anyone to see my sadness or how each step through the powdery dirt was growing heavier. When I looked up, Sparky was right beside me, matching my slow pace, and shaking with laughter. "Stop feeling sorry for yourself, you twit." She reached out. "Take my hand." I hesitated for a few seconds, but then I took it. It was the first time we had touched skin to skin. The sensation was electric. Energy surged through me. My ears buzzed and my teeth chattered. I was afraid to hold onto her but unwilling to let go.

Was this the end of me? Had Dr. Green won? "Am I splitting apart?" I gasped.

"Exact opposite," she beamed. "We're fusing. Hold on tight." My spirit slid out of my body and wiggled down my arm into Sparky's better, sturdier body. The old me deflated like a balloon and I exhaled the last vestiges of my timid, defeated self in a puff of sparkly bubbles.

Sparky dusted herself off and said, "This will be much simpler." I had to agree. Her quirky smile was now my smile. I looked out through her bright blue eyes that were so much like Paulie's and laughed from deep in my belly. Galloping like a wild horse, I ran to catch up with my new friends, kicking up a dust cloud of my own.

We found our classroom and were seated alphabetically. As my old self or as Sparky, I was assigned the desk behind Patrick MacDonald. Our teacher, a pretty blonde with a ponytail, welcomed us. "I'm Miss Fitch. I was a student teacher here last year, so I remember some of you from fourth grade. We have an exciting curriculum this year...." and on she went about math and biology. The confusion arose when we did roll call. We were required to stand up one by one and say our names. When we got to *M*, Patrick stood up.

"Patrick MacDonald."

Then it was my turn. I stood up and said, "Sparky MacGregor."

"Wait, wait, wait," said Miss Fitch. "That seat is for another girl." She called out my old name and asked if I was there.

"Yes, I'm here. But my name is Sparky MacGregor."

Miss Fitch chewed on the metal end of her pencil and perused the attendance list. "I don't have Sparky MacGregor listed."

"But I'm here and that's my name."

"She's from Scotland," said Gary.

"She has a sword and knows the Lady of Loch Tay," said Albert.

Miss Fitch let it pass and went on with the roll call. Then she distributed sheets of butcher paper and crayons. Our first assignment was to draw something that we had dreamed about over the summer.

I drew a red Pegasus, a flying stallion with blazing nostrils snorting fire. It was really good – a cross between the Mobil Oil flying horse and the song "Ghost Riders in the Sky." Flying was something I dreamed about all the time. Art was the way I broke the ice with all of my new teachers.

I sighed with relief when Miss Fitch looked at my work and said that I was a talented artist. She pinned my red horse to the display board at the front of the class. I wasn't completely in the clear, however. When it was time for recess, Miss Fitch said, "Sparky MacGregor, will you please stay behind? We need to go meet with the principal."

We took seats in front of Mr. Miller's desk. I sat at attention, hoping that he would see a pretty little Scottish girl, and not a ragged child with black circles under her eyes and ugly sandals with dirty socks. More than anything, I didn't want the school calling Mother. She must never know about Sparky.

"As I understand this situation," said Miss Fitch, "this student has changed her name to Sparky MacGregor." Then she uttered the fatal words: "Do you think we should call her parents?"

"No!" I burst into tears. Not very brave – I'd have to do better. I was bawling like a four-year-old.

Mr. Miller rubbed his chin and looked at me. "Do we have the right child?"

Miss Fitch looked in a file. "Yes, I have her photograph and her registration from her last school along with reports from Child Services and the State Police. This is her." Miss Fitch chewed her pencil some more. I could sense that these were kindly people, looking to do the right thing, but not wanting to break any rules. I had to solve this for them.

"It's my nickname," I said with a stroke of genius. "Other kids use their nicknames at school. Why can't I?"

"Well," mused Mr. Miller. "I don't see anything wrong with a nickname. Do you, Miss Fitch?"

"Not really. We can try it for a while and see how it goes. Is that all right with you, Sparky?"

I could have kissed both of them. Sparky was safe from my parents. Home and school should never mix. I hurried outside to play a mean game of kickball.

Chapter Sixteen

Teen Angel

By mid-afternoon, something wasn't right. Kids were falling asleep at their desks. The ones from the Navy base were fine, but my friends from the IB Apartments were groggy. Then Patrick turned around and vomited on the floor by my desk. His vomit was streaked with red. I wondered if maybe he had leukemia like Theresa.

Miss Fitch sent Donna to fetch the school nurse, Mrs. Lipsky. She arrived in her nurse's hat and looked the children over. She left with Patrick while the janitor cleaned up the mess. I was assigned to erase the blackboard to get me out of the way. From the front of the class, I could hear Mrs. Lipsky asking Patrick if his mother still gave him eight aspirins every night to make him go to sleep.

"Uh huh," he said.

"Is she giving it to Theresa, too?"

"I think so."

"And the other children? Are their mothers giving them sleeping medicine from Mexico?"

"Uh huh."

"Go to my office and lie down, honey. I'll be there in a few minutes."

There was a hurried conversation between Miss Fitch and Mrs. Lipsky. "What can we do?" Miss Fitch asked. "We don't even know what they're giving the children. Last year it was heroin."

"There's nothing much we can do but make sure the kids have enough to eat and that they drink a lot of water," Mrs. Lipsky replied. "It's always worse after the weekends when all of the brothels are running. Sometimes I think those women shouldn't be allowed to have children."

"They do their best. Mrs. MacDonald spends all her money on Theresa's medical bills. That's why she gives Patrick aspirin. It's cheap."

"It's a dangerous drug. It's making him bleed internally. If she's giving it to Theresa with her leukemia it could kill her. ...."

The conversation drifted away. After a while Patrick came back to class. He seemed okay. It was nearly time to go home when Mr. Miller came into the classroom. He whispered to Miss Fitch, who stood up frowning. She tapped on her desk with a ruler. "Class? Mr. Miller has come to inform us that there's been a shooting at Mar Vista High School. A boy named Billy Brown was killed."

"Shit," shouted Gary, slamming his desktop shut with a bang. The class erupted, everyone talking at once. "What happened?" "Who shot Billy?" "Why?" "Have they got the guy?" Questions ricocheted around the room while I sat in stunned silence.

Miss Fitch tapped her ruler again. "Class…class. Settle down. Let's hear what Mr. Miller has to say."

"I've known Billy since kindergarten. This is a tragedy," said the principal. "They haven't caught the shooter yet. They think he's hiding down in the wetlands near the border. You need to stay away from there. Avoid the high school and stick together on your way home – especially you kids headed for Caspian Way. Go straight home and lock your doors."

Miss Fitch added. "A police officer will let you know when it's safe to come back outside."

Our gang walked the long way home along Imperial Beach Boulevard. We took our time passing the scene of the crime. Cop cars, ambulances, and fire trucks were at Mar Vista. Lights flashed and radios squawked. High school students waited behind yellow crime tape for teachers to escort them off the high school grounds.

We were on the sidewalk a hundred feet or so from where Billy lay motionless under a blue tarp. Death stalked us all the way home. We talked about self-defense, weapons, and armor. We decided to gather all the aluminum we could find and bring it to the clubhouse as soon as the policeman said it was safe.

The police caught the shooter. It was on the news that same night. There'd been a gunfight in the wetlands and a Cuban drug smuggler was dead.

"Goddamn Cubans." Father smacked his hand flat on the dinner table, making the dishes jump. It startled Mother, who dropped a Rosarita's Mexican TV dinner face down on the floor. I had never heard of a Cuban, but this wasn't the moment to ask questions. Later, a policeman knocked on our door to say that it was safe to go to school in the morning. All clear. Life would go on without Billy.

No one in my family talked about the dead boy, but his death surrounded me. He had lived with his party-girl mother in Apartment A on the other side of the swimming pool. His funeral spilled into central courtyard with a great deal of crying. I was on my front step when the closed casket rolled past to the waiting hearse. I saw Kenny, Patrick, and Albert on their steps. Theresa gazed down from her bedroom window.

The other kids had known Billy pretty well, describing him as a nice guy who'd fallen in with a bad crowd when he got to high school. The day after the funeral, there was a memorial assembly at school. When we gathered at the clubhouse later, the atmosphere was heavy. I looked at my new friends thinking that the same thing might happen to one of us next. We'd have to keep our noses clean – stay out of trouble.

What else could we do? We were trapped – boxed in by the border to the south, the roadblock and "quarantine human sewage" signs to the west, the Mar Vista crime scene to the north, and Imperial Beach Boulevard with its bars and motorcycle gangs to the east. Our only escape was south into the patch of marshy wetlands – the Mexican sewer where Cubans waited.

Even Radio KGB seemed stuck on "Teen Angel" and other depressing tunes about kids who died young. Spirits were so low that no one was talking. I couldn't stand it – I had to do something. We needed a quest, something important to do together. I hurried into my apartment and dug *Miracle Sword* out of the closet. I'd never intended to show the kids my book, but we were in trouble.

The cars were out of the carport except for the '53 Chevy. I opened *Miracle Sword* on the hood, leafing casually through the pages. It didn't take long before the other kids grew curious. They gathered around me, pushing each other out of the way to see what I was doing. I turned to the page with a drawing of the Battle of Glenfroon.

"Cool," I said to myself. I hadn't been able to read it yet, but the picture was spectacular. "Look at this great armor. Bullets can't even touch you when you wear it." I could hear them breathing as they pressed in close to look at the armor. I had their attention. "I've gotta make some of this. Who wants to help?"

"I can make some swords," said resourceful Albert, "and I want a helmet."

"Let's make bows and arrows. I have some arrowheads," said Gary, pushing his best friend Albert out of the way.

"We need butcher paper if we're going to draw maps," said Theresa.

She was right. We needed access to the huge rolls of butcher paper that were in the art supply room of every school. Until then, we'd have to use the next best thing. "We'll use dirt," I said. "We've got lots of that."

Spirits brightened. From then on, we spent our recesses drawing armor designs and battle plans on the dusty playground. As soon as we got home from school, we focused our energies on gathering aluminum TV dinner trays and pie plates from dumpsters. Frozen chicken pot-pies were clearly big favorites at the IB Apartments.

Before long, we had a sizable stash of metal and armor construction was underway. Cutting the aluminum turned out to be tough because the scissors from school weren't strong enough. I brought kitchen knives from home. They worked pretty well, but I had to return them to the drawer every night before Mother started dinner. She complained to Father about how dull her knives were and made him sharpen them with a whetstone.

We started with simple things – bracelets and anklets – slicing our fingers on the sharp edges. Then we made daggers from TV trays and shields from Swanson pie tins. Some of us who were lucky enough to find Sara Lee cheesecake pans made crowns. We decorated our rusty bikes with shields and chains, transforming them into powerful warhorses with "rippling flanks and flowing manes" that pranced right out of *Miracle Sword*.

With our armor on, we were ready to set off on a great quest. We mounted our horses, leapt over Caspian Way, and galloped into the Highlands, shouting, "Ardchoille! Ardchoille!" We weren't defenseless kids anymore. We were the fierce and powerful Clan MacGregor leaping across vales and glens, giving our spirited horses their heads, loosening the reins and letting them run. Even the Tijuana River was transformed into a clear, cold Highland stream with green forest rising from its banks and, overhead, the fluttering wings of partridge and quail.

The spell was broken when Patrick shouted, "Shit, it's the cops." Two yellow-brown, open jeeps with guns mounted in the back were headed our way, sirens wailing. The Jeeps were pointed right at us.

"Shit, shit, shit," said Gary. "Let's run."

"No hope," said Albert. "They've got us."

"Stand your ground," I said. I felt invincible in my new armor. "I'll handle this."

A Mexican man in a brown short-sleeve uniform came out of each car. They stood together, arms crossed, looking us over. "You kids shouldn't be out here."

"The border's over there," I said, pointing toward the Tijuana fence. "We're okay. We're Scottish."

"What I mean is that river is full of piss and shit from Tijuana. You gonna get sick with typhus. Only people crazy enough to go through that water are them crazy-ass wetbacks and they get plenty sick, die with their bellies all swole up, screamin' in pain. It ain't pretty. Now, you kids ride back over that river before we take away your bikes. I'm gonna meet you over there 'cuz I got a business proposition. Better put those little kids in the jeeps. Don't want 'em fallin' in and dyin.'"

The bigger kids and I pumped our way back across the river while Theresa and the smaller ones rode in the jeeps with their bicycles mounted on racks on the back. Once on the other side, the kids and bikes were unloaded and one of the jeeps drove away.

"What's your name, li'l chiquita?" the man asked.

"I'm Sparky MacGregor and these are my lieutenants – Patrick, Rock, and Gary. We're from Scotland. I'm chief of Clan MacGregor."

"You can call me Pedro. I'm from Mexico. I ain't chief o' nothin'. We gonna do a li'l business, okay? You kids wanna make some easy money?"

"Duh," I rolled my eyes. The others nodded.

"Then here's the deal. I gonna give you some paper bags with addresses on them and you gonna deliver them at the IB Apartments. There's a lotta sick people in there cryin' for their special medicine. Can you do that?"

We nodded.

"I gonna give ya each a dime to deliver every bag. Good money for an easy job, huh? Come back tomorrow and get more bags. Bring some more kids. But don't come all the way across that stinkin' river. I'll be on this side. Don't worry 'bout the time, I'll see ya comin.'"

We lined up, eager to start on our quest. What could be better? We'd be helping sick people and getting paid for it. Pedro distributed the bags and the dimes. He said, "You look like good kids. That last kid, Billy – he kinda lay down on the job." Did he mean Billy Brown? I should have asked, but with money in my pocket, I forgot. We rode away. "Watch out for them MacCubans," Pedro shouted after us.

The deliveries were quick and easy. We just knocked on the door and a hand came out to take the paper bag. Sometimes they even tipped a penny. The group was transformed after our mission of mercy. Dusk was settling, but we were heady with the rush of adventure and reluctant to go home. Soon it would be time for dinner. Some of the mothers were already calling. The fathers were coming home. Their cars filled the carport. The first of the evening's wetbacks walked past us, casting a furtive glance and whispering, "Hola, bambinos." We watched him slide into shadows of the courtyard. More would soon follow.

We huddled together in the clubhouse to count our coins and decide what to do with so much money. Our mission had to stay secret so the MacCubans, or our parents, wouldn't steal our dimes. That's how I told the story in the space behind the dumpsters. I knew from years of being the "new kid" that nothing galvanized other kids like a secret mission. That worked especially well on the boys – that and giving them titles like lieutenant and prince.

We decided to put our profits into a dime bank that I happened to have and take turns hiding it at different apartments. I'd be first since I already had the bank in my closet at home. That settled, I insisted that the money be used to help those less fortunate than us.

Patrick said that his church, St. James, bought blankets for the Tijuana Orphanage every year at Christmas. "So the orphans don't freeze in the winter," he said. The wind shifted, sending a chill from the ocean. I shivered. It was easy to imagine orphans huddled together without a warm place to sleep. The group voted unanimously to donate everything we earned to buy blankets for the orphans.

Then the group voted to call us the "Kitty Queen Club," which was the name of a cat food. It was Theresa's idea. Nobody wanted to argue with Theresa, or she might bleed to death.

Chapter Seventeen

Sunday School

Billy Brown's death and my weak heart were weighing on me. I needed to talk to God. IB Elementary had a flagpole, but that was for little kids. Grownups went to church. St. James Lutheran was across the street from IB Elementary and a few blocks from the IB Apartments. Patrick and Theresa went to Sunday school there with a lot of kids from school.

I wanted to go, too. I'd never been to church – or not that I remembered. I'd tried sneaking into the Catholic Church once in Laguna Beach, but a nun grabbed my arm and told me I had to wear a hat. I didn't own one, so I stayed home. Mrs. MacDonald said I didn't need a hat to be a Lutheran, so I went to St. James on Sunday with the MacDonalds. I soon discovered that I couldn't get into Sunday school without a permission slip from my parents. I ran back home with the form and gave it to Mother to sign.

"Don't be silly." She crumpled the paper. "We aren't Christians."

This was news to me. "What are we then?"

"We're atheists," she said. "We don't believe in God."

I rolled my eyes. I believed in God, but I wasn't going to argue with Mother, who was steaming like Vesuvius after a night battling The Stink. She lit a cigarette, exhaling smoke. "We believe in science and reason. Didn't you learn that from Dr. Green?"

Confused, I ran back to the church and sat in a pew with the grownups. They were mostly Navy families with lots of uniforms. The church was cool and welcoming after running in the heat. It was pretty new – built like a ship, with arching wooden ribs and smelled like paint and wood shavings. I listened to Pastor John talk about the Gospel, while Mrs. Pastor John played the organ. I didn't hear God in his words until he spoke about their annual blanket drive for the Tijuana Orphanage. God was giving His blessing for our quest.

The following Saturday, I went with the MacDonalds to the St. James Pancake Breakfast. Church ladies were filling a woody station wagon with boxes of warm clothes to take to Tijuana. People were giving away sweaters and old clothes. If I'd had anything, I would have given it. But every time we moved, I was stripped down to one kid-sized box and the pair of shoes on my feet. Patrick introduced me to Pastor John and Mrs. Pastor John. She gave us each an oatmeal raisin cookie and a little white Bible.

I forgot to hide mine when I got home. That night Mother waved it in my face. "You've been at that church. I told you not to go." Technically, she'd told me not to go to Sunday school. I gave her the evil eye, but she wasn't done: "This is why you're scared of the dark. That damn pastor has filled your head with devils."

She surprised me by holding up a little bronze idol. It looked like a pot-bellied man with an umbrella on his head. "This is my devil chaser. Now you can turn out your light and go to sleep like everyone else." She set it on my chest of drawers.

I said nothing, waiting for her to leave, but she sat on my bed and lit a fresh cigarette. I saw tears in her eyes. "Goddamn it. Why do you have to be so pigheaded? Why can't you just follow Dr. Green's directions? We're all suffering because of you."

I tensed. I didn't know what she meant. It might have something to do with my last visit to the Lookout Mountain studio when I'd refused to shoot at another kid for one of their stupid movies. They'd punished me for that, although I'd forgotten how. Was that why we were living on the Tijuana sewer?

I wanted to ask, but questions were forbidden in our house. I was already treading water in Mother's bottomless pool of rage, but there was so much more that I needed to know. I blurted, "Why do I have to be a Bluebird? I hate it. I want to quit."

She slapped me before I could get my arms up to protect myself. "You selfish little bitch. You have everything and you just take, take, take. I wish you'd hurry up and die." She stormed out and slammed the door.

I sat frozen on my bed – afraid to move. I knew she'd be back, and she was. She pounded me with her fists, screaming, "You goddamn monster... I'm gonna kill you... Get used to the dark." She unscrewed my light bulb and slammed out the door. I exhaled, trembling, numbed by the beating. I heard Father calming her down.

"Weezie, Weezie... come here, Baby..."

"She's a bad seed... She's a beast... I hate this place."

Eventually Mother was quiet. When I heard Father snoring, I stood on my bed and screwed in a new bulb I'd stolen from the laundry room. I kept a stash of them under my bed for just this situation.

I picked up the strange figurine, wondering what Mother was talking about – devil chaser indeed. I wanted to throw it out the window, but Mother had called it *her* devil chaser. That meant she expected it back in good condition.

Up close, it had big lips and ears. It might have been a monkey in a hat. Its buggy eyes gave me the creeps, so I stuck it in a drawer. I dug out *Miracle Sword* and climbed into bed. I looked at pictures of the Battle of Glenfroon, imagining what it would feel like to be shot through the heart with an arrow.

CHAPTER EIGHTEEN

THE FAWN

"Rain's comin'," said Father the next morning. "Rain'll clean the air. Get rid of this godawful heat."

He was right about the godawful part. There wasn't a breath of wind. Even the swimming pool was too warm to play in. We owned one electric fan, so we'd gathered in the living room with the windows open trying to catch a bit of relief. My parents sat in their usual Sunday morning places at either end of the couch.

Father smoked and flipped through his Naval Reserve training manual on Hiroshima and Nagasaki. I'd already looked at the pictures of people who'd been burned into pillars of ash. Mother was poised like a cat, ready to spring into action at the first whiff of The Stink. I had decided to clean the dirt out of the living room carpet with a knife and discovered that passing it along the nap caused fleas to jump. I had them on the run.

"It'll be like a big toilet flushing," Father reassured Mother. "It'll wash all that Mexican crap out to sea – no more Stink. We'll go to the beach. How about that, huh, kid?" He threw a cigarette butt at me. "Want to go swimmin' in the ocean? Get your ugly butt eaten by a shark? Ha ha."

"Oh shit." Mother jumped to her feet. "It's Sunday. You've got to get dressed. You'll be late for school."

"What?" I gasped. Was she talking to me?

"You heard me. Get dressed … now! Jimmy, get the car."

I put on my school dress. I even brushed my teeth. Father drove too fast down Imperial Beach Boulevard, right past St. James Church. That was worrisome. I tried to be casual when I asked, "So where am I going to Sunday school?"

"The Art Museum," he said. My heart sank. That must be the name of the local Annex with my new Dr. Green. It had to happen sooner or later. To my surprise, Father drove to Balboa Park – muttering all the way about Miss Fitch and that goddamned meddling PTA. He dropped me off at the back door of the San Diego Art Museum and sped away. I stood on the steps, wondering what to do. I knocked on the door and a lady with a clipboard opened it. She signaled for me to come inside. "And your name is … ?"

"I'm Sparky MacGregor," I said.

"Oh yes … Lisa Fitch told me about you. I'm Mrs. Pendrake. I met your mother. Are you ready to paint?"

"Sure," I said. How did she know Mother? Paint? I thought I was going to church. "Am I supposed to paint God or something?"

"If anyone can, I'm sure it will be you," she smiled. I didn't know if she was kidding. I followed her downstairs to a corridor lined by classrooms and studios. Kids were in classes – painting, dancing, sewing, and even singing. If this was Sunday school, it looked great.

She led me to a studio with about twenty other kids. Each one sat at an easel with a big sheet of white paper. "Come on in," said Mrs. Roberts. I knew her name because it was printed on the blackboard next to a chalk circle divided into colorful slices of pie. "We're studying the color wheel. You're going to learn how to mix paints. Then we'll start doing sketches for your paintings. The best painting from each class will be exhibited in the Art Museum and auctioned off at the Patrons' Party next month. The winners will be invited to attend with their families. Now, take a few minutes and think about what you want to paint."

I stared at my paper. I didn't know how to paint God, so I decided to paint a fawn in the Highlands – a newborn deer half hidden by leaves. I started sketching. Then I experimented with mixing the paints on a wooden palette, using the color wheel. My colors quickly turned to mud.

Mrs. Roberts moved around the studio, commenting on each composition. "Don't try so hard with the colors," she said over my shoulder. "Think of this as a study in light and shadow. Your fawn is in shadow, peering into daylight for the first time. Learn to look at color with her new eyes – how exciting and frightening that must be for the little deer.

"Wherever you go this week, observe the way sunlight changes the leaves at different times of the day. See what weather does to color and light. A leaf might look green, but when you look closely, it has veins of purple and red – paint those."

While we cleaned our brushes at the end of class, Mrs. Roberts reminded us, "You can turn on your color anytime, anywhere." Father came an hour late to pick me up, but I didn't care. I sat on the steps of the museum, studying the way that sunlight struck a pot of geraniums.

The next day, I marveled at all the colors in the dirt I kicked up on the way to school. I turned on my color in class and watched through the window when clouds crossed the sun, changing the sky from blue to greenish gray. On the playground, I stared at dandelions poking through asphalt.

I thought about the colorless yin/yang wheel that spun in my head. "…
there is no life…there is no death…there is no white…there is no black…
there is no good…there is no evil…there is no God…" How could Mother expect me to believe that crap? How could I look at the amazing colors
of ordinary things and not believe in God?

I learned from Miss Fitch that the IB Elementary PTA had arranged to
send me to the museum's Accelerated Arts Program. All the kids had been
sent by their schools because they were good artists or actors or dancers
and couldn't afford lessons. Mrs. Pendrake drove me and some other kids
every Sunday after that. I'd get up early and wait for her brown Caddy on
Caspian Drive. She'd give us donuts and tell stories of how she used to be
a judge in the Navy JAG Corps. "You should think about being a lawyer,
Miss Sparky."

"I'm going to be an artist," I said. My artistic talent had gotten me farther than anything else. Why not become a world-famous artist?

Mrs. Pendrake stared ahead as we turned onto Coronado Avenue. Her
silence felt ominous. I braced myself. "You have to be realistic, honey.
Art can only be a hobby for people like you. Enjoy it when you're young.
You're going to need a real career to get you out of this place."

I rolled my eyes because I knew better. A fancy embossed invitation
had just come in the mail addressed to me. It was printed on thick white
paper and announced that my fawn had been chosen for the Patrons' Party auction. It read: "You and your family are invited to the Annual Gala
Exhibition and Auction of Children's Artwork at the San Diego Museum
of Art."

Mother had been forced to buy me a new dress and a pair of real shoes.
We ordered the dress from the Sears catalog. It was beautiful – yellow polished cotton with little pink flowers. The shoes were brown penny loafers
we bought from a street vendor. Mother bought a cocktail dress. Father
wore his suit and made my brother wear a bow tie. I was so proud of my
family – and of me.

The night of the gala was the first time I got to use the main entrance
to the museum. I'd always gone in the back. The museum looked like a
castle glowing in the dark. We parked with the rest of the families and
walked through gardens lit by fairy lights. I saw other kids I knew. They
were dressed up, too.

We climbed a long flight of steps to the tall glass doors with sculpted
arches where statues of old Spanish painters looked out over Balboa Park.
A banner down one side read: "San Diego Museum of Art" and on the

other side, "Welcome Young Artists – 1959." That was me – a young artist of 1959. Miss Fitch and Mr. Miller met us at the door with our nametags. Mine said *Sparky*. I threw it in the trash before my parents could see it.

The arched, red-tiled lobby was full of chattering, happy people in fancy clothes. I'd never seen so many pretty dresses and hairdos. There was a swan sculpted out of ice on the table. I had to touch it to believe it. The music started. Kids from orchestra class played classical music on the balcony. Waiters in white aprons passed trays of little snacks. There were martinis for the grownups and Cokes with ice for the kids.

The dancers from ballet class performed *The Firebird* on the landing at the top of the stairs. I watched spellbound. The girls in toe-shoes and tutus looked like real ballerinas. They belonged to this beautiful world of art and so did I. I helped myself to shrimp canapés and as many little sweet cakes called petit fours as I wanted. After the dance, Mrs. Roberts invited everyone upstairs to preview the student art before the big event – the auction.

I climbed the stairs ahead of my family. My eyes were on the fawn, which was framed and spotlighted at the top. I stood breathless in the admiring crowd – watching the wind rustle the leaves that I'd painted. I admired the light reflecting on the green surfaces, catching their purple-veined underbellies. The little fawn saw me. Her nostrils flared. She sniffed and flicked her ears, fearful of the crowd. "You're okay," I whispered. She was safely camouflaged by her coloring and spots that I had mixed with such love. I was the only one in the room who knew that she was Scottish.

"You've done it, Miss Sparky." Mrs. Pendrake swirled a martini glass. "You've painted God." She turned to Mother. "You should be very proud of your daughter."

Mother had a martini, too. Her nose was bright red. She stared at my fawn while Mrs. Pendrake moved on to admire the next student's work. "What did she mean, 'You painted God'?"

I shrugged. "Maybe it has something to do with the colors."

"Why did she call you Sparky?"

My stomach twisted. My mind went blank. "Dunno."

"Don't be so smug," Mother hissed. "I know you're up to something. There's going to be Hell to pay for this."

I felt like I'd been hit with a hammer. She was going to spoil my evening and there was nothing I could do to stop her. I hurried away, trying to blend in with the other parents, hoping Mother would forget about me.

I wanted to see the work of the other students – all of them. There were oils and watercolors, ceramics and mobiles, woodcarving and something called textiles. The possibilities for future projects seemed infinite. My resolve to become an artist strengthened.

A gavel struck. The auction was about to begin. My pulse raced. How much would my fawn sell for? I hoped it was a lot. As a famous artist, I needed to know about the value of art. I made it into the auction room and was headed for a seat when Father dug his fingers into my shoulders. "We're going home – now!"

I struggled to break his grip, but he had me from behind. "The auction … I can't leave now."

He propelled me toward the stairs. "See what you've done?" Mother stood at the bottom, sniffling into a handkerchief. "You've upset your mother. Now there's gonna be trouble."

CHAPTER NINETEEN

POMEGRANATE ROSE

Father wasn't wrong about Mother. "You think you're such hot stuff," she screamed. "I had a scholarship to the Art Institute of Chicago when I was sixteen. *That* was a big deal. San Diego's a backwater, so don't you get all high and mighty thinking you're somebody special."

She tore apart my bedroom looking for everything that had ever been taken from her during her life – oil paints, brushes, canvases. She was convinced that I was the thief. I managed to toss *Miracle Sword* and the dime bank through the window to Patrick before she started rummaging through my closet. "It's all gone," she wailed after finding nothing but dirty socks and underpants. "Every time we move all my stuff disappears." She searched my drawers and found the devil chaser, holding it up to prove her point that I was a thief. I crouched on the bed, arms over my head, ready for her blows. I thought about what Mrs. Pendrake had said about needing a serious career. If Mother was an artist, then it was time I considered becoming something else – a lawyer, or maybe a doctor.

Father *was* wrong about the weather. It didn't rain. Instead the searing hot Santa Ana winds swept in from the Mojave Desert, scorching every bit of moisture from the air. The wind dried the dirt around the settling ponds, the unpaved paths, and playing fields into fluffy brown powder that coated our hair and eyelashes. It stuck to our clothes and shoes, turning everything gray, including our cracked lips. Dust blew up my nose and into my eyes and ears. When I washed, it left muddy streaks on my face. With my black hair, I began to look like a wetback.

When the winds gusted above forty miles per hour, the school closed. I was stuck inside the apartment with my family, staring out the window at flying dust. No one could ride a bike in a storm like this one. I wanted to see what the wetlands looked like in a sandstorm, so I slipped out the back door and fought my way to the carport.

The clubhouse was buried. Blue Balloon had vanished under a foot of dirt. I felt my way to the end of the carport. I couldn't see anything from there, even my feet. I stumbled over the curb and got turned around. I panicked, freezing in place. If I went the wrong way, I could fall down the embankment into a pond full of sewage. Pedro would find me dead when the storm ended. It could be weeks.

A horn sounded behind me. I followed the faint headlights of a car back to the safety of the carport. It was my next-door neighbor, Mrs. Smith – Kenny's mother. "They have parties every night," Kenny had told me when I asked about the honkytonk piano and the weird noises coming from the room next to mine. He said that the room belonged to his four sisters and they had different boyfriends every night. "The old man keeps a baseball bat on top of his piano and the old lady knows how to use it when those greasers get out of hand."

"Hi, Mrs. Smith," I tapped on her window. I wouldn't ordinarily speak to Mrs. Smith, but I was glad to see her. She parked her pink Cadillac and waved at me. She had pink hair and a miniature poodle dyed to match. She seemed glad to see me, too.

She tucked the little dog into an oversized pink purse and opened the car door. "This is just terrible. I didn't think I'd find my way home and I only went to the store. Come into my kitchen. I'm going to make the girls some lemonade." She opened a pink umbrella. The wind blew it inside out. She held me tightly against her as we ran for her back door, the one next to ours. We tumbled into her kitchen in a cloud of grit and dust. The wind slammed the door behind us. It was the first time I'd been inside their apartment. It was a mirror image of ours except for the pink furniture and Mexican girls in muumuus working at sewing machines. The girl Kenny had introduced to me once as his sister Rita was there, except Mrs. Smith called her Mary.

"Here you go, dear, a nice cold glass of lemonade." She handed me a frosty glass, tinkling with ice cubes. "Mary, would you pour a martini for Mr. Smith?"

That was the first time I'd seen Mr. Smith, although I heard him every night on the piano. He was stretched out on the sofa in rumpled clothes, snoring. Maria put the frosted glass on the coffee table without attempting to wake him.

"You're such a pretty girl," said Mrs. Smith, eyeing me. "Have you ever had a bubble bath?"

"Sure, lots of times," I lied.

"We have jasmine, sandalwood, pomegranate, mango…the girls take a bubble bath every night, don't you, girls? And we have shampoo to match. You don't want your skin and your hair smelling different. The boys don't like that."

The very idea of taking a bath should have set off warning bells, but I was captivated by the idea of perfumed bubbles. I let down my guard.

"Candy," Mrs. Smith called to another Mexican girl. "Honey, draw Sparky a bubble bath, extra bubbles. Let's see what kind of skin she has under all this dirt. I think it's very white, don't you? Then we'll do her fingernails and toenails with passion pink. Girls, show Sparky your fingers." They all wore the identical shade of bright pink.

"I might even trim your hair." She ran her fingers through my hair. "Has it ever been professionally cut?"

I shrugged. I didn't think much about my hair.

"Hmmm…" Mrs. Smith looked at my glass. I hadn't taken more than a sip of lemonade. It had a bitter flavor and I didn't like it. "Did I make it too strong?"

"No, it's fine. Can I take it with me to the bathroom?"

"Of course, you can, dear."

Candy called down the stairs that everything was ready. Mrs. Smith led me to a bathroom that looked like every girl's dream – pink tub, pink toilet and sink, pink walls and tiles. There were Barbie dolls and stuffed animals. Radio KGB played "Love Potion No. 9." The pièce de résistance was the mountain of pink bubbles. I could bury myself in there. I'd never seen bubbles like that except in Sandra Dee movies – and every girl wanted to be Sandra Dee.

"You have a nice bath now. When you're done, put on one of these clean muumuus and we'll do your nails." Three pretty floral muumuus swung from a hook on the back of the door. She closed it and I turned the lock. I peeled off my filthy clothes, eager to jump into the bubbles. I didn't know what the scent was, but there was a matching shampoo called Pomegranate Rose. I lathered it into my hair. I played in the bubbles until the water got cold, then let some out and turned the hot tap on. Twice, Mrs. Smith knocked to see if I needed any help.

"I'm fine," I replied, returning to my game of Lady of Loch Tay meets the huzzbee prince.

"How's the lemonade? You want some more?"

"No, thank you." When the hot water ran out and the bubbles were nearly gone, I got out of the tub. My body was still coated with foam and I wiped steam from the mirror to look at myself. I hadn't spent this much time naked since I could remember, and I noticed for the first time that my nipples were more prominent than they used to be. When I felt them, they were hard, tender little lumps. I quickly dried myself using a fluffy pink towel. I debated drinking the lemonade. I was thirsty, but I had a bad feeling about it, so I poured it down the sink. I pulled on a muumuu and went downstairs.

"Just as I thought, you have lovely skin, very white," said Mrs. Smith. While Mary did my nails, Mrs. Smith trimmed my hair, layering it into pretty waves. The snoring had stopped. Mr. Smith was awake. He was staring at me and I didn't like it. I crossed my legs, wishing I'd put my underpants back on. He gulped down his martini and poured another from a Mexican glass pitcher like the one Father used.

Mrs. Smith fluffed my hair and stepped back to look me over. "You look beautiful, honey. You must be sleepy by now. Wouldn't you like to lie down?" She scooped up my dirty clothes and put them in a paper bag that she gave to Mary. "Take Sparky upstairs and show her your room." I didn't want to lie down, but Mary was climbing the stairs with my clothes. I hurried after her, holding my muumuu so Mr. Smith couldn't see up my skirt. I was on high alert now, hoping he would start playing the piano. I had the terrible feeling that he was hunting me.

I expected the bedroom that shared a wall with mine to be a mess, but it was bright and clean. There were four beds with ruffled pink bedspreads. A pink stuffed poodle sat on each pillow. The rug was white and fluffy. I was distracted by its soft feel under my bare feet just long enough for Mr. Smith to grab me from behind, pinning my arms. He pressed his body against me, stroking my skin with his thumbs. "Such pretty skin... so white..." he shoved me face down onto the bed and jammed his knee between my legs so that I couldn't kick.

I was suffocating, with my face buried in a pink poodle. Mr. Smith pulled up my skirt and ran his hand up my thigh, then up my side, pinching my nipple. I struggled to lift my head, barely able to gulp enough air. I caught a glimpse of Kenny standing in the doorway.

"So white... so soft.... Ouch." Mr. Smith went flying sideways.

Mrs. Smith hit him again with the baseball bat. "You pervert," she screamed. "She's not for you. Kiko Aguilar will give us a hundred bucks for a tight little virgin whitey like this one."

She was winding up for another blow when I managed to wiggle free, grab my clothes, and run right into Kenny. His arms were stretched across the opening, like he was blocking it.

"Kenny, grab her." shouted Mrs. Smith.

I pushed against Kenny, who was about my size, but he didn't budge. "Is that the best you've got?" he leered, and I felt my blood boil. I kicked him in the knee and pushed him out of the way so hard that he fell on his behind. I ran down the stairs and out the back door into the Santa Ana winds.

Grit stung my face and body as it blew up my muumuu. I was barefoot, practically naked, stubbing my toes on rocks as I felt my way along the outer wall of the carport and into what should have been the safety of the clubhouse, but the clubhouse was filled with wetbacks. They stared at me with tired, dirty faces. They beckoned for me to shelter with them, but I shook my head. I needed a place to change and that wasn't going to be it.

I felt my way to Father's Mercury. It wasn't locked. I climbed into the backseat and ditched the muumuu, pulling on my own clothes while the wind howled, and grit peppered the windows like tiny bullets. I thought about crying, but how stupid that would be? Instead, I imagined flying over the desert in the yellow biplane, buffeted by howling winds and swirling sand. Suddenly the car door opened. Kenny got in. I started to hit him. "Get down," he said, pulling me flat onto the seat. "Shhh!"

"Kenny, you get her." Mrs. Smith was nearby, shouting. "Bring her back for some nice pink lemonade." We could hear Mr. Smith, too.

Kenny and I lay head to head – our hair touching. "I knew you'd get away," he said. "I had to put on a show for those two."

"Sure, you did." I scowled at him.

"This is for you." He handed me a bottle cap that changed everything. It was the new Dr. Pepper that I'd been searching for. "I have two of them. You can have that one. It's an extra."

The kids in IB collected bottle caps and Kenny was the undisputed bottle-cap king. There wasn't much else to collect around there. "That man isn't my father," he said. "And the witch with the pink hair isn't my mother."

"Where are your parents?"

"Who knows? These two found me in Tijuana. I look pretty white and you heard what they said about Mexican greasers liking tighty whities like me – and you." We didn't say anything more for a long time. We just lay there listening to the storm. What could we say? We were trapped in a Santa Ana windstorm, surrounded by hostile forces of nature that were less frightening to us than the people in our lives. Eventually we sat up and Kenny said, "I want to go to Scotland, too."

"Sure thing," I replied.

He struggled to open the car door against the wind, "Stay away from that pink lemonade. There's bad stuff in there."

By the time I got back to Apartment C, I was filthy again. No one noticed my pink fingernails or my haircut or even seemed aware that I'd been outside, which was fine with me. Later, when Mother found the pink muumuu smelling of Pomegranate Rose in the back of our Mercury, she let Father have it with both shrieking barrels. I said nothing.

The Santa Ana kept us prisoners in our apartments for three days and nights. Sometimes Kenny and I ran the short distance across the courtyard to Patrick and Theresa's. We'd design armor and play with our bottle-cap collections. Mrs. MacDonald slept all day, so we had the run of the apartment if we kept quiet. It would have been a good time to work on our armor, but the aluminum was stashed in the clubhouse and we were afraid to go there. We reckoned that the Mexicans had probably stolen it by now. They needed armor as much as we did.

When the winds finally died down, Imperial Beach had become a colorless landscape buried under a foot of gray dust.

"Good," I thought out loud. "It snowed in the Highlands."

By sundown a refreshing cold wind rolled in from the ocean and the tidelands came alive with wetbacks again. They must have been waiting on the far side of the river and now moved as quickly as they could toward California. They raised a cloud of dust, particularly the ones on motorcycles, in cars, and in trucks.

It was Saturday night again and the IB Apartments were ablaze with red lights and loud music. Mrs. MacDonald sat at her open window in a strapless red dress, looking as glamorous as the rest of the party girls. When she saw me in my window, she shook her blond curls and blew me kisses like Marilyn Monroe. Mrs. Smith stood under her pink porchlight. She welcomed bikers who pulled onto the sidewalk. I could see the logo on the back of their jackets that looked like a snarling wolf. The kids had called them Lobos Locos or "Crazy Wolves." Soon enough, the usual racket started up in the bedroom next to mine – only this time I heard terrified high-pitched barking followed by soul-piercing squeaks that made my hair stand up.

I didn't have to see it. I knew that the little pink poodle was being stomped to death. I held my breath and waited. A few sad whimpers later, footsteps ran up the stairs. I could imagine Mrs. Smith with the baseball bat. "You murdering grease ball," she screamed. The bat smashed against something solid. I heard a long slow moan of pain. "Take that, you Mexican pig. And that ... and that."

The honkytonk piano never stopped playing as if nothing was happening – even when an ambulance came. A man with a swollen, purple face was rolled out on a gurney under my window. I watched him through my blinds. His rolled-up eyes looked dead. Blood trickled out his ears. Later, two policemen stood on the stoop with Mrs. Smith while she made googly eyes at them and gave them money. They left happy. Soon Lobos Locos came back, parking their motorcycles on the sidewalk. The grunting started again in the room next to mine.

All the while, Mr. Smith kept playing his happy tune. I hunched on my bed shivering, my heart racing. I couldn't erase that horrible, bloody face or the howls of the dying poodle. I put on my full armor and spread out my weapons on the bed – a pair of blunt scissors from school, a lighter, a can of hairspray, and a butter knife. They didn't seem like near enough.

The bed next door was thumping against the thin wall. What if it broke and the Lobos Locos came through the hole? I pretended to be a TV actor. I told myself that this life was just a movie. My real life was in Scotland where I'd be safe once I unlocked the secrets of *Miracle Sword*. That old book had already given me Sparky and I was only on page sixty-two.

Eventually, I heard Father snoring, so I screwed in a new light bulb. I had to steal new ones a couple times a week from the carports and laundry rooms. Everyone always blamed the Mexicans. I pored through *Miracle Sword*, searching for a way to escape Imperial Beach. I fell asleep the way I usually did – face down in the book, drooling on the pages. Kenny told me later that the Mexican guy would live – he just had a busted skull. Mrs. Smith made him buy her a new poodle. She dyed it pink too.

I quickly forgot about them in the excitement of Little League Baseball starting up. The ballpark abutted the wetlands on a corner of land between the IB Apartments and Mar Vista High School. On game days, the border opened. Mexican families loved baseball games. They brought truckloads of watermelons and huge tubs of corn-on-the-cob that they boiled and salted. The House of Hotdogs sold hot tamales for 5 cents. I would sit in the stands eating tamales and listening to the Mexicans talk about the day when one of their own would make the big time and play pro ball. Pedro came to watch the games in his jeep. He'd park and meet us under the stands with our deliveries.

"You're a pretty girl, chiquita," he said once, handing me my dime. "Why don't you wash off that dirt so boys can see you?"

I gave him the evil eye. I didn't want boys to see me, not as a girl anyway. The dirtier I was, the safer I felt. Miss Fitch had sent a number of notes home to suggest that my personal hygiene needed improvement.

She recommended that I take more baths, but that wasn't going to happen. I wasn't about to take off my armor or clothes ever again.

Baths were dangerous, they always had been. It was a reality of my childhood that had been reinforced by my experience with the Smiths. And that was the trouble with vacuuming away memories – I forgot to be careful. I missed the warning signs. I should have known better than to get suckered into a bubble bath, even if it was pomegranate rose.

Nothing was ever more ominous than being told to take a bath because it meant that one of Father's "special business friends" was coming to dinner. Those were the times that Mother scrubbed me with a hard-bristled brush. When my skin was scalded and pink, she'd take red, baby-doll pajamas out of her dresser drawer and make me put them on. I hated them. They were too tight and transparent.

I would fight and bite as Mother pushed me into them, smacking me with a hairbrush until I submitted. Then she'd slick down my hair with Wildroot Cream-Oil and hiss in my ear, "You be nice to Mr. Gambolo." She'd pinch me and shove me into the bedroom where a fat old man named Gambolo, or Iserio, or Pocano, sat in his undershorts, chewing on a cigar. Father's special friends had been scrubbed from my memory before I got to Imperial Beach. I needed to believe that things were different now.

After the game, I jumped on Blue Balloon and raced with the warriors to the IB Apartments to make our deliveries. "Ardchoille!" we screamed, flying into the future.

CHAPTER TWENTY

TENT OF WONDERS

T he Halloween Carnival at Mar Vista High was the IB event of the year. It was only a day away and I wasn't going to miss it. We'd been sneaking onto the high school grounds on spy missions dressed in our armor. We watched high school kids putting up booths. They taunted us, "Hey kids. Halloween isn't until tomorrow. Nice costumes, ha ha."

We threw sewer balls at them and were chased away by Coach. "You delinquents get out of here and stay out," he shouted. We ran through the big hole in the boundary fence where it fronted IB Boulevard. Then we headed off to steal carnival posters that the high schoolers were putting up. We crouched low, keeping behind the bushes – following a convertible with teenagers riding on the trunk. They jumped off to glue posters onto telephone poles, bus stops, and fences. We snuck along about 100 feet behind, taking the posters down and rolling them up before the glue dried. I thought they'd be perfect for decorating the Kitty Queen Club. They were big and bright, featuring JoJo the Dog-Faced Boy in his red uniform. But when we tried to unroll them later, they were hopelessly stuck together. When they dried, we could only use them as swords.

On Halloween day, carnival trucks pulled onto the Mar Vista playing field. Roustabouts set up the Tent of Wonders next to a Ferris wheel and bumper cars. "Just wait until you see it after dark," Patrick exclaimed. "It's beautiful."

On the big night, I hurried through dinner and headed to the clubhouse. Kenny, Patrick, Theresa, and a dozen kids were already dressed in their armor. Pedro was there, handing out our parcels and dimes. We went trick-or-treating early to deliver the bags of medicine and get treats from our neighbors. Halloween wasn't much of a big deal at the IB Apartments. Pickings were slim, mostly extra pennies and nickels, but we made a couple of dollars. We put the larger-sized coins in a glass jar where we kept all our tips. They wouldn't fit through the little slot for the dime bank.

I stowed the jar in my closet and hurried back to the clubhouse to put the finishing touches on my costume for the carnival. Theresa had stolen a big jar of Mrs. MacDonald's lanolin face cream to which I'd added a bottle of Mother's blue shoe dye. We'd read a chapter in *Miracle Sword* about the Picts who painted themselves blue before battle. It had scared away the Romans, so it should work against Cubans and greasers. We were spreading it on our arms and faces when a family of wetbacks came through.

"Hola, bambinos," said the father. Children peeked from behind his knees.

"Hola," we said.

Hurdy-gurdy music suddenly echoed around the carport, startling all of us.

"Que pasa?" he asked nervously.

"It's Hal-low-een," said Rock, helpfully. "That's why we're blue."

The woman spoke hurriedly. It sounded like she wanted to turn back. The children clung to their father's pants, looking scared. A horn honked and a convertible overflowing with witches, goblins, and ghosts sped into the carport – teenagers. They spilled out of the car, laughing and whistling – dancing around us on their way to the carnival. Soon after, a dozen Lobos Locos crossed Caspian and pulled onto the sidewalk with an ominous roar. They wore werewolf masks and revved their bikes with hairy hands and long bloody claws. They jumped off and headed through the courtyard doing wolf howls.

That was it for the wetbacks. The family melted back into the shadows. "Adios," I shouted. "Vaya con Dios." I didn't know what it meant. I'd heard it on *Zorro*.

"Let's get moving," said Patrick. "They're opening in ten minutes."

The dark bleachers of the Little League ballpark were the first stage in our plan. They were usually the exclusive territory of the high school kids. They smoked, kissed, and drank from bottles in paper bags. Boys and girls went under the bleachers to kiss lying down or climbed onto the roof of the IB House of Hotdogs. Grade school kids like us were usually chased away, but not on Halloween. The teenagers had gone across the street to the party. We crossed Caspian where it curved into IB Boulevard and ran to the bleachers. The dirt around the hotdog shack was known as the mother lode for bottle-cap collectors. Some of the kids, serious collectors like Kenny, went down on their hands and knees, scratching in the dirt.

"Come on, you idiots," Patrick whisper-shouted. "Get up on the roof before the greasers see you." We scrambled to the top row of seats and jumped onto the roof of the House of Hotdogs. We stood among empty beer bottles and cigarette butts, gaping at the high school across the boulevard. We watched huge crowds mill around in the dark. Lights started to flash randomly in pink, yellow, orange, and purple. Then music swelled and lights coalesced, forming circles around the Ferris wheel and tracing the minarets of the Tent of Wonders.

Patrick was right. "It's beautiful." I exclaimed. Spotlights danced over the crowd showing everyone in costume. Mar Vista looked like Oz – better than Munchkin Land and the Emerald City combined. The Ferris wheel started to turn, gaining speed while the crowd cheered. Teenage girls screamed when the wheel whooshed them into the air.

A microphone squealed. "Ladies and gentlemen, step right up to the amazing, the stupefying Tent of Wonders. In a moment we will raise these damask curtains and you'll see a collection of Oriental oddities that have been exhibited in the palaces of kings." He sounded like somebody famous – a world traveler. I hung on every word. "If you're brave enough to enter the Tomb of Terrors, you'll find the most horrifying collection of living freaks in the world. Yes, yes – these pathetic human creatures are alive. But heed my warning! They are extremely dangerous. Approach them at your peril. Talk to them if you dare. They're chained for your safety. If you get too close, we will not be responsible for what happens." All eyes were glued on the tent, but the curtains remained closed.

"You will see slothful Mathilda, the five-hundred-pound fat lady, the fattest woman in the northern hemisphere."

"I met that fat lady on the train," I bragged. "She has a tiny little head."

"Shut up," said Patrick.

"You'll meet Belinda the Mermaid – half woman and half fish captured off the coast of Zanzibar. I warn you, do not approach this vicious abomination, this creation of the devil. Mothers watch your children. The chains are in place for your safety."

I gasped. The gold damask curtains were rising slowly. The crowd surged forward. Amber light from within lit their excited faces. "And if that isn't enough, you'll see JoJo the Dog-Faced Boy, raised by wolves in the wilds of Siberia." The howl of a wolf startled the crowd. "That's JoJo. He's getting restless. Buy your tickets before he goes wild. We don't want him attacking any more children, not after what happened last week in San Ysidro."

Wallets were out and purses open. Then he said, "Tickets to the Tent of Wonders are only twenty-five cents for adults and five cents for children. That ticket is good for a ride on the Ferris wheel. It's the bargain of the twentieth century."

We were stunned: "Five cents?"

"Crap," exclaimed Gary.

"We need those nickels and pennies," said Patrick. "We need the money jar."

I chewed my lip. No way around it – I'd have to go back to the apartment. "I'll get it. You wait here." I said. I climbed back down the bleachers and dashed across Caspian without looking. I had to get up to my room without getting caught. That meant crossing the living room without being seen.

I took off most of my armor so that the crinkle of aluminum wouldn't give me away and snuck through the back door. Father, Mother, and my brother sat on the couch watching *Wagon Train* with their backs turned to me. I slithered across the room on my stomach using the huzzbee technique I'd developed in the swimming pool. Nobody saw me and I was able to slip up the stairs. I was opening the door to my room when Mother grabbed my hair.

"Where the hell do you think you're going?" She shook me and slapped me a few times. She looked at her hand – the palm was blue. Then she saw the wall. "What in God's name?" I had left a blue smear up the stairs and onto the landing. Blue streaks stained the floor and the walls wherever I had touched them, including one complete handprint on my bedroom door. "You're going to take a bath and then you are going to clean up every bit of this mess. Got it?"

She pushed me into my room and shut the door. I heard her start the bath water. "Don't you even think about sneaking back out. If I catch you again, you'll be sorry." And that was that. I was trapped. I couldn't go out the window – the drop was too far. I couldn't get back downstairs because they would see me for sure and, besides, I'd gotten off easy so far with just a few slaps.

I stood in the middle of my room, trying not to touch anything. Pebbles struck the window. I pulled open the blinds. Carnival lights flashed over the roofs and behind the warriors who stood in the courtyard. Hurdy-gurdy music blared when I opened the window.

"Where's the money jar?"

"I'm grounded."

"Can't you get out? Need a rope?"

I knew that I wasn't getting out. It took all of my energy to keep from sniveling. I had an idea. "Wait a minute." Rushing to my closet, I pulled out the jar. It was about halfway full – more than enough to buy tickets and some ice cream. I put it inside my pillowcase to keep it from breaking.

It hit the ground with a crunch and broke anyway. Fragments of glass and coins scattered all over the sidewalk. Kids rushed to scoop them up. They swore as they cut their fingers, but nobody cried.

"Thanks, Sparky," Patrick shouted. I watched them run in a mob across the courtyard, all discipline forgotten in their mad race to the Tent of Wonders.

I let loose my tears of self-pity in the bathtub while Mother scrubbed me down with the hated bristle-brush. She kept scrubbing, but the blue dye didn't come off. I cried myself to sleep with my hands and hair covered in Saran Wrap. It was hot and itchy, but I was afraid to take it off.

I was still blue in the morning when I snuck out of the apartment and crossed the street to Mar Vista. It was a typical Saturday morning and there wasn't another human in sight. A flock of seagulls cawed and squawked over half-eaten hotdogs, pretzels, and waxed paper that littered the ground. They barely moved aside when I made my way to the rides. Up close, the bumper cars looked tired. The exposed metal parts were rusty. The paint came off on my fingers like chalk. I sat in one of the Ferris wheel cars, swinging it, pretending that it was about to sweep me into the air. It squeaked on a rusty hinge, its paint faded and chipped. I recalled the movie sets in the Lookout Mountain studio. On film they looked like castles, forests, pyramids. In real life, they were nothing but painted cardboard.

The curtain to the Tent of Wonders stirred in the breeze so I went in. The tent seemed smaller than it had the night before, worn out without the music and the lights. I wondered if the "pathetic human creatures" were still inside. The Tomb of Terrors was open. It was darker and a little bit scarier. JoJo's empty cage was there with the door ajar. Up close, I could see it was made of wood and chicken wire. I tripped over a chain and followed it to the wall. It was plastic, sewn to the canvas and held in place with black tape. A sign painted on the canvas said, "Belinda the Mermaid. Beware!" I pulled on the flimsy chain. How could that hold a vicious creature from the deep? She must not be very strong.

The Tent of Wonders and the Tomb of Terrors weren't scary at all. I pretended to be Belinda until I heard the scrape of a chair on the other side of the canvas. Someone tuned a radio to the news. I smelled coffee.

It was time to go.

CHAPTER TWENTY-ONE

THE BLUE BELLS OF SCOTLAND

When the rainy season finally hit, the deluge did have the effect of Father's giant toilet flushing. But he had not taken into account what would get flushed where. Within the first few days of the monsoon, a tidal wave of garbage, sewage, animal carcasses, tar, bottles, cans, old mattresses, and car parts surged into the Tijuana River, depositing a five-foot wall of debris on both banks. Then tidewaters flooded the estuary, spreading garbage and sewage everywhere. The old Stink was nothing compared to the new Stink.

"Nothing stinks like Tijuana in the rain," said Kenny. We were sitting in the backseat of the Mercury with our bottle-cap collections spread on the seat. "Mexicans dump their crap in the street and wait all year for the rainy season to wash it down here. After a while it gets washed into the ocean."

"Do you remember Tijuana?" I asked. "From when you were a kid?" Kenny had a lot of bottle caps from Mexico. I picked up a pretty orange one with a black bull on it. Kenny didn't like to talk about Tijuana. That was fair enough. I didn't like to talk about Chicago or Seattle. But since all of their garbage was now in our backyard, I thought I should know something about the place. I probed a little deeper. "What's it like?"

"Lots of homeless kids in the Zona Norte." He took the bottle cap from my fingers and put it back into proper order. We played quietly until Gary, Rock, Patrick, and Theresa climbed into the car. After a while, we made so much noise that Father came out and chased us away. When the rain let up for a few minutes, we crossed to the far side of Caspian and looked down into the great swirls of refuse that floated where high tide met the flooded river. When the tide ebbed, garbage was washed out to sea like Father had said, only to be replaced by the next massive discharge from Tijuana. It was like a toilet flushing, filling up, and flushing, over and over. Fortunately, other things were afoot to take our minds off of the new Stink. IB Elementary was gearing up for the holidays and I had been selected as the lead artist to design the school's Thanksgiving mural.

"I'm so excited," bubbled Miss Fitch. "Sparky is in charge of choosing a name for our class and picking who will be on the painting team. Last year the mural was painted by Mrs. Hannah's Bananas, the year before, Mr. Stoltz's Colts, and before that, Mr. Kerry's Berries..."

Gary, who was pretty quick, had his hand up. "Does the name have to rhyme with Fitch?"

I had been running the unfortunate possibilities through my mind – Fitch's itches, twitches, witches, bitches. It wasn't good. I had my hand up.

"Yes, Sparky." There was only one possible choice in my mind. Most of the class was still blue. Mrs. Lipsky had looked us over the day after Halloween and sent notes home suggesting a special soap that nobody could afford. Fortunately, it was fading – slowly. "How about Miss Fitch's Bluebells of Scotland."

Our teacher looked relieved. "That's a lovely name. Can you tell me what a bluebell of Scotland is?"

"Well," I said. "It's a bell and it's blue..."

"It's a flower that grows in the Scottish Highlands. Tomorrow, I'll bring you a picture and we'll start learning about the biology of flowering plants."

By recess, the blue kids had become the cool kids. Everyone wanted to work on the school mural. There were a lot of perks to being on the painting team, including access to the roll of butcher paper in the supply closet and time away from class. For me, choosing the team was easy. If you were blue, you were in as a Bluebell of Scotland. We had kids on the team from kindergarten through sixth grade. Miss Fitch said that I was very "egalitarian." That sounded like a good thing.

A huge piece of butcher paper was spread on the floor of the auditorium. Miss Fitch gave me a box of Polaroid pictures of murals from previous years. I looked them over and found them depressing – too much black with darkly dressed Pilgrims and Indians in mud-colored buckskins, I had other plans. I dressed my pilgrims in kilts and, to make the effect of tartans, covered them in squares that I filled in with every color except black or brown.

Once I had painted a few pilgrims and drawn the outline for the rest of the mural, the Bluebells of Scotland were unleashed with paints and brushes. It was their job to paint the rest of the squares any colors they wanted. Most of them couldn't paint within the lines and primary colors blended together in the full palette of the color wheel.

It looked so good that I drew squares on the Indians' clothes and even in the sky. The Bluebells used every possible color on my carefully drawn leaves. We had so many kids working on the project that every square inch of the eight-foot long mural was covered in one-inch squares of color. Somehow it all worked, even though the only clearly identifiable structure was an orange pumpkin.

Mrs. Pendrake loved it and made sure it was photographed for the *North County Times*. The result was described in the newspaper as a cross between a Gustav Klimt and Jackson Pollack. After Thanksgiving, the mural hung in the San Diego Art Museum until Christmas. An eight by ten-inch color photograph of it was tacked up in the trophy case next to the principal's office.

IB Elementary prepared for Christmas. The Bluebells of Scotland were put in charge of painting the Christmas nativity scene. I had free access to the supply room, which meant that I was often alone in there with boxes of pencils, reams of foolscap, rolls of butcher paper, and endless light bulbs. In the name of the Clan MacGregor, I helped myself.

After school, we stretched out long sheets of butcher paper on the floor of the clubhouse and drew pictures of Highland battles. On the tablets of stolen foolscap, we designed full body armor, complete with moving joints and elaborate decorations. Soon, my lieutenants and I were coming to class wearing breastplates under our clothes. We carried shields. Miss Fitch agreed to this only as long as we hung them with our coats at the back of the room. She made it very clear that swords and other weapons were not tolerated at school.

We learned Christmas carols and I sang a solo verse of "What Child Is This?" for the big school concert. We had punch and cookies with the parents and teachers after the show. We finally walked home late at night in a chattering cluster of parents and kids. For the next two weeks, we'd be on holiday break.

I should have been more careful, but I was happy. In a few days, it would be Christmas. The whole school had participated in the St. James Church blanket drive and on New Year's Day, the class that raised the most money for blankets would go on the bus to deliver them to the Tijuana Orphanage.

We had raised over thirty dollars in dimes for our medicine deliveries. The Bluebells of Scotland were sure to win.

CHAPTER TWENTY-TWO

FOLLOW THE PIPER

Father bought a fake Christmas tree at the PX and brought it home in a box. "It's a nice one from Japan, Fatso. Let's put it together." He put up a center pole that had holes for the branches. We got it assembled after a few false starts and it looked pretty good although it smelled like plastic.

Out came old boxes with strings of lights that needed to be untangled and tested, packages of ornaments and tinsel. My brother and I fought over how to put on the tinsel while Father sorted the lights. Mother was in the kitchen peeling potatoes. A roasting chicken filled the apartment with good smells. I was laughing, being silly. My brother and I jumped up and down cheering when Father plugged in the colored lights. Then Father sat at the kitchen table and lit a cigarette. "What d'ya say, Weezie? Shall we give it to her?"

I was surprised. "What? A present? But Christmas isn't until Friday."

Mother looked me over skeptically. "Do you want it or not?"

"Yes…of course I do!" I felt giddy.

"I don't know," said Mother. "You haven't been a good girl this year. If we lived in Norway, you'd be lucky to get a lump of coal for Christmas."

Father looked at his watch. "Just give her the box. We've got a time schedule."

I was delighted by the big, shiny, pink box that Mother slid in front of me. I pulled the white satin ribbon and lifted the lid. Wrapped in pink tissue was a filmy, pale green nightgown. It had a matching robe that tied with a green satin ribbon. It was breathtaking. I'd never seen anything so beautiful. This was something Sandra Dee would wear.

"It's called a peignoir set," said Mother.

"Every girl should have one," said Father.

I danced around the room, holding it up in front of me in the hall mirror. "I'm going to put it on."

"Oh, no, you don't." Mother grabbed my collar. "You're filthy and you'll ruin it. First, you take a bath." She filled the tub with steaming water. I locked the door, pulled off my clothes, and scrubbed myself down. I even washed my hair and cleaned under my fingernails. I hadn't spent this much time in a bath since Mrs. Smith's bubbles.

I pulled on the negligée and admired myself in the mirror. Did I look more like the Lady of Loch Tay or a movie star? I turned from side to side, posing. Then I noticed that my nipples were visible through the filmy material. I touched them and felt a burning tingle between my legs. It was pleasant, but ominous. Shadows of other Christmases crowded onto the edge of my vision. I had to lean against the sink to keep from vomiting.

Instinct told me to rip off the peignoir, put on my dirty clothes and run away. I fingered the material. It was lovely. When I looked up into the mirror again, I looked grown up. I was five feet three inches tall and ten years old, nearly a teenager. Everything was different now. My parents had given me a lovely gift that showed how much they loved me.

What was wrong with me? Instead of being grateful, I was acting like a scared little brat. I was being selfish and silly. I slid my arms into the flowing robe, tied it and bounded down the stairs.

A whiff of English Leather was the only warning I had before Vito grabbed me from behind. Someone shoved a needle into my arm. I broke free, swinging my fists, but the room was spinning. I struck wildly, ready to kick, claw, and bite. I staggered. My feet got tangled in strings of Christmas lights and I crashed onto the coffee table, upending it.

"Stop her," Mother yelled. "She's going to knock over the tree."

Two men tackled me. They rolled me in a blanket and tossed me in the back of a van. Vito climbed into the front seat and I recognized another of the Dr. Whites when he turned around to stare at me. "Isn't this the kid you cold-cocked in Laurel Canyon last year?"

A cold wave of outrage jolted me, thrusting me into the place where Christmas memories were stored. I knew what was about to happen. I was going to be a party favor. Children were going to die – maybe me. I struggled to move, but I was helpless.

Last Christmas, it had taken four of them to hold me down and still I'd screamed until someone stuffed a sock in my mouth. They'd laughed when I gagged and nearly vomited. Then they started sticking me with their big red things. They didn't think it was so funny when my leg got loose, and I kicked one of them in his ugly sac as hard as I could. Someone whacked me on the head. I lost consciousness just as someone else was saying, "You can't kill that one. She's got the mark on her."

I'd woken up in a hospital. Mother was telling a doctor how I was a bad kid who'd jumped out a window and cracked open the top of my head.

That had been a year ago. I'd forgotten about it at Grandma and Grandpa's. Then Father had promised me that things would be different in Imperial Beach. I'd believed him.

"She won't be any trouble tonight," said Vito from the driver's seat. "Look at her."

"What'd you give her? She looks dead."

"Cuban blend. She'll be okay for the party. We'll keep her doped up this time, or she fights, remember?"

"Little bitch nearly castrated Joey Trumbull. I took both of them to the ER."

I shivered, hot and cold at the same time. "Fitch's Bitches," I tried to say. The van hit a bump and my body jerked. Someone next to me moaned. Someone else was crying.

"She's wakin' up. Give her more of that Cuban whatever."

"Nah, might kill her. Who wants to fuck some dead kid?"

"Joey Trumbull comes to mind."

I drifted off and awoke to the scent of cinnamon. I was being carried past garlands of fresh pine, bright with fairy lights. Wreathes draped the walls. A log snapped and blazed in a stone fireplace. Nanny Black's white cap and moustache came into focus. He laid me on a bed of pine boughs and lit a cigar. "This is your sacred bower, Goddess Godgyf. It is my honor to serve a thirteenth-generation witch."

He hummed, puffing smoke while braiding ribbons and flowers into my hair. He arranged my peignoir, crossing my arms and placing my hands on my breasts. "You look good enough to eat." He stroked my cheek. I heard the bleating of goats. *They're all going to die.* I dozed until someone shook me.

"Godgyf, wake up." I struggled to open my eyes. I saw the face of an angel.

"I'm Minerva." The girl looked about my age. She was blond and wore the same peignoir set. I tried to get up, but my feet were far away, on someone else's body. Another face appeared, a red-haired girl with terrified green eyes. She also wore a peignoir.

"Lots of kids are here," said Minerva. "Vito gave us special names for the party. This is Elf, or something like that."

The redhead burst into tears. "I don't remember my name ... Elfie, Elfin ... I don't know. I'm so scared."

"Shhh! They're coming."

I woke again with men standing over me – some wore Navy whites and some, khakis. "Hey Joey," laughed Vito. "Here's your Christmas present."

Joey Trumbull bent down to my face. "That's the one who busted my balls." He poked me in the ribs a few times. I couldn't move no matter how I tried. My brain was disconnected from the rest of me. He unzipped his pants. I tried to scream, to shout, spit, to curse him in Gaelic, but could only moan. "I'll nail the little cunt this time."

"First you pay the piper."

Joey pulled out his wallet and counted bills into Vito's hand. How many times had I lived through this scene before?

When I woke again, my nighty was pushed above my waist. I wanted to push it down, but Joey Trumbull lay on top of me, pounding me with his red thing and muttering, "Good little cunt, good little cunt." I could feel nothing.

Minerva ran past me, shrieking, "Help me! Help me!" I saw other little girls in green peignoirs and men with no pants on. Fauns danced through the room playing flutes and drums. I tried to follow them with my eyes, but the room spun. I had to get away but couldn't move. I closed my eyes, willing myself to die.

"Sparky, Sparky...hey, kid." It was the marble-sized head of the Fat Lady on a long stalk, protruding from one of Joey's ears. A second head came out of Joey's other ear. The two of them yelled at me in tinny little voices, "Kid, don't give up. Don't ever give up. They win if you give up. You can get out of here – follow the piper."

I searched the room. Sailors and naval officers were everywhere. A goat screamed, then a child. A dozen little girls were running around in terror. Uniformed MPs stood at the door with their arms crossed, blocking their escape. I forced myself to concentrate. I floated out of my body and followed the notes from the flute as they danced up through the smoky air in search of a crack in the ceiling. There had to be a way to the freedom of open sky.

From a great height, I looked down on my body. The hairy ass of a sailor pounded away on me. My nightgown was up under my arms, my legs and arms spread, my palms up as if in surrender. My hair floated around me on a pillow. I looked like an angel. I moaned in defiance.

"You like this, don't ya, baby?" snorted the sailor. Fury rose in my chest. I lost the sound of the flute and fell back into my body – the last place I wanted to be. I panicked, staring out through my own eyes like a terrified animal. I searched the bedlam for the music of the flute again. I couldn't find it.

The sailor's ears sprouted fat-lady heads. A dozen tiny pairs of eyes zeroed in on mine. "The tinfoil, rip it off," squeaked twelve little faces.

"Do it with your brain." With all the power of my mind, I fought to control my fear. The sailor was pumping faster, getting ready to scream. "Tinfoil. Now!" the heads shrieked. The walls of the room were covered in foil. My body was wrapped in foil. The man who had just shouted and collapsed on top of me was wrapped in foil. "Free yourself. Leave all this behind."

I tore foil from my arms, freed my hands. Then I ripped it from my face and head – kicking my legs free and unwrapping the rest of my body. The more I tore away, the lighter I became. I floated upward until I was out of my body altogether. "Don't stop. Follow that piper – now." A flute-playing faun danced past. My ears zeroed in on the melody. I followed the creature to a forest path just as its cloven hoof disappeared behind a tree. I raced around the bend and ran right into him.

"What are you doing, little girl?" He tapped the flute against the palm of his hand.

"Following the piper like the fat ladies said."

"Not this piper." The faun rolled his eyes. "Those pipers."

I heard the howling whine of bagpipes. A dozen pipers burst through the underbrush, wearing kilts in the red and green tartan of MacGregor. Following them on a warhorse was handsome, black-haired Robin Abroch MacGregor. I'd made it to Scotland. He scooped me up and hoisted me onto his saddle. "Take the reins, Sparky. You're in control here."

I nestled against him the way I used to do when I still had Daddy. His arms felt strong and safe around me. I put my head on his chest to hear his beating heart. Whenever I saw tinfoil grow up his arm and onto my skin. I tore it off. I had to stay diligent in my mind, alert to the dangers. He set me down at the edge of the loch. "There's someone who wants to see you," he said.

I waded into clear, cold water and saw the reflection of brave Sparky wearing her kilt and armor instead of the terrified girl in a peignoir. The Lady of Loch Tay rose from the water, barely rippling the surface. She stroked my hair and led me to the shore. We sat together on the sand. She whispered, "You are my favorite warrior, little Sparkler."

"God, what a man," screamed the next sailor, rolling off me.

"I'm no good," I sobbed in the lady's arms. "I'm not brave enough. When they hurt me I cry."

"You're strong. You're a MacGregor. MacGregors never give up. We survive despite them. You will grow up. You will survive."

"But they're killing me."

The screams of a child intruded. It rippled the waters of Loch Tay with a foul wind that darkened the sky and forest. Then came something worse – a howl of mortal pain.

"Minerva…Minerva…." I wept, holding tight to the Lady, burying my face in the folds of her gown, choking on my tears. I was helpless. I had no control over anything. They could do whatever they wanted with me and the other girls. Tinfoil grew up my arms and over my chest. It covered my face until I couldn't breathe. I didn't care. I didn't want to live anymore. Why didn't they cut out my heart, too?

The lady tore it away. "There is nothing you can do to save that poor girl. You're just a child yourself. These children won't survive, but you will. I promise."

The music of flutes and drums started again. Someone drew a star with warm liquid on my forehead, over the scar of Mepa's upside down cross. A man in a purple robe said, "Godgyf, you have been anointed by Satan in the blood of an innocent."

I screamed soundlessly, wanting to get Minerva's sacrifice off of me, but I couldn't. The Lady dipped her robe in the loch and washed away the blood. I sobbed in her arms. She quieted me like a mother, whispering, "What happens down there isn't real. Only this is real. Remember that, Sparkler – only this is real." She placed a silver dagger in my hands. "This is magic. It will protect you until you're big enough for the real Miracle Sword. You must grow up and be strong, so that no more children will have to die."

I held up the dagger. "I'll save them, Lady, all of them. I promise."

The light faded. I knew it was time for me to leave. I had one last question: "Why didn't they kill me too?"

"You have something special." The lady smiled, melting back into the water. "They think that you belong to them."

"Do I?" The Lady was gone. A pale light shimmered below the surface. I splashed into the water, making ripples and waves. "Do I belong to them?" I beat the water with my silver dagger, shouting, "Who am I?" The loch shattered like a mirror and I fell to Earth with the broken pieces.

The new grunt had fat lady heads sticking up all over his body. "Happy New Year," they screamed in unison.

I woke up in my bed at the IB Apartments. There was no sign of my peignoir set. I never wanted to see it again anyway. Father came in with a cold glass of Tang. "School tomorrow, but first – one last little treat for you, Fatso." He handed me the glass. "This is from Vito. It's something new called LSD. Let's see what it does for you."

I was desperately thirsty and gulped it down before I thought about what Father had just said. As soon as he left, I was up trying to turn on the light, but the light bulb was missing. I pulled on some underpants and an undershirt, then dug in the closet for a bulb. I reached up to screw it in and the bed lurched. Everything in the room began to move. *Suckered again.* When would I learn?

The usual grunting and bumping in the room next to mine was so loud that it roared like a train through my head. I crouched down with hands over my ears. I heard scratching on the glass of my window. A thousand pairs of fiery eyes stared at me. "You've got something special. You belong to us," they hissed. Mr. Smith's honkytonk sounded hyped-up and edgy. Notes poured into the air and broke into other notes, coming at me rat-a-tat-tat like machine gun bullets. Ready to fight, I pulled out my weapons – the butter knife, scissors, cigarette lighter, hairspray, and now my silver dagger. An army of creatures hovered under my bed and in my closet. "You belong to us." A tattooed arm burst through my wall. The tattoos danced, twisting like snakes that slithered onto the ground.

A powerful hand grabbed me by the hair and pulled my head against the wall. I didn't think twice. I cut it off with my dagger. Piano notes in bright colors flowed like blood through the hole, pelting me in the face while creatures outside shrieked, "Olé! Olé! You are ours." They slapped the window with their tongues and claws.

Another arm burst through the wall and I burned it with the roaring flame of the cigarette lighter. It flared green and curled into ash like the Wicked Witch of the West. An angry face appeared in the hole, I sprayed it with hairspray that burst into flames like a flamethrower. I turned to do battle with the creatures at the window.

Their tongues were sliding through the glass, wrapping themselves around my arms and legs. "Ours, ours. You look good enough to eat." I fought to free myself. I threw everything I could find at the window until it broke. A wall of yellow paint gushed into the room and swirled around, dancing with the notes, pelting me with pennies and nickels. The paint flowed out through the hole in the wall into the Smiths' apartment, taking the notes and the monsters with it.

I covered the hole with a pie tin and hammered it into place. I took an iron stake from under my bed and drove it into the wall with a sledge-hammer, hitting it over and over until I drove it through into the other room. Then I set to work cutting up aluminum. I was up all night, muttering Gaelic curses, throwing bricks at the monsters, and making armor.

I woke up when the alarm clock went off. It was time for school. I was lying on the floor. Other than the mess I'd made, my room looked normal. There were no holes in the wall. The window wasn't broken. I searched through piles of clothes and papers but couldn't find my silver dagger. Was it real?

I caught my reflection in the mirror. Huge eyes with dark circles stared back at me. I'd lost weight over Christmas break and my clothes hung loose. When I came downstairs, Father thought I looked so funny that he took my picture. "Smile, Fatso." His new Polaroid flashed. I glared at him. I couldn't even muster an evil eye.

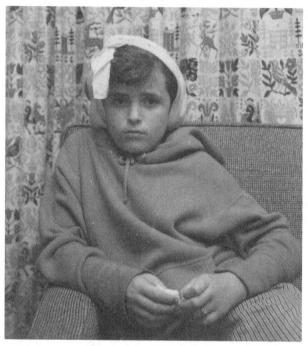

I met up with Patrick and the other kids for the walk to school. The dime bank was in my lunch pail. A thick fog blanketed IB that felt like an extension of my mind. I dreaded the moment when someone would ask me where I'd been. But the kids were quiet. We cut across Mar Vista, each lost in our own thoughts.

CHAPTER TWENTY-THREE

CHILDREN OF THE MIST

P atrick emptied the dime bank on Miss Fitch's desk. "Three hundred and thirty-six dimes," he announced. "That's $33.60 from the Bluebells of Scotland."

She stared at the pile of dimes and exclaimed, "Goodness. That's so much money. You should have won the contest." She took a breath but didn't ask where it had come from. Instead, she exhaled a soft whistle that amplified and reverberated in the hung-over echo chamber of my head.

I kept my face down, watching fish swim in the wood grain of my desk. I felt numb, certain that I would never muster a smile again.

"It's too late for the contest. Mr. Kerry's Berries got to go to Tijuana," she said. I knew that already. I'd seen the photos on display by the principal's office. Miss Fitch chewed her pencil. I felt her stare drill into my brain as if she knew it was my fault that we hadn't delivered our dimes in time.

We'd waited until the last minute to turn it in because Pedro promised us a Christmas bonus. I had just put the last of the bonus dimes in the bank when Father called me downstairs to assemble the Christmas tree and mother gave me the peignoir set.

That meant the money stayed in my closet and never reached St. James. The Bluebells were knocked out of the contest and it was my fault. I turned my head and stared out the window, watching the fog flatten the world into blank white paper. Guilt was added to my book of misery.

Mr. Miller came to the classroom after recess to congratulate the Bluebells. "I've given the money to Pastor John. St. James will deliver the blankets on their next trip to Tijuana. We will give you a special mention in the school display box." He paused. The unspoken question of how we had acquired such a large amount of cash hovered over his head like a thought bubble in a comic book.

I had a bubble over my head, too, but it was empty. I'd sent legions of little brooms and vacuum cleaners scurrying behind my eyeballs to erase my memories of that terrible Christmas. Doors were slamming shut to memories of cinnamon and pine, then double-locked, triple-locked, and pounded with nails. Soon, only my feelings would remain as question marks, without reasons. Eventually, those too would fade.

My eyelids felt heavy. I put my head on my arm and woke up when Patrick vomited bright red blood at my feet. Mrs. Lipsky escorted him from the classroom, threatening to call his mother and "read her the riot act." That made Patrick cry.

Gary shouted, "Mrs. Lipsky, you can't call his mother."

Mrs. Lipsky did call Mrs. MacDonald, but not for Patrick. A short time later, during lunch break, Theresa collapsed on the playground, her arms and legs twitching violently. I ran over and saw Mrs. Lipsky kneeling by the fallen girl. "It's a seizure. Call an ambulance and get that MacDonald woman down here."

The ambulance came, all sirens and flashing lights. Mrs. MacDonald and Mrs. Lipsky disappeared into the back where Theresa lay, impossibly small beneath a mound of blankets. They drove off in a fury of sound and dust, leaving us standing in the silent fog. Patrick had fallen asleep in the nurse's office. He didn't hear anything about Theresa until he wandered back to class much later.

"Oh no, poor Patrick," said Miss Fitch. She took him to the principal's office. "We'll be back in ten minutes. Sparky, you're in charge."

"Me?" I protested. I wasn't in charge of anything. Instead of going to the front of the class like I would on a normal day, I laid my head down again and felt like I might stop breathing. The class should have erupted into pandemonium, but it didn't. Gary, the lead troublemaker, sat quietly, carving his initials on the desktop, Kenny played with his bottle caps, Linda and Sandy whispered in the back of the room. When Patrick and Miss Fitch returned, we were motionless, soundless. Patrick took his seat without looking at me. I saw that he'd been crying. I turned away and stared out the window.

The silence was terrible until Miss Fitch taped her ruler at the front of the classroom and said, "Sparky, take three other students down to the supply room. Get a big sheet of paper and whatever paints you want. The Bluebells are going to make a get-well card for Theresa – something bright and cheery to hang on her wall at the hospital. Patrick can take it to her after school."

My head jerked up – a quest. Even better, an art project. Soon, we were in the supply room, arguing about the theme and the colors. Gary and Albert wanted to do a battle scene with swords and men in kilts. Donna and I wanted to paint the Lady of Loch Tay. As a compromise, we tore off two pieces of butcher paper.

CHILDREN OF THE MIST

The boys painted the battle of Glenfroon with lots of blood and arrows while the girls painted the Lady of Loch Tay hovering over a blue pond surrounded by fairies and flowers. We spent the rest of the school day on the floor with pencils and paints. Mr. Miller gave us permission to stay late after school to finish. Kids from other classes came by to help. Then he drove Miss Fitch and Patrick to the hospital.

Walking home without the MacDonalds, we played a game called, "Children of the Mist." The MacGregors were notorious for emerging from the mists of Scotland to steal cattle and disappearing back into the fog before they could be caught. I told that story as we ran around the Mar Vista fields, playing tag. We heard Coach shout, "Get off this property, you delinquents. I'll have you all put into juvie."

We looked at one another, questioning whether this latest threat was real. We knew he probably couldn't see us since we couldn't see him, so Gary shouted, "You'll have to catch us first."

With that, we gave the Highland war cry that had sent shivers of fear throughout the Scottish countryside, "Ardchoille! Ardchoille! Ardchoille!" Then we ran.

Chapter Twenty-four

Tunnel to Scotland

Time, rain, and high tides flushed the garbage from Tijuana out to sea. When the fog lifted, we took to our bicycles again, plunging downhill to the settling ponds, over dirt dikes, and into the estuary. I didn't care about the foul mist or the stink or the damp ground that made for slow going. I pedaled hard, working up a sweat and howling like a Highland wolf.

I wanted to forget Christmas. We all wanted to forget that Theresa was still in the hospital. Mrs. Lipsky had told us that she'd bled inside her brain. She was in a coma. No one was allowed to visit her – even Patrick.

Pedro had warned us that there might be quicksand after the rains, so we stopped far short of the Tijuana River. Our deliveries were getting heavier. The medicine came in brick-sized parcels now. It was wrapped in brown paper that fit in our lunch boxes. We were delivering about twenty parcels a day.

We sat on our bikes, winded and panting, waiting for Pedro. Then Patrick asked the question I'd been dreading: "Where were you on Christmas break?"

Kenny said, "We came looking for you. Your dad said you went to a party."

Linda frowned. "We thought you ran away with the money."

They waited, drilling me with their eyes. I'd spent days trying to think of what to tell them, but my head was a muddle, my thoughts dissolving faster than I could form new ones.

I wanted to tell them the truth, but the truth was insane. When I caught mental flashes of Nanny Black's mustache or tiny heads growing out of Joey Trumbull's ears, I had to close my eyes and hum the visions away. I didn't want my friends to think I was crazy.

"I-I didn't take the money," I stuttered. "It was in my closet."

"We couldn't get it."

"We lost the contest."

"We should have won."

"I went to Scotland," I said, avoiding their eyes. "The Lady of Loch Tay gave me her silver dagger."

"Then where the hell is it?" Patrick challenged. "Show us this silver dagger."

I stared at my shoes, wishing that he'd just hit me and go away. My voice was a raspy whisper. "Father gave me LSD and monsters took it."

"Bullshit," Patrick threw down his bike and kicked it. I'd never seen him so angry. "That's just one of your goddamn lies." His lip trembled. He was close to tears. "Tell us the truth, for once."

I couldn't look at his red, angry face. "It's kinda true," I mumbled.

"Oh yeah? We're never going to Scotland and you're a goddamn liar."

His words cut me deep. "I don't tell lies. I tell stories." Everything good in my life – even Sparky – came from stories, but he did have a point. Stories were lies, technically.

"It's not fair," said Gary. "You make us believe you. Then you disappear."

I might as well disappear forever. I was going to die of a weak heart anyway. In a year or so Mema would look in her hatbox and be surprised to find the 5 x 7 color school picture that I'd put in there. "Weezie, who is this child?" she'd ask.

Mother would frown. "I don't remember her name – she had so many."

"Just tell us where you were," said Rock, breaking my reverie.

"I saw two men put you in a van," said Kenny.

"Who were they?" Linda asked. "Where did they take you?"

What could I tell them about Christmas? I closed my eyes, squeezing them until time slowed and rolled backwards into the memory of cinnamon and pine. A faun danced past, waving his flute. He winked at me. "Follow the pipers – don't you remember?" he said. "And what did the Lady of Loch Tay tell you?"

"Only this is real," I murmured.

"Look at me, goddammit," Patrick shouted in my face.

A dozen tiny fat-lady heads sprouted from his ears, their voices squeaking, "Rip off the tinfoil and get away."

"What tinfoil? Where is it?" I screamed in my mind.

"It's in your head," they shouted. "Rip it away with your brain." I fell into the well of my mind, tearing tinfoil from my arms and legs, growing lighter. I began to float, whispering, "Only this is real.…only this is real." Patrick was gone. The warriors were gone. The wetlands spun around me, blurring into the green of the yin/yang wheel. I heard the men in purple robes chanting, "There is no joy…there is no sorrow…there is no truth… there are no lies…there are no enemies…there are no friends…"

"Bullshit," screamed the fat lady.

"Only this is real…Only this is real," I repeated. And there it was – the growl of bagpipes so loud that the sand roiled and buckled under my feet. I was sucked into the ground, spiraling through space until I blinked and hovered above Loch Tay. My breath rippled the water. Below the surface the Lady smiled.

"Sparkler, you've come to see me again."

"Lady, please take me to Scotland. I've hurt my friends. I have to get away from here."

"You must do it yourself. Draw a circle on the ground. When you've filled it in exactly the way it looks in Scotland, a tunnel will open. Jump through and I'll catch you."

"Can we all come to Scotland?"

"Of course." Her light faded.

"Where's my dagger?" I shouted.

"It's safe with me." Before the Lady vanished, I glimpsed a flash of silver.

I came out of my trance with a war whoop, startling everyone. My dagger was safe, and I'd found the way to Scotland. I jumped off Blue Balloon and did a victory dance. It was so obvious. How could I have missed it all this time? I had to show my friends.

I searched through clumps of refuse until I found a long, strong stick. "We can get to Scotland and I know how," I declared. I drew a big circle in the sand. "This is our tunnel. All we have to do is to draw it perfectly so that it matches the other side in Scotland. Then it'll open and we can jump into Loch Tay."

I filled the circle with details of the Scottish landscape the way that the Lady might see it when she looked up through the water. Father would call this a fish-eye's view of the pond. I drew overhanging trees, clouds, flying birds. The Bluebells crowded around the circle. We'd already done three art projects together. We were a well-honed team. I had their attention, even Patrick's. He looked miserable, but I could tell he was interested.

"See how it looks? Pretend that you're under water, looking into the forest. It's just like looking up from the bottom of the swimming pool."

"How will we know when we have it right?" asked Linda.

"The sand will turn into water and you'll see sunlight shining through from the other side. When that happens, jump and we'll be in Scotland in a few seconds."

"Will we see the Lady of the Lake?"

"Will I get a bow and arrows?"

"Do I have to wear a kilt?"

The questions didn't last long. The warriors spread out to find sticks. They covered the wet sand with circles, filling them in with fanciful landscapes. We stayed long after Pedro handed out our packages. We forgot that in winter it grew dark early until the first wetbacks approached. "Vámonos bambinos," they said with a flurry of hand gestures that signaled it was time for us to go home.

We rode back toward Caspian, but no matter how hard we pedaled, the going was slow, and people swarmed around us. There were men, women, children, mothers carrying babies. They warned us to hurry because motorcycles were coming. The Lobos Locos would knock us down and steal our lunch boxes if they caught us. Patrick urged the warriors to pedal harder. I muttered Gaelic spells that made our bicycles take flight.

It was raining by the time we finished deliveries and went home. I fell asleep to honkytonk, the yips of Mrs. Smith's new pink poodle, and the rumble of thunder.

Chapter Twenty-five

Welcome to the Magick

Torrents of rain kept us out of the estuary. IB Boulevard flooded and the school playground was under an inch of water. Raw sewage floated into town.

The school was making us stay inside to take comprehensive IQ tests instead of our usual classes. Miss Fitch explained that this was the State of California's response to the Russian launch of Sputnik. We were making our contribution to the space race by sitting at our desks and working through endless test booklets with No. 2 pencils.

After school, we sprawled on the floor of the carport, drawing tunnel designs on butcher paper until it got too wet. It was the best we could do until the ground dried out. Pedro brought our deliveries to the carport. "Stay outta the marshes cuz they really dangerous right now. Crazy wetbacks're drownin'. We got quicksand and lotsa typhus."

I'd make it home in time for dinner. Afterward, while the family sat on the sofa watching *Wagon Train* or *Cheyenne* or *Maverick,* I stretched out on the floor, drawing tunnels on paper bags, receipts, tin can labels, cardboard boxes – any paper I could find. On Friday nights, however, *Zorro* had my undying attention. I was in love with Don Diego de la Vega.

"Put on a dress tomorrow," said Father when he turned off the TV. "I'm taking you to Sunday school."

On Saturday? I didn't argue. He must mean art class. I was up early and ready to go. Rain dripped through the canvas roof of the Mercury as Father drove past St. James Church. We also sped past the exit to Balboa Park and the Art Museum. My stomach tensed. "Are we going to the Annex?"

"Shut up or I'll tell Dr. Green that you went to church."

"So?"

"So, shut up." Father took an exit too fast, skidding on the wet road, pressing me against the door. It was unlocked. Should I jump out now and get it over with? Father grabbed my arm. "Don't even think about it."

The new Annex was at the top of a long, winding road. There might have been a view of the ocean. I heard surf breaking, but all I saw was rain.

We entered a stone building with a cross and a rose above the door. "Is this a church?"

"Don't you recognize your Rosicrucians?"

"From the radio?"

The door opened. A stranger in a white coat with a Dr. Green name tag shook Father's hand. "Jimmy!" He seemed older than the other Drs. Green. He had wavy white hair and a moustache. "So, this is your daughter. You must be very proud of her." He led us to an office. We sat at the desk across from him. Father lit a cigarette while Dr. Green opened a file with my name on it, muttering, "Hmmm…oh my."

Father fidgeted. He exhaled a plume of smoke and flicked ash on the floor. "Look, here's the thing. Weezie's driving me nuts, what with the girl's weak heart and all."

"Her heart is fine."

"What do you mean? I thought she was dying."

"That's Weezie's idea. Your job is to keep her alive." He leaned forward to look at me over the top of his glasses. "There's a pretty girl under that dirt. She's been able to handle the psychological splits and the physical abuse. She survived our little holiday Saturnalias – not many do. We're going to put her in our Sex Magick program." Dr. Green gave me a creepy smile and splayed his fingers, forming wings like some corny magic trick. "Picture it, Jimmy – young people like her will lead our revolution with music, drugs, and sex. We need pretty girls that we can control. She's tall. She'll be like one of Herr Hitler's Vril girls. Can she sing?"

I was hovering at the ceiling, searching for fauns and pipers, trying not to hear. Father pinched me and I jumped. "You sing at school, don't you, Fatso?"

I shrugged, "Dunno."

Father scowled. "I still think you should take her. Weezie hates Imperial Beach and the kid's out of control."

"Your wife likes the money, doesn't she? If we take the girl, you don't get paid."

"What about Weezie? She's family, isn't she? Her grandfather was the Grand Commander or whatever your Templars call it. What about her brother, Wally?"

"Weezie had a lot of promise when she was young, but her mind's cracked. She's not strong like Wally – or this one. The truth is we don't need her anymore. If it weren't for Wally and the girl, we'd cut her off." His eyes were on me. "Stand up, child."

Father pinched me and I stood.

Dr. Green grimaced. "Look at those legs. She's covered with bites. What are those – fleas? No wonder she's anemic. What are you feeding her?"

"TV dinners, chicken pot-pies, Oreos, peanut butter. Weezie isn't much of a cook."

"That skirt's so short I can see her underpants. Tell your wife to buy her some clothes and get a cookbook. There's no excuse for malnutrition in the State of California."

"Who's going to pay for all that? We need more money. I want a raise."

"Nonsense. We're the NSA, not Fort Knox. And that reminds me…" Dr. Green slid a stapled report across the desk, "we have this little embarrassment to discuss. We know all about that pedophile operation you were running on the side. You thought we wouldn't find out about your Italian friends?"

Father looked through the attached photos and blanched. I recognized some of the "special business friends" he'd brought home to see me.

"This stops immediately. And the girl's appearance had better improve or you're out of a job."

"Now just a minute. I've done everything you've asked. You can't just throw me out."

"Watch me. Let's see how well you do on your own." Dr. Green slid another file across the desk.

Father eyed it suspiciously. "What's that?"

"Emergency room records. We took care of the CPS and police cases in Washington and Illinois, but then this little surprise showed up from Laguna Beach. I'm afraid that California has tougher child protection laws."

"That wasn't my fault. The boys got a little rough. Kid wound up in the ER again."

Dr. Green pushed the button on his intercom. "Send in Nanny Black."

I was disgusted by Father's words and glad to leave with the new nanny. Anything was better than this. I scarfed up the warm chocolate chip cookies, knowing they were drugged, and held out my arm for the shot. This time, I welcomed the flush of drugs that muted my humiliation.

I woke up smelling of soap and shampoo. I wore a white blouse, a full skirt with pictures of Paris on it over a petticoat that crinkled when I sat up. I had on clean white socks and shiny brown shoes with straps. My hair was in a ponytail. I was in an unfamiliar bedroom with a dressing table, a mirror, and a book called *Here's to You, Miss Teen!*

I preened in the mirror for a while, admiring my hair. I wondered what a Vril girl was and why Dr. Green had said that I might be one. There was nothing else to do, so I read the book. I learned that a girl should take a bath and change her socks and underwear every day. A teen needed seven pairs of socks and underpants. Did I have that many? I didn't think so. She should brush her teeth each morning and night. I thought about the notes that Miss Fitch kept sending home, urging Mother to improve my personal hygiene. Was this what she'd meant? Did my parents wash this much? I'd never thought about it.

1961 – 62

The door opened. Nanny Black brought eggs, bacon, orange juice, and toast with peanut butter and honey. I wolfed it all. Nanny brought me more toast and a glass of milk. I ate that, too. I felt better than I had for a long time. Nanny led me to a classroom. Other children were already there – pretty girls and handsome boys in new clothes like mine. I'd never seen any of them before. They looked like Mouseketeers from *The Mickey Mouse Club* on TV. Was this someone's birthday party?

"Here's our new girl." A muscular man with a surfer's tan and blond ponytail welcomed me. "I'm Dr. Brown. You can call me Chip. Welcome to Sex Magick."

A lady dressed as a pixie danced into the room, releasing a cloud of balloons with colored strings. "Hey kids, do you know who this is?"

"Tinkerbell!" kids shouted, jumping to grab at the strings. I took one and found an empty desk at the back of the room. I dreaded what was coming and wanted no part of this hyped-up chaos. I needed time to mull over what Dr. Green had said about Mother and how he had dressed down Father. What did he mean that my weak heart was Mother's idea and that I wasn't dying? Was that good news or bad news?

Dr. Brown clapped his hands. "Tell the new girl where we're going today."

"Disneyland! Yay!" The kids bounced, balloons bobbing. Disneyland? That sounded way too good. I had grown up watching *Wonderful World of Disney*. I never imagined that Disneyland was a place I'd actually visit. I rubbed my temples. My head hurt. I had a very bad feeling about this.

Dr. Brown handed me a nametag that said, "Hi! I'm Suzy Q."

"What's this for? My name is Sparky."

"This is your Sex Magick name," he smiled showing big white teeth. "Hey kids, let's help Suzy Q learn her name."

"Suzy Q…Suzy Q…Suzy Q…." The kids laughed and bounced their balloons. What was wrong with them? They all had name tags with silly names like Bobbi Bee and Kitty Cat. They made a lot of noise, but I could tell from their wild eyes that they were scared. What did they know that I didn't?

Dr. Chip Brown sat down with his elbows on my desk, chin in his hands. "You're way too serious, Miss Suzy Q. You've got to loosen up and have some fun. Chew on these." He did the same abracadabra finger display as Dr. Green, fanning his fingers into wings. Was this some kind of secret message? Jellybeans spilled onto my desk like magic. He watched me pick one up and chew it. The drugs kicked in before I swallowed. I saw his face broaden until he became the grinning Cheshire Cat. He stood up, "Okay, kids. The bus will be here in a few minutes, so let's go over the rules."

I quickly understood that my job was to go alone into the crowds at Disneyland and find a man to be my daddy for the day. I was to do whatever it took to get him to buy me a ticket for Mr. Toad's Wild Ride. Most importantly, I had to get him to go on it with me. When the car drove onto railroad tracks and into the headlight of an oncoming train, I had to take off my clothes or get him to kiss me or something else that a normal daddy shouldn't do. There would be cameras waiting. There had to be good photos of me being bad if I wanted to get back on the bus and go home.

On the ride to Anaheim, we sang Disney songs and Dr. Brown passed around more jellybeans. I laughed and shrieked with the other kids. We were let off at different places around Disneyland. I showed my name tag and was admitted to Frontierland. It was raining, but I didn't care. I felt huge, invincible – like Alice in Wonderland after she ate the "tall" side of the mushroom.

I should have kept a handful of jellybeans because I was very hungry. I smelled hamburgers cooking. A sign at the Golden Horseshoe Saloon said, "Frontier Burgers, 50¢." It looked warm inside. I tried to go in, but a man with a coonskin cap blocked my way. He looked at my name tag. "Hold up there, little Suzy Q. Where's your ticket?"

"My what?"

"You need a ticket for the Golden Horseshoe Revue. It's about to start."

I choked up, shivering. "I'm cold. I want a frontier burger." I was ravenous. The street skewed sidewise. I'd faint if I didn't eat.

"Go to the cashier and buy yourself a ticket."

"I'm starving. I don't have any money." I started to cry in big sobbing gushes like my heart had ruptured. Was that really me making all that noise?

"I'm sorry, little girl. If you can't buy a ticket, you've got to step out of line. Where are your parents?"

"My parents?" Real tears of grief surged from my ocean of pain. Father wanted to give me away and Mother wanted me to die. "I'm an orphan," I wailed. "I'm all alone. Nobody loves me."

I turned to leave and bumped into a man in a suit. He flashed a white handkerchief. "No need to cry, little girl."

I blew my nose on it and handed it back to him. "Will you be my daddy?"

"Let's get you your frontier burger and find your parents."

I was back on the bus at four o'clock with ticket stubs for lots of rides. I had managed to be photographed on Mr. Toad's Wild Ride with two different daddies. I'd pulled up my skirt on cue for the cameras and hoped that was enough.

The bus was half empty when we left. Where were all the other kids? I thought about asking Dr. Brown when he came down the aisle to collect our name tags but decided that I didn't want to know. There was no singing on the way back to the Annex where Mother was waiting to drive me home.

CHAPTER TWENTY-SIX

SPUTNIKS AND ANGELS

On Sunday morning, I woke up in stripes. The rain had stopped. Sunlight streamed through the Venetian blinds, casting shadows on my bed and lines across my walls. The sun brightened, lighting every floating speck of dust on fire. I blew out a breath, making the dust motes dance. Seagulls screamed outside my window. I'd never get back to sleep. I might as well get up.

I grabbed the clock – six a.m., too early to go out. We'd been warned by Pedro never to come down to the estuary until the Border Patrol had "cleaned up." I took that to mean "taken all the bodies away." I lay back in bed, willing my mental vacuums and brooms to scrub away every memory of the Magick Kingdom – riding Dumbo and whirling in the Mad Hatter's teacups, dizzy in the rain and plunging into the dark maze of Mr. Toad's Wild Ride with a man's hand up my skirt.

I had survived the day and that's what mattered. Chip said I was a natural for the program and that we'd move on to bigger challenges next time. I didn't want a next time. There was nothing from Disneyland that I wanted to keep. It was as ugly and phony as Lookout Mountain and the Tent of Wonders. I urged my mental scrubbers to clean faster. There was no such thing as magic.

A pebble hit my window. Patrick and Kenny were outside on their bikes. Other kids were coming too. It was a glorious day. It had been nearly two weeks since we'd been able to draw tunnels in the wetlands. Forgetting Pedro's warnings, I got dressed and dug out the rolls of butcher paper with the tunnel designs we'd drawn during the rainy season. I tiptoed out the kitchen door, ran to the carport and strapped them to Blue Balloon's handlebars with rubber bands. With a war whoop, we mounted our bikes and plunged downhill and across the ponds to the wetlands, thrilled to feel the wind on our faces.

It took a while, but we found a patch of sand that was dry enough to make drawings. We stacked our bicycles in the reeds and unrolled the butcher paper with all of our designs, holding it in place with rocks. Then we found sticks and began making tunnels in the sand. Soon, the ground was covered with circles and Scottish landscapes. Every time a circle was completed – with trees, forest animals, and sometimes fish – we would gather at the edge, ready to jump. So far there had been no glowing lights, no water, no Lady of Loch Tay. We'd have to work harder.

We fanned out into the reeds, searching for more flat, sandy patches. The reeds had grown up taller than we were. I couldn't see my friends anymore. Suddenly, Sandy screamed. I ran toward the sound of her voice. I rounded a clump of reeds and bumped into Albert. Patrick and Gary joined us with other kids. We found Sandy pointing to a mass of black jelly where the reeds had been crushed. "What's that?"

"It looks like a jellyfish." Gary poked at the clots with his stick. I leaned close, my stomach in a knot. I knew that terrible smell – human blood. I tried not to let my terror show. Gary's stick snagged a tiny hand.

"Oh shit." Fear became rage and I plunged my hands into the pile. I pulled out a baby. She was tiny, rubbery, and cold. She was attached to the jellyfish by her belly button. I cleaned the blood from her face. "Come on. Breathe. Breathe." I clutched her in my arms. She couldn't be dead. We ran back to our bicycles. I wrapped her in the butcher paper.

"There's Pedro's Jeep," said Albert. "Let's go."

I put the baby in my basket and held her with one hand as I pedaled. All the way, I talked to her, naming her Conchita, willing her to live. "You're okay, Conchita. You'll grow up to be beautiful and smart."

Pedro saw us coming. "I told you kids. Don't come out here so early. ..."

I pushed Conchita into his arms, trembling so badly I could barely speak. "Give her a blanket. She's too cold."

"Sorry, lil' chiquita. It's too late for that. She's dead." He tried to put Conchita in the back with another body.

"No," I sobbed, pummeling him with my fists. "She's just cold. Take her to the hospital. Take her now."

"Okay, okay. But from now on you kids stay away until we clean up out here. Got it?" He put Conchita on the seat beside him and started the engine. We followed the jeep toward Tijuana on our bikes as far as we could go. Then we broke away and rode home.

On Monday, the Blue Bells of Scotland voted to do another mural for the school – this one was dedicated to Conchita. Miss Fitch didn't ask who Conchita was, but she gave permission for us to gather paints from the art supply room.

We laid a fresh piece of butcher paper at the back of the classroom and I penciled in a church like the one I'd seen on *Zorro*. In front of the church,

I drew Mexican people having a fiesta, with a piñata that looked like a burro hanging from a tree. Men wore sombreros and played guitars and maracas. Women danced in elegant mantillas.

In the middle, a tiny baby smiled from the arms of her mother. The Blue Bells painted the piñata bright pink, the tree purple with yellow leaves. They decorated the people with colorful clothes. I painted a baby angel in a long, pink dress, floating in the sky. We were about to paint in the sky when Mr. Miller came into the room and changed everything. He and Miss Fitch left with Patrick. We stopped painting. We stopped everything, willing time to halt, hardly daring to breathe. Even Gary sat still.

Miss Fitch came back without Patrick. She tried to put on a brave face, but it couldn't be done. Theresa had died.

When Miss Fitch could catch her breath to speak, she told us more about how Theresa had had the best medical care that the State of California could provide and that everything possible had been done to save her. "The bleeding wouldn't stop. She never woke up. She never saw your beautiful paintings."

I swam out of my body and floated to the ceiling, looking down on Miss Fitch sobbing at her desk. Kenny pounded his head and Gary rammed his penknife into the wood before leaping up and punching the wall until his hands bled. Other kids were crying. I was the only one who wasn't reacting. I was sitting quietly, staring up to where I hovered above myself.

"We'll paint both of them." I said, standing up. "Theresa and Conchita will be best friends in Heaven."

I ran to the back of the room. Color flowed from my brushes onto the paper while I painted another, bigger angel floating next to the tiny one. She had blue eyes and blond pigtails. I dressed her in Theresa's favorite sweater and put a golden crown on her head.

Then the Blue Bells painted the sky midnight blue and added a sputnik with a comet's tail, a smattering of small white stars, and a sliver of moon.

CHAPTER TWENTY-SEVEN

OFFICER FRIENDLY

Patrick didn't return to class for a week. I went by his apartment every day but didn't see him. I waited for the funeral, thinking that they would bring Theresa back to the IB Apartments like they did with Billy Brown. But Patrick and his mother had gone to bury her in a place called Tarzana. Kenny and I were sitting on my doorstep sorting bottle caps when Patrick finally came home. He looked haggard and pale. I'd never noticed how his face was covered with freckles. They really stood out against his white skin.

"Let's go riding," he said. We ran to the carport, mounted our bikes, and galloped down into the wetlands, standing on the pedals with our arms in the air. We raced expertly across the narrow dirt dikes and onto the tidal flats shouting, "Ardchoille, Ardchoille!" Soon others were riding and shouting behind us.

The next day, Patrick walked to school with Kenny and me. He stood motionless in front of the angel mural displayed next to the principal's office with tears streaming down his cheeks. He stayed there even after the bell rang and Miss Fitch had to go fetch him for class.

The mural had become a shrine where students and teachers left flowers. Pastor John brought candles from St. James – thin tapers that we lit and stuck into a shoebox filled with sand. Kerry's Berries and Hannah's Bananas wrote poems. Other classes painted pictures of angels, stapling them to the edges of our painting.

Most of it was for Theresa, but the kids remembered Conchita, too. Most of IB Elementary knew about us finding her body. Word had gone around among the kids with the speed of a whisper. No one said a word to parents or teachers because we weren't supposed to go to the wetlands. We'd been warned by a succession of smiling policemen who came to the school to lecture us about where we shouldn't go and what we shouldn't do. Whether they were old, young, fat, or thin, they all wore nametags that identified them as Officer Friendly.

"It's dangerous to go anywhere near Mexico," they'd say. "That open Tijuana Sewer is really dirty. You could get sick with typhus." The officers were emphatic that children should never go anyplace in the marshlands where the reeds grew because wetbacks hid in them. Terrible things could happen if they caught us. We tolerated the lectures in silence. We were more leery of policemen than of Mexicans. Police had been involved in my life many times already and hadn't done me one bit of good.

That day, a new Officer Friendly whose official police nametag said "Jones" came to our class to warn us out of the estuary. "There's quicksand and flash tides. You could get sucked under and drown. People die down there all the time, even very young people." He looked young himself, standing at attention with his hat on. He stared down his nose at us like we were roaches and we glared back, giving him the evil eye.

This guy was no match for the warriors of Clan MacGregor. We knew he'd really come to ask about how we'd found Conchita. Maybe if he'd been a bit friendlier and less of a stick, we might have answered some of his questions, but we were silent. It was an uncomfortable fifteen minutes before Officer Friendly-Jones left, telling us that he was on his way to Mar Vista to search the high schoolers' lockers for drugs. "You kids wouldn't know about any drug smuggling around here?" he asked. "There's a lot of brick cocaine showing up in Imperial Beach."

"No, sir." We shook our heads.

At recess, I saw police cars pull into Mar Vista with their red lights flashing. Officer Friendly-Jones and other cops were busy opening lockers and dumping the contents into boxes while the teachers watched.

I was familiar with cocaine and wanted nothing to do with it. I'd seen way too much "coke" at the Saturnalias. There was also plenty of it at what Mother called "Navy parties," where open barrels were filled with white powder. Groups of sailors and officers with their wives and kids were encouraged to help themselves, cramming it up their nostrils with thin bamboo sticks or snorting it through rolled-up dollar bills. Father ranted against Cubans in general, but he liked their rum and cocaine. He always said that the Cuban gunrunners put on the best parties.

I liked the Cuban parties, too, because kids were invited and not treated like party favors. In fact, we were often given presents, like a facemask and flippers that I got to keep. I stayed away from the cocaine. I was much more interested in the open crates of handguns, machine guns, and hand grenades packed in shredded excelsior.

The labels on the green boxes said, "Property US Navy." It was an open secret around IB that Cubans were trading drugs for guns up and down the Southern California coast. The raw sewage that kept people away from IB's beaches worked out well for smugglers. Cubans and sometimes Russians ran the drugs through the surf at night. Then they'd hold a big Navy party in one of the hilltop houses in El Toro, Topanga, or Laurel Canyon with lots of Cuban pulled pork and tortillas cooked on an outdoor grill. I could eat all I wanted. The sailors brought long, green gun boxes and stacked them by the door. Father would make them pry open the lids before they could have any cocaine or Cuban barbecue. I'd eat pulled pork and watch him poke around inside the boxes, counting the guns that smelled like grease.

My favorite house was in El Toro Canyon near Laguna Beach. It had a huge deck with a view of the ocean and an outdoor swimming pool. As the adults got high and acted silly, kissing each other and dancing to *son cubano* records, the kids played Marco Polo and huzzbees in the pool. After dinner, when my lips turned blue and my skin wrinkled, I'd wrap myself in a towel and wait for the party to end. I knew that wouldn't happen until the Cuban host with the laughing eyes and big smile turned serious.

With a snap of his fingers he selected boxes from the stacks. Weapons were pulled out and loaded. He picked up a gun, cocked it, and aimed down the canyon, saying, "I gonna shoot me some jackrabbits for *guiso de conejo*" – rabbit stew.

It was pretty easy to shoot rabbits. The desert canyons were infested with them. One shot and dozens leapt from the bushes. Their white tails bobbed as they fled. The drunken grownups laughed while the Cuban slaughtered bunnies that lay bloodied and jerking on the ground. After he'd satisfied himself with the guns, more cocaine disappeared up the noses of my parents and their friends. Finally, when it got dark, Mother shooed me into the house to change. It was time to go home.

Our car swerved down the twisting road at breakneck speed while Father ran his hand up Mother's leg. "You put both hands on that steering wheel, you hear me?" she shrieked with laughter.

Tires squealed. The car skidded on every hairpin turn. Father took both hands off the wheel, steering with his thighs. On the flat, straight stretches, the road came alive with jackrabbits. They ran alongside us, leaping into the road, and freezing in the headlights. They stared at us with glowing red eyes as we mowed them down.

"Bonzai!" Father shouted.

CHAPTER TWENTY-EIGHT

THE FLY BALL

Our angel mural faded. Easterly winds blew away the drawings and poems. The deaths made it more urgent than ever that we find our tunnel to Scotland. We covered the elementary school playground in circles, then spread over to Mar Vista High. More kids were wearing pie-plate armor and I'd started a fad for aluminum earrings cut from TV dinner trays. They were bloodying earlobes all over the school. We were getting out of there soon. As soon as one of us drew the perfect tunnel, we'd all jump to a beautiful world far away.

No one had successfully jumped yet, but we weren't stupid. We knew it wasn't going to be easy to reproduce a view we'd never seen. It required patience, determination, and luck – virtues for which the MacGregor clan was famous.

I got close once, plunging all the way into the waters of Loch Tay. It happened out in center field during a softball game. Miss Fitch had tried to get me to play first base or shortstop to develop my infield skills, but I begged for center field because nothing ever happened there. Very few kids could hit a ball that far, so I could ignore the game and draw tunnels.

The game started, but I paid no attention. I drew the largest possible circle in the soft, dry dirt, filling in intricate details of trees, clouds, birds, and flowers. The game rambled on with the usual walk after walk. I worked on three tunnels at once, drawing circles and imagining every detail of Scotland on the other side. I imagined what factors such as motion might be doing to my image, because the wind was probably blowing over there, shifting things around. Then I wondered if maybe it was raining, or snowing. I covered one tunnel drawing with raindrops. I added some intricate snowflakes to the next one and waited for an effect. I thought I saw the ground shimmer a little, as if I was close to getting it right. I was focusing hard on jumping when Miss Fitch yelled, "Sparky, duck!"

My head exploded and I tumbled headfirst into a black pit of freezing water that had no bottom – an endless well without light or air. I was falling through the tunnel, plunging through empty space to the very core of the Earth, spinning at dizzying speed on my way to Scotland. My brains were jumbled. I was paralyzed. I couldn't breathe. I was going to die before I got there.

I struggled to move my arms and legs, to open my eyes and take a gulp of air, but I was helpless, falling deeper into darkness instead of light. I wanted to live and breathe. I wanted to see Scotland. I was nearly dead when the Lady of Loch Tay pulled me to the surface and lifted my head above water. She held me in her arms, wiping the water from my face and whispering, "It's okay, Sparky honey. You can breathe now."

I took a deep, gasping breath and opened my eyes. Hovering over me was a luminous, blurry face. Wisps of blond hair were backlit by sun so brilliant that it burned my eyes. Fairies with shimmering wings buzzed around her head. I could hear the warriors in the distance shouting, "Sparky's down."

"I jumped," I tried to say, but my voice was weak, my throat scratchy. I rolled onto my side and vomited. I fell backwards and passed out.

I identified the sounds and smells of the nurse's office before I opened my eyes and groaned. A man in a suit was thumping my ankle with a rubber hammer.

"She's awake," said Mrs. Lipsky, the nurse.

"I'm glad you're okay." Miss Fitch sounded relieved. "That fly ball came right down on top of your head. You went face down in the dirt. You had so much in your mouth and nose that I was afraid you'd choke to death."

Mrs. Lipsky stuck a thermometer in my mouth. "It's a good thing Miss Fitch took that first aid course. She just saved your life."

"Who would have thought that Bubby Suarez could hit a ball that high?" said Mr. Miller. "Maybe he'll go pro."

My classmates were gathered at the open door, babbling about the incredible sound the softball made when it bounced off my skull and how Miss Fitch had carried me to Mrs. Lipsky's office.

Mrs. Lipsky was on the phone with Mother now, getting permission for the doctor to give me a shot for the infected sores on my legs. He was filling an evil-looking syringe. Everyone was busy, excited and proud of themselves. I didn't say a word. I was heartbroken.

I'd almost made it to Scotland. I'd gotten it right and the Earth had opened. I'd been in the tunnel, but Miss Fitch had pulled me back. She must have caught me by the ankles, wrenching me out of the arms of the Lady of Loch Tay. Tears ran down my cheeks. Miss Fitch wiped them away with a wet gauze bandage. "There, there. It's going to be okay." She held a bag of ice to my head. "You've got a concussion, that's all."

I drifted off after the shot in my butt, waking up to hear the doctor talking to Mother. "Nasty crack on the noggin. She'll be groggy and confused for a few days. Then she'll have quite a bump. It's a good thing that Miss Fitch acted so quickly and cleared out her airways. She could have suffocated." The doctor showed Mother how to put ointment on my legs and told her to keep them clean.

Mr. Miller drove us home. He was full of praise for Miss Fitch and repeated the story of how she'd saved my life.

I sulked in silent resentment. Next time, I was going all the way.

CHAPTER TWENTY-NINE

THE SCOTTISH SOLDIER

The fog in February thickened into soup. The good news was that it kept the Stink from rolling in at night and Mother's mood improved. She bought me seven pairs of white cotton underpants with the days of the week on them. I had just put on "Monday" when she handed me a bag with a dozen pairs of white socks, a new toothbrush, and a copy of *Here's to You, Miss Teen!* I had forgotten about that book, vacuuming it away with my memories of Disneyland and the Annex.

"Dr. Green says to read the book and clean yourself up," said Mother.

She might be sleeping well, but I wasn't. At sunrise when the thumping and bumping noises died down next door, my window shook to a new sound – boom…boom…KABOOM. I was up, wide awake, my heart pounding. Was it the Russians? I ran to my parents' bedroom. Mother was snoring in bed, but Father stood by the window with binoculars. "Come here." He pointed. "Look out there." I could usually see the ocean from his window. Now, there was only fog. Boom…kaboom and a flash of red. "Goddamn battleships are shooting the bejeezus out of our old tin-can boats." I didn't know what he meant. I didn't care – just as long as it wasn't the Russian invasion that we'd all been afraid of.

At breakfast he said, "Navy's using my old ship the *Lyman* for target practice. Damn shame, blowing her to smithereens like that." He'd been an officer on the *Lyman* before he was on the *Dortch*. He liked to tell stories about the brave little destroyer escorts who went up against the Japanese fleet and chased them away. For several days, battleships pounded the dawn while I cowered under my covers, making armor and imagining that the Campbells were attacking.

The bone-chilling fog kept us out of the wetlands. We found an old camouflage tarp that had washed up on the access road after a flood tide and hauled it to the carport. We stretched it over the dumpsters to make a tent. It was wet and stank of diesel. Albert found an old gooseneck lamp and I screwed in one of my lightbulbs.

We huddled around the lamp for warmth, our breath steaming, while I read *Miracle Sword*. The book wasn't helping morale. King Jamie had ban-

ished the MacGregors, calling them a "wicked and unhappie race." Mac-
Gregors were being hanged and beheaded all over the place. We stared at
an illustration of a fancy party at the Campbells' Castle Finlarig. Ladies in
ball gowns stood on a terrace that overlooked an open pit dungeon where
MacGregors were chained, half-starved and dirty, but defiant. One by
one, they stared up at the raised sword of Black Duncan Campbell before
their heads were chopped off.

The bodies of other MacGregors swung from trees on Judgment
Hill, their necks stretched. It was gruesome. I felt like crying but kept on
reading. It had to get better, but it didn't. There was even more depressing news for the clan : Any woman caught with a MacGregor man was
dragged through the streets naked and branded on the face with a key.

I shivered, sprouting goose pimples. "It's too c-c-cold," I said through
chattering teeth. I sniffed the air. Wood smoke drifted from the estuary.
The wetbacks were keeping warm in the reeds by burning brush and drift-
wood. On clear days we'd seen their smoke rising from clumps of rushes.
The others smelled it, too.

"We need a campfire," said Gary.

"We can cook some marshmallows," said Linda.

"First we need firewood," said Patrick.

Gary jumped up. "I know where to get it." The kids were off in a flash,
collecting rolled-up *North County Times* newspapers from back stoops.
We had an impressive pile in no time. Gary poured on a can of lighter fluid
and struck a match.

Flames leapt to the carport roof and the sudden rush of fiery wind blew
the ball of burning papers under our Mercury. I stood paralyzed, watching
flames scorch the paint. Our car was about to explode. Quick-thinking
Albert grabbed the hose and sprayed water under the car, extinguishing
the flames while the rest of us ran away.

At that moment, Father came out to get his paper. Burning pages of the
North County Times flew into the kitchen. Mother screamed and stomped
out the flames. Father swore and stormed into the carport. He caught Albert holding the hose and frog-marching him to Apartment F. He banged
on the door, shouting, "Charlie, open up, you SOB." It was opened by a
fat man in an undershirt with tattoos on his hairy arms. "Give this little
bastard of yours what's comin' to him," said Father. Albert's old man was
one of Father's Navy-night buddies.

We crowded into Patrick's bedroom next door to Albert's and listened
through the wall. We heard slaps and Albert crying followed by the clank

of a heavy buckle. Charlie was going for his belt. "Not like the old days, eh, Jimmy?" Charlie sounded wistful. "A man could keep his home shipshape without no namby-pamby social workers and Child Services butting in. What'd my damn kid do this time?"

"Set fire to the garage." Father's lighter clicked. I imagined him lighting a cigarette. "Burned up my paper. Nearly burned up my car."

"Well, well – didn't think the little so-and-so had it in him."

"Chip off the old block, you sonofabitch," Father laughed.

The belt snapped and Albert screamed – once, twice, three times. "Go to your room. You're grounded until I say so." A door slammed. Charlie sounded winded, "How 'bout a cold Bud. I got some of that good vitamin B in the fridge." Bottle caps bounced on the floor.

When Albert showed up for school the next morning, he had a black eye and swollen nose. News spread and Albert's heroism became legend. Even some Mar Vista kids called through the fence at recess, "Way to go, Bertie."

The fog was unrelenting. We gathered under the tent again after school and used the gooseneck lamp for light and heat. Our fire-building days were behind us. We had a new problem – not only were things looking bleak for the MacGregors, but I was running out of book. It ended in mid-sentence on page two hundred and six, leaving us beheaded, branded, and with our necks stretched on Judgment Hill. That was only ten pages away. Something new had to turn up soon or we'd be too discouraged to get ourselves to Scotland.

Fortunately, a message from God arrived on my birthday, compliments of Miss Fitch and Radio KGB. Miss Fitch's special man friend was the famous DJ Tommy McCloud. She'd shown us an 8 x 10 glossy of him, smiling behind a big microphone with the letters KGB on it. We listened to him play records and make funny noises every afternoon.

My eleventh birthday fell on a Friday. I'd told a few friends about it, but nobody said much. Birthday parties were for little kids. The IB kids didn't talk about their birthdays or expect anything special. I wasn't even sure that my parents remembered. Some years they did and some they didn't. Grandpa and Grandma always sent me a card with five dollars tucked inside.

We were in the carport listening to "Alley Oop" on the radio. I was under the tarp, "ooping" with the chorus and deciding how to spend my five dollars. The old radio was acting up. It squealed while Albert fiddled with the antenna and dials. The song faded out and Tommy McCloud boomed on air.

"Hey fans, it's time for a special KGB Happy Eleventh Birthday to a girl warrior, Miss Sparky MacGregor. This next song is for you, kid. Keep on fighting."

"Did you hear that?" Patrick ran over to the radio. "Turn it up."

"Here's Andy Stewart, all the way from Scotland with his new hit single, 'Scottish Soldier.'" There was a pause and I imagined Tommy McCloud positioning the needle on the rim of the shiny new record. Beautiful music flowed into the carport.

There was a soldier, a Scottish soldier
Who wandered far away, and soldiered far away,

I tried to slow time so that I could catch and hold every word. I couldn't. It ended too soon, but I got the message. This was definitely a sign from God. A lump swelled in my throat. Tears stung my eyes. He hadn't forgotten me. We'd soon be in the Highland hills if we kept drawing tunnels.

That night, my family did have a party with birthday candles stuck in blueberry muffins. They were delicious. My parents gave me a red portable record player and I was thrilled. Mother had joined a Record-of-the-Month club and I'd been listening to *Pal Joey, South Pacific, Sound of Music*, and *Flower Drum Song* on the big hi-fi in the living room. I'd wanted a record player of my own so I could play records in my room.

I was disappointed to discover that the long-playing LPs from the record club wouldn't fit on my little turntable, but I had saved the five dollars from Grandma and Grandpa. I had enough to buy five forty-five-speed records of my own. I'd begin my collection with "Scottish Soldier." Until then, I could listen to the old seventy-eights, like "Ghost Riders in the Sky," and "One Meat Ball," that I'd found in the dumpster.

The day after my birthday, a package arrived from mother's mother, Mema. I'd written to her in a flood of guilt, apologizing for taking *Miracle Sword* from her hatbox. To my surprise, she hadn't been mad at all. In fact, she'd started writing letters about our family history, sharing what she knew about our other ancestors. It wasn't much, but it was something. I'd mailed my latest letter to her the day before to ask if she knew what was in the missing pages of *Miracle Sword*. Our letters must have crossed in the mail, because her brown paper parcel sat on the breakfast table. I untied the string and peeled it open. The gift inside was wrapped in plaid paper that looked like MacGregor tartan.

"Well, unwrap it," said Mother, suspicious of anything that came from Mema.

I took my time. It wasn't every day that I received a present that was wrapped so beautifully. I removed and folded the paper. Inside was my first forty-five–speed record. The shiny blue jacket was printed in gold lettering – very classy: "Black Watch Pipes and Drums, 42nd Scottish Highlanders at the 1958 Edinburgh Tattoo."

"Weird name," said Father. "Tattoo?"

"Yeah, weird." I did my best to sound nonchalant, as if I didn't care, which was tough because my stomach was turning somersaults. Bagpipes! I stayed casual, tossing the record beside my plate of scrambled eggs – a safe distance from my brother's sticky hands. My parents read the newspaper and ignored me. As soon as I could get away and still look bored, I hid the wrapping paper and ribbon under my mattress with *Miracle Sword*. The poor book was falling apart. I tried to keep it flat and dry, but there was black stuff growing on the pages. I tucked my record inside the record player and snuck out the front door with it.

The clubhouse was empty. We'd learned our lesson about going into the wetlands too early, but now kids were showing up way too late on Saturdays. We'd never get to Scotland by being lazy. There was still work for us to do. I had to get their attention and knew just how to do it. I had to be quick, appearing from the mist like Clan MacGregor, then disappearing before my parents caught me making noise.

Fortunately, Father had *Pal Joey* cranked up pretty loud on our hi-fi. Mr. Smith was playing honkytonk. Otherwise, the apartments were quiet. I plugged in my record player and slid "Black Watch Pipes and Drums" from its sleeve, careful to touch only the edges. I wiped it with my shirt, before fitting it onto the special turntable adapter for forty-fives. I lifted the needle to the record and cranked the volume up to the maximum. I had to wait through the rustling sounds of an excited audience, followed by the swelling roar of applause. They were seeing something thrilling that was coming my way – that was for sure.

The long crescendo whine of bagpipes started in the distance, growing louder until the carport thundered with Scottish drums, and "Scotland the Brave" echoed around the buildings. I saw pipers and drummers marching down Caspian Way. They turned sharply into the carport, swaggering toward me, swinging their kilts and sporans. Sashes of MacGregor tartan were draped across their chests and they wore tall, black fur hats.

The first piper winked and marched right through me. Dozens more just like him followed. The magnificent sound roused my innards. If I could have turned the volume up even louder, I would have. I wanted the whole world to hear it. I hadn't even played to the end before Patrick showed up with jam on his face. He was followed by Linda, Kenny, Sandy, and a new kid named Cookie, who came in her bathrobe and slippers. The rest arrived by the time I'd played it a second time.

The music changed everything. The bagpipes sang to us of survival – courage over adversity. The MacGregors had suffered terrible defeats, but they'd never surrendered. We were Scottish soldiers, too. If we went down, it would be with swords raised shouting, "Ardchoille!" We would never surrender.

It was still too foggy for the wetlands, so we rode our bikes toward the dirt fields of Mar Vista. A convoy of jeeps nearly mowed us down when we tried to cross IB Boulevard. They skidded around us and turned onto Caspian Way, then disappeared down the access road and into the fog. There had been a lot of activity in the wetlands since New Year's. We knew that it had something to do with the military, but we'd have to wait until the mist cleared to check it out. Until then, we'd draw our tunnels at the high school. By the time Pedro found us at Mar Vista, we'd drawn a dozen tunnels.

"You bambinos're lookin' pretty sharp today." He handed out our dimes and bricks. They were getting heavier. "Hope you kids been eatin' your Wheaties."

CHAPTER THIRTY

THE PIE SHOPPE

Early Sunday, Father drove me to the San Ysidro bus station where he bought me a ticket. I looked it over. "Oceanside? Is this some new kind of Sunday school?"

"Just get on the bus." He pushed me ahead of him up the steps and pointed to a seat. "Sit here." He gave a dollar to the driver. "Let her off at the Oceanside Pie Shoppe. You know it?"

"Sure do. That's our thirty-minute lunch stop."

"Just make sure she gets off." He turned to me. "You got that, Fatso?"

"Can I have some money, too?" I hadn't eaten breakfast and I was hungry. But Father was off the bus. The door closed and we were on the road. I listened to my stomach growl, wondering how far it was to Oceanside. Why was I going there? Could it be another painting class? I hoped so.

I looked around the bus which was about half full – mostly old ladies. They didn't look like artists. There were a few sailors. I thought about pulling the "daddy" routine when we got to the pie shop. We passed a Page Boy Drive-in. I smelled burgers and fries. We turned onto the Coast Highway and drove past groceries, restaurants, food carts, and bodegas. I tried not to think about food.

The fog cleared north of San Diego. Eucalyptus trees and tall palms swayed. Sun glinted on the Pacific. Sailboats flew downwind with rainbow-colored spinnakers. I would learn to sail someday. I'd ride the wind and tides to Treasure Island or maybe Japan. The glare off the ocean made me sleepy. I dozed with my head against the window and woke up when the bus parked in front of the Oceanside Pie Shoppe. "This is where you get off," said the driver. There were other buses parked in a row. The one next to us was marked, San Ysidro. "That's the one you take back."

The old ladies headed for the toilet. I slid into an empty booth and gazed longingly at the glass case behind the counter. I'd never seen so many slices of pie – wedges of apple, cherry, pumpkin, peach, strawberry, and every kind of cream pie I'd ever imagined. I was hungry enough to eat them all.

I pinched my tummy – no fat. Why did Father call me Fatso? I searched the room for a daddy candidate – someone good for a burger, fries, and a piece of pie. A man in a raincoat and fedora came in. He sat at a booth the next row over. Perfect. He could be my daddy today. I started to get up.

"Don't even think about it, Suzy Q." A blond man with a ponytail slid into the seat across from me. It was Dr. Chip Brown from Sex Magick. What was he doing here? I had a sinking feeling that this wasn't art class. I gave him the evil eye. I didn't want to go back to Disneyland – ever. "Then you're in luck." He spoke, answering my thoughts, but his lips didn't move. "No Disneyland today." My mouth dropped open. Was he a ventriloquist? "No, I'm not a ventriloquist. I'm talking inside your mind with my mind." He made the now familiar sign with his hands, splaying the fingers to form wings. "It's Magick." I felt dizzy. I must be hallucinating. "No, you're not hallucinating. Look around inside your brain. What do you see?"

"Food," I said, staring at a piece of lemon cream pie. "I'm starving."

"Then concentrate. I want you to create two simultaneous parallel realities."

"I've gotta do what?"

"Just cooperate. Fall into your mind. I've seen you do it to escape from the Saturnalia and Lookout Mountain." I closed my eyes. "Keep your eyes open. Look at me." Chip was unrelenting. I did want to escape – from *him*. I squinted, willing him to dissolve until he shimmered and buzzed. The pie shop exploded, sucking him through the roof and into bright sky.

I could still see every detail of the real pie shop, but in my mind, I was standing in a park. "Excellent," he said. "You've just split. You are in two simultaneous realities. This is called duality." I ignored him and concentrated on the park. People with blank faces laughed. The grass was too green, the clouds too white. There was a playground with kids on swings and pushing each other on a merry-go-round. Dogs barked and moms rocked prams. Chip sat on a bench, looking relaxed. "This is good – a happy place is a decent start. Keep going."

I stepped onto the grass. A black plastic case sat in the middle of the lawn. It looked familiar – Mepa's record player. I hadn't seen it since Seattle. The lid lifted. A record was turning soundlessly. "Did you put that in my head?" I wondered.

Chip's voice came from the record. "This is how we'll meet in your mind."

"Can you see everything inside my head?"

"For now I can. You'll learn to keep me out when you get better at this. You're doing fine. If you pass this next test, I'll be your handler for the new psi program.

"The pie program? Handler? I don't understand." I said aloud.

"Stay in your mind. There's no need to speak. It's psi – P-S-I, not pie. Psi is a special gift that runs in families. It's very rare. Your Uncle Wally has it. I have it. We can make people do things by planting ideas into their minds. When two of us are together, the psi grows stronger in both of us. Just imagine what a room full of people with this kind of power can do."

My stomach growled so loudly that he must have heard it. "Can I eat now?"

"You passed your test at Disneyland. You got two random men to break the law and do something immoral and illegal by messing with their minds. That's psi. That's how we tell who has it and who doesn't. It's too bad we can't use their photos from Mr. Toad's Wild Ride. Those guys are too ordinary."

"They didn't really do anything. I tricked them."

"Who cares? We were testing you, not them. You get us compromising pictures of anyone in the future, and we'll own him. Sex Magick is all about illusion – just like Disneyland. Besides, you're psi. You can't help it. You were born that way."

"Can I eat now?" I asked. He splayed his fingers again, looking at me expectantly. I wondered if I should do it, too – form two wings with a circle in the center. I decided not to.

Clearly, he believed that magick was great stuff. I wasn't so sure. I thought back to the Tent of Wonders. It had looked amazing from across the dark road with hurdy-gurdy music and swirling lights, but it was just a yellowed old tent in the daylight.

I thought of the rust and flaking paint on the Ferris wheel. Illusions looked shabby up close, even at Disneyland. The glint of sun on the ocean – that was real. There was no illusion to rolling surf or wind-filled sails because God made those. My attention was drawn to hamburgers sizzling on the grill. The old ladies were eating. The bus drivers were eating. Everyone in the restaurant was eating – except me. "Can I have a burger now?"

Chip handed me a nickel.

"It's not enough. A burger's twenty-five cents."

"Go play the jukebox. Press zero seven. See what you think of our new music from England. It's called the Mersey beat. We've tweaked the frequency. It makes girls like you go crazy."

I got up, feeling the weight of the coin in my hand. I wanted something in my stomach more than music. I decided to buy a glass of milk and gulp it down before he could stop me. I walked toward the counter, ready to order. I held out the nickel, but the counter dissolved. The pie shop became the mind park again. A jumble of voices rose from Mepa's record player like rumbling thunder.

I looked around. Men in MP uniforms were seated at a picnic table. They weren't looking at me, but they were thinking about me and not in a good way. "Yes, it's a test," said Chip from his park bench. "If you play the jukebox like I told you, life will get better for you. You'll move ahead in Sex Magick and develop your psi. You'll grow up to be a judge or a senator – maybe a movie star. If you don't?" he nodded toward the men. "They're just waiting for you to screw up. They are not your friends. They don't think you're special like I do. They don't believe in psi."

The men were looking at me now. I recognized them from the Saturnalia. They were the MPs who'd stood at the door to keep girls from escaping. I recalled the bleat of goats, the pipes of the faun, and the screams of little girls. I saw myself pinned beneath a half-naked sailor. I knew what would happen to me at the next Saturnalia if I faltered now.

I started to sweat – my heart pounding. In the park of my mind, thunder rumbled. Storm clouds darkened the sky, wind whipped my hair. Chip was speaking, but thunder drowned out his voice. The MPs turned into cartoon tigers with dripping fangs and razors for claws. I'd never get past them. I had to pass this test if I wanted to live.

I forced myself to calm down by mentally turning the dials on the record player. "Very good," Chip said. "Now, it's time for you to choose. It's them or me." I walked to the jukebox, put in my nickel, and punched 07. When I got back to the table, a cheeseburger, fries, a chocolate shake, and a bus ticket back to San Ysidro waited. No pie? I looked around, but Chip had gone. I tucked into the French fries. The music started:

Boom, boom, yeah, yeah, yeah
Boom, boom, hey, hey, hey

I liked the song. It made me feel like jumping up and dancing. The tune stayed with me all the way back to San Ysidro where Mother waited in the Mercury. "You're late."

"I was on the bus. Sorry."

She put the car in gear and burned rubber out of the parking lot. It didn't take psi to see that she was furious. But I was tired. I yawned, a big mistake. She punched me so hard that my head hit the window.

"Owww... what was that for?"

"You think you're such hot stuff. You've got those toadies at the Annex telling you that you're special – that you've got those 'psych' powers."

117

"It's psi – P-S-I...ow!" She punched me again. We were at a stoplight. I tried to open the door, but she reached behind me and locked it.

She grabbed my hair, shaking my head. "You're nothing but a cheap little piece of shit. If I'd had that abortion, I'd be rich and famous by now. When you were born you sucked all the psych out of me. You stole my life."

"You can have it back," I shouted. "I don't want it. Take it." I fumbled with the lock, but we were moving again. "I don't believe in all this Magick crap. I'm a Christian."

Another punch. "You filthy ingrate. We give you everything and you turn up your nose. I wasn't supposed to have another baby after Nicky."

"Who?" My head jerked up. I felt like I'd been punched again. What was she talking about? "Who's Nicky?" I demanded.

"They took away my baby and left you. I should have gotten rid of you before you were born. I'm glad you've got a bad heart. I'm glad you're dying."

I crouched on the floor, wedged under the dash – out of range of her swinging fist. When I was sure she couldn't hit me, I shouted, "I'm not dying, and I just passed my psi test. You flunked and I passed. I'm going to be a doctor. I hate you." Mother sped up and swerved through traffic, sobbing like a crazy woman.

CHAPTER THIRTY-ONE

LOST BOY

"Time to get to work," said the voice in my head. I sat up in bed. It wasn't even daylight and Chip was in my mind, bugging me. Now I'd have to wake up enough to shut him off. He kept talking: "This is your own fault. Four in the morning's when your defenses are lowest. You keep me out the rest of the time."

"Go away," I groaned, but I knew what to do. I had to visualize the park, go there, and close the lid on Mepa's record player. I might as well go to the bathroom and pee first.

"You do that. And while you're at it, brush your teeth. You're not very sexy with greasy hair and green teeth."

"Go away. I don't want to be sexy. I hate sexy."

"That's happening whether you like it or not. It's called puberty."

"Shit, shit, shit." Wide awake now, I stormed through the vision of the park and slammed the lid on Mepa's damned phonograph. I kicked it a few times, then covered my head with my pillow. Was this a nightmare or was Chip really getting into my head? Or worse – was I turning into Mother? How could I tell if I was going crazy?

What he'd said about puberty was true. My body was changing – and I was growing rapidly. I'd gone from being an average-sized kid to a tall girl, gaining six inches over the past year. My clothes were too short and too tight. I wasn't nice and flat-chested anymore. Linda and Sandy were wearing training bras even though they were flatter than me. I couldn't ask Mother to buy me a bra and I'd made my promise to God never to need anything. I used what I had – chicken pot-pie plates.

Miss Fitch noticed that I was wearing a pie-plate brassiere under my clothes – I could tell by the way she frowned and chewed her pencil. It was terribly uncomfortable, but I was ashamed of what was happening to me. The other kids remained oblivious. All the warriors had taken to wearing more aluminum armor in anticipation of the big jump to Scotland. The more I read to them about the treachery of Clan Campbell, the more we felt the need to buff up our weaponry. The Campbells might be lying in wait to attack us the minute we stepped through the tunnel. It would be foolish to be caught unprepared.

Our designs became more elaborate. We learned to cut and shape the metal and fit it to our bodies. One day at recess, I overheard Miss Fitch and Mrs. Hannah wondering where we managed to find all that aluminum. It was no mystery. Between the apartment dumpsters and the piles of trash in the wetlands, we had a never-ending supply.

Warm winds from the Imperial Valley finally swept the mist from the wetlands. We mounted our bikes and rode across Caspian, forming a battle line along the rim of the hill. The view below was shocking. The wetlands had been transformed. Trucks, jeeps, cranes, and men were scattered all the way to the border. We saw Pedro's jeep waiting on the far side of the Tijuana River. A line of trucks clogged the access road. There was only one way to go – downhill and over the settling ponds.

"Ardchoille!" shouted Patrick.

"Archoille! Archoille!" The brave MacGregors flew over the narrow dirt dikes, taking the steep incline to the wetlands at a thundering gallop. Men in khaki uniforms turned in surprise. "Hey, stop. You can't come down here." They waved their arms and shouted as we galloped past. We leaned forward on our horses, dodging bullets, arrows, and cannon fire. We were on a mission to save the sick by delivering their medicine. Nothing could stop us, not even the US Army Air Force.

"Crazy kids. Don't you know that's Tijuana down there? Turn around."

Of course, it's Tijuana, nincompoops. We pedaled harder and faster, raising our swords as we hit the river at full gallop, howling like wolves. Once across, we slowed to a canter and then a trot, riding up to where Pedro chewed on a toothpick. We dismounted and asked him what was going on.

He shrugged. "They lookin' for some badass drug smugglers. They settin' a trap for 'em. Gonna shoot 'em down, right outta the sky."

"The smugglers are using airplanes?" It was Gary's dream to be a pilot. He had a dreamy look on his face.

Pedro shrugged. "They ask me what I think. So, I say, 'Yeah, that sounds good. Gotta be airplanes flyin' 'cause I don't see nobody smugglin' nothin' down here.'" While he was talking, he handed out the bricks of medicine. We put them in our lunch boxes and loaded those on our bikes.

"Take a look," he said, handing me his field glasses. Naturally, everyone started shoving. They all wanted to take a look. Pedro had to teach us how to line up our "good" eye and then focus for the "bad" eye. I finally got the binoculars away from Albert and looked at the mountain of gear the soldiers had. Most everything was still in boxes stenciled with USAAF, but there were two partially constructed towers and a platform with a shiny round metal drum on top.

"What are those?" I pointed.

"Them bugle things are sound detectors. Army had 'em around here during the war. The round thing is a searchlight. These Army boys gotta have somethin' to shoot at. Ain't no Japs or Krauts so they gonna shoot down smugglers. Now get going before it gets dark and they shoot you."

He shooed us back across the river. We couldn't go very fast uphill in wet sand. The packages of medicine had gotten even heavier and they slowed us down. We had to stand on the pedals as we worked our way between men and boxes. I was afraid we might be stopped, but the USAAF had lost interest in us.

Men stood around the hood of a jeep, studying plans while other men in camouflage unloaded gear. No one even looked up. We slowed to a leisurely pace, threading our way past the piles of equipment and taking a good look. The ground was strewn with stuff that looked like the insides of our hi-fi. Albert was clearly tempted. He would have stopped, but I poked him and told him to move it. If he wanted some of that stuff, we could come back later and pinch it.

An officer winked at us. "Hey there, kids. You want some gum?" Poison! That was enough to get everyone pedaling harder. Our steeds sprouted wings that carried us home in time for deliveries and dinner.

After dinner, Father left with Charlie, Albert's dad, for Navy night. They went twice a month to get drunk and study atomic bombs. Mother was always snoring in bed by the time he staggered home. This was my chance to talk to him alone.

I had stopped dreaming about Chip – I could keep him out of my head most of the time. I was dreaming about Nicky now. I'd asked Miss Fitch what kind of name Nicky was. She said it was short for Nicholas. Did I really have an older brother? What happened to him? I was waiting on the stairs in my pajamas when Father came in. He jumped when he saw me. "Fatso. What d'you want?"

He was drunk and I had the advantage of surprise. I shot him right between the eyes when I demanded: "Where's Nicky?"

"What? …" he staggered and sat down hard on the stairs. "Who told you?"

"Where is he?"

"How dare you! He's nowhere.... There is no he...." Was Father crying? "Nicky was everything you're not. You have no right...none at all." I'd never seen him like that. I was rattled and hesitated too long.

"Jimmy?" Mother stood at the top of the stairs. She was sober. I was trapped between them. "What's wrong? What'd she do now?" I ran down the stairs past Father before he could grab me. I was out the back door, not knowing anything more about Nicky – except that he was real.

I hid in the '53 Chevy, sleeping for a while, until I woke up shivering. No one seemed to be looking for me. The IB Apartments were quiet, settled for the night. I wanted to sneak in and go to bed, but when I approached, the kitchen light was on. I peeked in the window. Mother and Father sat at the table, smoking. Empty wine and beer bottles were scattered on the counters and floor. Mother sat with her back to me.

Father's face was a teary mess. "How'd that kid find out? Who told her?"

"It's that goddamn Chip and his 'you're so magic' psych program." Mother tapped her ashes onto a plate of butts. "She wants to be a sex goddess. She wants to be a movie star – the next Marilyn Monroe. Fat chance..."

"But she knows Nicky's name. What are we going to do?"

Mother was on her own jag. "Dr. Green called today. That creep told me to stop our side business with the Italians. We're supposed to buy her food and clothes with our own money. 'No more of those spick pedophile friends of yours,' that asshole says to me. 'We've got bigger plans for that girl.'"

"But Weezie, how could she know Nicky's name? That's what I wanna know... She said Nicky, clear as day."

"I'll tell you how. The little bitch stole all my psych – that's how. It was mine – my father gave it to me." Mepa? I recalled the bearded old man lying dead in a wooden box. "Then he goes and marks her forehead. He helped that little witch suck the psych right out of my body. She cost me my baby, and my fucking father rewards her for it."

The cross that Mepa had carved into my forehead was on fire. I pressed my hand over the scar above my left eye to stop the pain. Lights flickered and spun around me. Suddenly I was in the vision park under a brilliant blue sky. Children laughed on the swings and pushed the merry-go-round. I wasn't cold anymore. Mepa sat on the bench instead of Chip. He stared at me with his crazy gray eyes that were so much like Mother's. He held up a knife.

"No!" I screamed and ran into the house. My parents barely registered my mad scramble until I reached the stairs.

"You'll never speak of Nicky again," Father shouted after me.

CHAPTER THIRTY-TWO

FREDERICK'S OF HOLLYWOOD

Mother didn't notice the changes in my body, but Father did. He stared at my chest over the top of his morning paper. "Hey Weezie, look at Fatso."

Mother looked me up and down. "She looks like a hooker."

"She's growing a rack as big as yours." Father whistled. "Wait until the boys get a look at those knockers. They're all gonna want to come and play."

"Forget it," said Mother. "Dr. Green said no more of your Italians. We're out of that business."

I cracked my boiled egg, struggling to maintain an air of nonchalance. No more of Father's "special business friends" pawing me was good news but having breasts as big as Mother's wasn't. I buttered my toast. I couldn't let my parents detect my rising panic. If they sensed how much they were humiliating me, it would make them worse. They eventually tired of their game and started picking on my brother, who wasn't so good at ignoring them.

I headed outside. Mother's hooker comment had frightening implications. I needed to be alone to think. It was a warm Saturday morning – too warm for the pie-plate brassiere. I wore shorts and a red tee shirt that had been loose on me the previous summer. Now it stretched over my bulges in uncomfortable ways. I had one other tee shirt, but it was just as tight. Even worse, it was white, and my nipples showed through it. I wasn't ever wearing that one again. Unless I got some new clothes, I was running out of options.

I went to the carport for my bicycle and rode aimlessly up and down Caspian Way, which was still deserted. I pondered the meaning of my parents' words. Were they predicting my future? Did I have anything to say about it? I knew what a hooker was – the party girls that watched their kids play in the IB swimming pool were hookers. They were glamorous women who sat in their windows in tight clothes and sexy underwear, jangling charm bracelets and inviting men to come in for a good time. The young Mexican girls who lived next door with the Smiths were hookers, too.

What was I in this scheme of things? Vito called me a party favor. I wondered what the difference was between a party favor and a party girl. I decided that it had to do with being paid. Chip and his Sex Magick sounded like more of the same kind of slavery – only as a Vril girl.

Mrs. Pendrake was right. I needed a serious career if I wanted a way out. I'd have to become so powerful that no one could force me to do anything I didn't want to. I'd become a lawyer or a judge – maybe even a doctor. But how could I do that with these despicable knockers? Did girls even become doctors? What could I do with no money for college or medical school? I'd have to work and go to school. Was I strong enough? Smart enough?

The morning was getting on my nerves. It was too quiet. I'd just seen an episode of *Twilight Zone* where a girl woke up to find that everyone else on Earth had been vaporized by aliens. What if that happened to me? Could I stand to be alone forever?

I thought about throwing pebbles at Patrick's window or seeing if Kenny was out on his front step yet but hesitated. They were boys and I was a girl. If I was changing into a woman, they would soon be changing into men. Nothing would ever be the same between us once we had adult bodies. We would look like the high school kids who kissed on the Little League bleachers. The thought of kissing Patrick or Kenny felt all wrong. I shook my head. Yuck! What was I thinking?

From Caspian, I looked down to the wetlands. The Army spy gear was covered with tarps. The men would be along later. From my window, I'd watched some of them walking through the IB apartments last night, whistling at the girls in their windows. The Friday night parties had gone on until dawn. Everyone was sleeping now. After lunch, the party girls would put their hair in curlers and wash sheets in the laundry room. Later they'd sit by the pool, painting their nails and watching us swim.

The kids knew to stay quiet in the morning. The only sound on Caspian was the squawking of gulls. I pretended they were vultures waiting for me to die. Their cries heightened my sense of loss. I hated the way that things were always changing and how each change was like a death. It made sense when I was moving from one place to another, from school to school, closing doors behind me and forgetting. But now my own body was changing while I stood still. It had turned me into a time bomb that wouldn't stop ticking.

Life wasn't fair. I should have been born a boy – Mother might have loved me then, and I would be a doctor for sure. My role models, with the exception of the Lady of Loch Tay, were all men. I didn't even like the word *woman*.

I rode my bike through the carport and onto the grass of the courtyard, trying to imagine what it would be like to sit in one of those windows every night wearing sexy underwear and jangling a charm bracelet. Maybe that wouldn't be so bad. I'd bleach my hair blond like Mrs. Smith and Mrs. MacDonald. I'd wear pretty dresses and paint my nails bright colors, but what came next? What did they do when a man came in for a "good time"?

Unwanted memories of the Saturnalia sickened me. I felt dizzy. I sat on the grass with my head on my knees, wanting to throw up my past along with my breakfast. Someone called out, "Sparky?" It was Mrs. MacDonald, Patrick's mom, dragging a cardboard box through her front door.

I stood up, feeling silly. "What're you doing?"

"My spring cleaning – getting rid of some old things that don't fit anymore. A girl gets older and she puts on some weight," she laughed. "Right?"

"Sure." I slumped my shoulders to hide my new curves.

"Can you give me a hand getting this to my car? Can we put it on your bike?" We loaded the box onto my handlebars, and I pushed it to her pink Nash Rambler. She opened the trunk and we slid it in together. I liked Mrs. MacDonald. She was always good for a peanut butter sandwich after school, or to watch us play huzzbees. I'd hardly seen her since Theresa died – except at night in her window. Sometimes she'd look up to my window and wink at me. "Got to take these old things to the Goodwill," she said. She opened the box and I saw a charm bracelet.

"That's beautiful," I gasped.

She held it up. It sparkled in the light, reflecting the sun. "Give me your arm," she said. "Let's see how this looks on you." She snapped it on my wrist. "I have so many of them. The Lobos Locos guys are always giving them to me. This one was Theresa's favorite." We both had tears in our eyes as I jangled the charms. "You should keep it. It would break my heart to give it away to a stranger. Theresa would want you to have it. There, it's settled. It's yours."

"Thank you," I said, unable to take my eyes off the shiny charms.

"You've grown so tall this year. I think you're as tall as I am." In fact, I was a bit taller. I still had my eyes on the bracelet and barely noticed that Mrs. MacDonald was pulling clothes out of the box. She held up a gray felt circle skirt with a pink poodle on it. "This doesn't fit me anymore. I was saving it for Theresa, but now..." She held it up to my waist. "It's a perfect fit. Take it. You can't say no, because Theresa is watching from heaven."

I wasn't about to say no to a charm bracelet or a poodle skirt – the hottest fashions of 1960. I looked up and said a quick thank-you to Theresa. Mrs. MacDonald pulled out pink and gray sweaters that matched the skirt. "Why don't you just take the whole box. You were Theresa's dear, dear friend and I want you to have the things I was saving for her. It'll make me happy to see them on you."

We moved the box to the backseat of the Mercury a few cars over. She hugged me and burst into tears. I said, "Thank-you, Mrs. MacDonald." She kissed my cheek and hurried away.

The top on our convertible was up. I was feeling pretty private when I changed out of my too-tight tee shirt and into one that fit. It was even a little big for me. I had some room to grow. It was pretty and pink, and it smelled like roses. I found a pair of pedal pushers that I put on. Finally, I dumped the box out onto the seat and discovered the mother lode – several matched sets of new brassieres and panties with the price tags still on them.

They were too beautiful to touch with my grubby fingers, so I lifted one of the sets by its plastic hanger. The brassiere had two matching panties. The tag read, "Frederick's of Hollywood: Push-up Bra and Panty Set." The bra was red satin with ruffled black trim. The panties were cut low in the waist and high on the leg. One pair was red with black trim and the other black with red trim. They were lacy and elegant, unlike the cotton Spanky pants that I usually wore, the ones with the days of the week printed on them.

I carefully lifted three more brassiere and panty sets from the pile, hanging them up on the coat hooks above the windows. There was a black set with tiny pink hearts like polka dots, an emerald green ensemble with white stars, white lace trim, and tiny white bows. The last was pure white lace with tiny panties that didn't look very comfortable.

I tried on the red bra. It fit me perfectly. At the bottom of the box, I found a pink satin sachet tied with a yellow ribbon that made the clothes smell nice. Grandma had given me one once, but I didn't know what had happened to it. I decided that from now on I'd keep a sachet with my clothes.

I couldn't let my parents see me carrying a box into the house, so I decided to make several trips, carrying a few things each time. First, I had to take off the charm bracelet and hide it, but not until I'd had a good look at it. It was too dark in the car to see it properly. I walked down to Caspian and sat on the curb.

I shook my wrist, jangling the bracelet. It made a wonderful tinkling sound. Several of the charms were little bells disguised as a tiny house, a Christmas tree, and a girl in a poodle skirt. There was a little poodle head with pink rhinestones for eyes, a steamboat, an alarm clock, and a goose. There were also some Mexican coins – old silver pesos.

I heard a car door slam. An engine revved to life. Panicked, I ran to the carport in time to see the powder blue Chevy pulling out of the parking space next to ours. I'd thought for a terrible moment that I'd been caught out by Father, but our Mercury was still parked in its place. My secret was safe.

I quickly stuffed everything back into the box, including the bracelet, and stashed it behind the dumpster. Then I began carrying in the clothing in paper bags that I hid under my bed. The Frederick's of Hollywood bra and panties sets, and the charm bracelet, went under my mattress with my best treasures.

Now that I was wearing a bra and a shirt that fit me, I felt safer. I hurried out to find Patrick and Kenny. I didn't think any more that day about becoming a woman. I was a kid again. Soon a band of us were riding our bicycles up and down Caspian, making as much noise as we could.

In early afternoon the Army guys started showing up with more crates and cables. They pulled off the tarps. We could see wooden towers in a straight line, parallel to the border. They were mounting sound detectors on them that looked like bullhorns. Albert and the other boys stood mesmerized by the sight of a diesel generator. I knew what a diesel generator was because Albert had explained it in boring detail the day before.

"It's like a car motor." He droned on and on. We ignored him and drew pictures of battles, weapons, and tunnels. "Except that you put in diesel fuel, which is cheaper than gasoline. You don't turn it on with a key like a car. It has a separate starter motor that runs on a battery. ..." and blah, blah, blah. "It's going to power the equipment so they can catch the smuggler planes."

I was dubious. I hadn't ever heard any planes. Exploding tin-can boats, yes – but no aircraft. Apartment C was so close to the border that I surely would have heard something flying over. There was no question that the Army Air Force was serious, though, because every day we'd seen more men and equipment. "They're wiring up the searchlights," said Albert. "Connecting them to the generator."

By the time Pedro brought our deliveries, we were back to drawing tunnels in the sand.

"What'll they do to the smugglers?" Patrick asked him.

"Shoot 'em down," said Pedro. "Kill 'em dead."

"I don't see any guns," I said.

"They probably have an atomic ray gun," said Gary. He'd been to see the sci-fi movie, *The Blob*. He argued continually about the effects of atomic radiation with Rock, who'd seen *The Brain from Planet Arous*. I hadn't seen either one, so I wasn't particularly concerned with man-eating mutants. I did get upset when the boys started drawing aliens in the tunnels. I didn't say anything because maybe they were right. Who was I to judge?

The sooner we jumped the better. It was springtime, the perfect season for flying away to Scotland where flowers other than geraniums bloomed and birdcalls other than the screech of seagulls filled the air. In science class, we were studying the anatomy of plants. Miss Fitch gave me the job of drawing each flower specimen on the blackboard. Our tunnel drawings were soon decorated with the detailed illustrations of flower parts: petals, stamens, anthers, and sepals.

One morning in May, we arrived at school to a buzz of excitement. Rumors circulated that something important had happened at IB Elementary. Once we'd hung up our shields and settled into our seats, Miss Fitch filled us in.

"Class, do you remember the week of testing that we did in January?" We looked at one another, trying to remember back that far. "Well," she tilted her head, "the results of the Comprehensive IQ Tests have been analyzed by the Board of Education and the list of the ten smartest students in California has come out. We haven't seen it yet, but one of those students is right here at Imperial Beach Elementary. Isn't that exciting?" She bounced up and down a few times, clapping like a kid. Miss Fitch could look very young for a teacher. "They're sending someone all the way from Sacramento to announce the name. I sure hope that it's one of our Bluebells, but we'll have to wait a week to find out."

The teachers could talk about nothing else at recess. We could hear them gossiping while we ate our peanut butter and jelly sandwiches at lunch, speculating on who the smartest kid could possibly be. Was the winner a Kerry's Berry or Hannah's Banana? No one seemed to consider a Bluebell of Scotland – us least of all. We didn't think of ourselves as smart. We were the tough kids at school.

CHAPTER THIRTY-THREE

THE SMARTEST KID IN CALIFORNIA

The day Mr. Peterson arrived from the Board of Education didn't start well for me. I'd been having scary nightmares and suspected lingering effects from Father's glass of Tang. So did he. He'd asked me about it several times since Christmas break. "Having weird dreams, Fatso? Bright colors? Hallucinations? Strange noises?"

I always answered, "Nope – slept like a baby."

The night before Mr. Peterson's visit was the worst. I dreamed that an arm smashed through the wall and grabbed baby Nicky. I stabbed it with my silver dagger until it spurted yellow blood that flowed into a ribbon and snapped at me with rattlesnake fangs. It pulled Nicky through the wall, sealing it.

I woke up shivering. My sheets were soaked with sweat. I felt naked even though I slept with my black Frederick's of Hollywood bra and panties under my pajamas. I spent the rest of the night making armor and playing my bagpipe record.

I'd learned to block Chip's early morning intrusions. I kept him out of my psi by mentally stuffing Mepa's record player under the park bench so tightly that it couldn't open and start to play. I nodded off at dawn to the sound of battleships blasting tin-can boats – boom…boom…kaboom. When I woke up, my "Black Watch Pipes and Drums" had a big scratch across it. I was too upset to eat breakfast. I hurried out the door before Mother saw me.

I usually drew the flower parts on the blackboard before botany class, but Miss Fitch asked Cookie to do it instead. She could see that I wasn't feeling well. I'd been run-down – moody and puffy. I had cramps in my tummy that came and went – making me think I had to poop, but there was nothing there.

When Miss Fitch was called to Mr. Miller's office to meet Mr. Peterson, I was face down, asleep at my desk. Kenny and Patrick had to fill me in later on what happened. She'd left Gary in charge and the room erupted into chaos. When she returned, she ignored the paper airplanes and brought order, sorting everyone into their seats. She pulled a spitball out of her hair and addressed the class. "I have exciting news! The student with one of the highest IQs in Southern California is right here in our class – a Bluebell of Scotland!" Everyone was silent, staring at one another.

"Who is it?" asked Rock.

"I don't know yet. They wouldn't tell me, but the representative from Sacramento is on his way to our room right now." Fortunately, she looked behind her at the blackboard. Someone had drawn The Blob devouring a naked lady. She knew who the culprits were. Gary and Rock had been doing this for a couple of weeks. "You two clean this up. Now."

They were quick with the erasers and the board was clean in time for Miss Fitch to write, "Welcome, Mr. Peterson," before he swept into our classroom with the principal, the vice principal, the head of the IB School Board, and Mrs. Pendrake. He shook Miss Fitch's hand and congratulated her for having a top-ten student in her class. A reporter from the *North County Times* snapped pictures with a flash bulb. Even that didn't wake me up. Mr. Peterson looked at his clipboard, cleared his throat, and announced that the smartest kid in Southern California was – me!

He was met with stunned silence and puzzled looks. Nobody in class knew me by my real name. Miss Fitch asked to see his clipboard. "Oh, you mean Sparky MacGregor," she said. The students snapped to attention, turning to stare at me. Later, Kenny said that I looked like a drooling tin can. Gary said I looked like I'd been eaten by The Blob.

"Sparky... wake up," Patrick hissed, poking me. I drifted toward consciousness and heard the class whisper-screaming, "Sparky, Sparky..."

I heard Miss Fitch explaining, "Sparky MacGregor is her nickname. We like to encourage children to be creative here at Imperial Beach Elementary. She's a very talented artist and we're extremely proud of her. Did you see the pictures of the Thanksgiving mural at the San Diego Art Museum?" Miss Fitch winked at me. She was stalling, giving me time to come to my senses.

I rubbed my eyes. I had no idea why she was talking about me. I felt hot and sluggish. My tummy hurt even worse. The vice principal, Mrs. Ackerman was German. She was not as patient as Miss Fitch. She rapped her knuckles on my desk and uttered Mother's terrible words: "Be nice to Mr. Peterson."

A switch flipped in my brain. I floated out of my body because I knew what came next. Mr. Peterson was clearly one of Father's "special business friends." Dr. Green had said there wouldn't be any more of those awful men at our home, so now they were coming to my school. I went on the offensive, throwing Mr. Peterson the evil eye and muttering the most terrible Gaelic curses I could make up. If I'd had a broadsword, I would have run him through with it.

Mr. Peterson's eyes widened. "Do we have the right student?"

"Oh, yes," said Miss Fitch with a bright smile. "She's the one."

"I have her files right here." Principal Miller tapped a thick manila folder. "I can share them with you later, but this is definitely your student." I was surrounded by grownups and felt defenseless. I wanted to cry. I increased the volume of my curses. The class egged me on.

Mr. Peterson looked confused. "What on Earth is she saying?"

"It's Gaelic," said Miss Fitch. "Or something like Gaelic. It's a made-up language the students use when English isn't enough to express their feelings. I believe that she's cursing your immortal soul or something like that. But never mind. Let's all go outside and see the tunnels to Scotland that the children have drawn. It's become quite a project – very creative."

This was the part I feared the most. The class would go outside and leave me alone with this strange man. "Sparky, you and I will go with Mr. Peterson...and yes, you can all go...yes, you can take your shields." I stopped cursing, relieved. I wasn't alone – twenty kids were forming a line, getting ready to show Mr. Peterson our tunnels.

We walked around the school, examining the circles that extended all the way to Mar Vista and across the road into the wetlands. "We're going to jump to Scotland through these tunnels," Patrick announced while the photographer took our pictures. "We just have to get the drawing right."

"We're Scottish," said Gary. "We're MacGregors."

"Are you now?" said Mr. Peterson. "Tell me all about it."

"Come along, students," said Mrs. Pendrake. "You can tell your stories to Mr. Peterson in the new library."

In addition to the "smartest kid" announcement, Mr. Peterson had come to dedicate our new library. None of us had paid much attention to the construction work at school until he cut the red ribbon and we entered a room lined by shelves of new-smelling books. When we were seated at long oak tables that smelled like cut wood, Mr. Peterson made a speech thanking Mrs. Pendrake and the PTA for collecting the books that had been matched by an equal number of books from the Board of Education. In addition, the library would be subscribing to *Life Magazine*, *Look*, and *National Geographic* courtesy of the *North County Times*.

I'd never seen such riches. I stared at the shelves, reading titles and authors, trying to peek through the covers into the magic that each book waited to share. I could barely keep from pulling out a book and starting to read. I was reaching toward the nearest shelf when Mr. Peterson said, "We dedicate this library to the memory of Theresa MacDonald."

Mr. Miller was holding a framed photograph of the mural that the Blue Bells of Scotland had painted for Theresa and Conchita. The original had faded long ago, but someone had taken this picture while the colors were still bright. Mr. Miller handed it to Mr. Peterson, who handed it to Mrs. Pendrake. She hung it on the wall behind the librarian's desk next to Theresa's school picture. Mrs. MacDonald was at the back of the room with Miss Fitch, crying into her handkerchief. She smiled and waved at me when she saw me looking. I was wearing the green satin brassiere and matching panties, although no one knew that but me.

Mrs. Pendrake said, "I declare the Imperial Beach Elementary School library open." We applauded and lined up for our new library cards. While the warriors chattered away with Mr. Peterson about our tunnels and Albert demonstrated his superior knowledge of diesel engines and radio receivers, I stared at the photograph, willing the two angels in the sky to flap their wings and escape into the magical world of these books. "You can be whatever you want to be," I whispered. "Come on, Theresa, come on, Conchita. Fly! You'll be happy in the books. It'll be like going to heaven."

A strange thing happened. Not only did Theresa and Conchita take flight, but each of the stars did as well. Even the painted sputnik flew off the paper and circled the room. I looked closely at the angel faces. I recognized Minerva's bright blue eyes and Elfin's red hair – the little girls from the Saturnalia. "Hurry up. Get into the books. You'll be safe there." They heard me and disappeared. From then on, I drew tunnels with angels and stars, and searched for the girls in every book I read.

CHAPTER THIRTY-FOUR

THE TICKET

Miss Fitch promised me that good things would come from Mr. Peterson's visit, but I wasn't so sure. I didn't like being the focus of attention at school. I'd felt safely anonymous in my aluminum armor, but now the teachers seemed to be on a crusade to improve me. They were nice about it, but even ones I barely knew like Mr. Kerry and Mrs. Hannah started recommending books to read and records to borrow.

I had no doubt that I'd been given a golden ticket with the opening of the library. A new world spread before me every time I opened a book. Some of them were used, but most were fresh from the publisher. I liked nothing better than the smell of a new book and I was careful to open each one in the middle, then in quarters, pressing down the pages the way that Mrs. Pendrake showed me.

She also taught me to use the card catalogue that provided access not only to our library, but to the vast world of books owned by the California Board of Education. If I wanted something that wasn't in our library, I could order it for free and have it in my hands in a few days all the way from Sacramento. I treasured every printed word and illustration about the world beyond Imperial Beach.

I could also get records. I checked out forty-five speed records ranging from the Boston Pops to the New York Philharmonic. At night while my family watched television, I was head down in a book, having adventures on a pirate ship or traveling the Silk Road in a caravan. I read and re-read *Wind, Sand and Stars* by Antoine Saint Exupéry, particularly the part when he was lost over the Sahara Desert. He'd been a pilot in the war and flown over Africa like Paulie had. I pored over maps of the world and read books by Robert Louis Stevenson, Rudyard Kipling, Jack London, and Zane Grey. I discovered the Brontë sisters and Jane Austen. My theft of light bulbs became legendary. Mother would take my light bulb away every morning and I'd replace it at night with a new one from the carports, porches, or school. Nothing could keep me from reading.

I preferred adventure stories, but I also studied self-help books like my copy of *Here's to You, Miss Teen! A Guide to Good Grooming and Poise*. It was illustrated with drawings of teenage girls in ponytails talking on the phone, playing records, and taking bubble baths. Since we only had one bathroom and the door didn't lock very well, I wasn't about to take my clothes off to bathe. I did start washing my hair with dish soap in the kitchen sink and pulling it into a ponytail with rubber bands from the newspaper. I spent a little more time making earrings and bracelets than armor. I even wore my new charm bracelet to school. At first, I was afraid that Patrick would recognize it and say something, but he didn't.

On the Sunday after Mr. Peterson's visit, Mother drove me to San Ysidro to catch the bus to Oceanside. She told me to wait at the pie shop for the shuttle to a new Annex. This time I had 25 cents in my pocket.

The café was nearly empty. I sat in a booth chowing down a slice of apple pie and thinking about my life. Mr. Peterson would be back in a few weeks to speak with me about opportunities for my education that the State of California was ready to offer. I was eager to hear what he had to say. My parents had made it very clear that they had no intention of paying for college. My brother would go to a university, no question – but after high school I was on my own. Grandpa and Grandma had told me that there was money in their wills to put me through college. I'd asked Father about it. "Forget it, Fatso," Father said. "Nobody wants damaged goods."

Well, poop to that. The representative of the Board of Education was coming all the way to Imperial Beach because he saw something of value in me. I experienced a glimmer of hope for the years ahead. I quickly dampened my thoughts, realizing that hope was something to be buried, hidden under a mountain of lies. Suddenly I was too sleepy to finish my pie. The room slanted and my ears buzzed. My head drooped onto the table. I had to close my eyes.

"You think you're smart, do you?" I heard Chip in my mind. "I know you're hiding something. You're keeping secrets." I snapped to attention and sat up. He was somewhere in the pie shop – close enough that I couldn't shut him out. I hurried to finish the pie, stuffing my cheeks in anticipation – but of what?

I looked around anxiously. Kids sat at every booth now. They were well dressed like me. I wore my poodle skirt and the fluffy pink sweater from Mrs. MacDonald – I didn't remember putting those on. The room got louder. It sounded like our class with Gary in charge, but no one was speaking. I was hearing their thoughts. They were worried. Psi was thick in the air.

The jukebox lit up. I looked over, expecting to see kids pumping in nickels, but no one was there. The music started on its own: Boom…boom…boom…boom… The walls vaporized. We were spun into the whorl of a twister and sucked over a cartoon rainbow into bright yellow sky. Our hearts synchronized to the pulse of the beat. Our visions coalesced. We were in the park – separate but melded together. Mepa's record player had been replaced by the jukebox, its neon lights flashing to the music. Bluebirds chirped. Monarch butterflies flitted between blossoms. We had flowers in our hair.

Chip stood on the bench tossing handfuls of jellybeans. Kids grabbed and ate them as if they were starving. I swallowed the mouthful of pie that I'd stored in my cheeks, ignoring the candy, and pulled unwanted daisies from my ponytail. The music amped up and the kids sang along. They took off their shoes and danced barefoot on the grass – everyone except me. I felt as sad as they seemed happy.

"I don't belong here," I said.

Chip's head grew huge in front of me. "This's what happens when you try to keep secrets. You get left out. Eat a jellybean and join the party."

I didn't move. I liked the music and dancing barefoot looked like fun. I really wanted to feel like dancing, but I didn't. My heart wasn't cooperating. My feet were stuck to the ground. "I don't feel like dancing. I don't belong here."

"You better hope that you do belong here." The music tempo sped up, becoming so loud that my teeth rattled.

I held my hands over my ears and screamed, "Where's Nicky? What did you do to him?"

The music stopped. "What's this all about?" I recognized Dr. Green's voice. He was standing next to Chip, wearing a white coat.

"It seems she's found out about the other child."

"Weezie's kid? How can that be?" Dr. Green scowled. "Talk to those parents. This shouldn't have happened."

"There's more. She's keeping something back from me. She's keeping secrets," said Chip. "We've fine-tuned the scenario. She has responded well to the remote viewing, but she's building walls to keep me out. There are things about her that I don't know."

"She's resisting? Is that good or bad?"

"Both. She's harder to control as a subject, but independence makes her more resourceful. It made Wally a great agent – and he's also difficult, as you know." They looked at me. I felt like a rabbit in the lights of an on-coming car. I barely knew my Uncle Wally.

Dr. Green asked, "What do you suggest?"

"We'll take her back to basics," said Chip.

"This is like breaking a spirited horse, isn't it?"

"That's right. We'll put her on the wheel for a good dose of yin/yang until she gets it."

I came to life. "No!" I turned and ran through the park – headfirst into a wall. It knocked me on my butt. I shook my head, stunned.

My clothes were gone. I was wearing a hospital gown. The trees and grass faded until there was no park – just a plain white room with speakers on the wall and a mirror. "Goddamn Sex Magick bullshit," I screamed. No wonder Mother's mind cracked. These creeps would make anyone crazy. I stood up and pounded on the glass, shouting at the men I knew were standing behind it. "Let me out. I'm leaving."

"Can she see us?" Dr. Green sounded surprised. "Did she hear what we said?"

"Of course, she did. She's got psi," said Chip proudly. "I told you, she's the real deal."

It took two Nanny Blacks to chase me around the room, catch me, give me a shot, and tie me down to the wheel. The yin/yang started to spin. Voices chanted through the speakers: "There is no good…There is no evil…There is no God…There is only the Prince of Light…There is only the Prince of Air…" I was spun into green – but this time I didn't surrender. Instead I ripped the tinfoil from my head like the Lady of Loch Tay had taught me. I fell into my mind and screamed, "Ardchoille!"

I jumped through the Earth to Scotland.

CHAPTER THIRTY-FIVE

MR. PETERSON

"Sit down, Sparky." Mr. Miller nodded to a chair. I sat, holding tight to the seat by hooking my toes around the legs to keep from floating away.

Mr. Peterson looked up from my file. "Your family certainly moves a lot," he said, smiling. "I have your records from several states. You're a remarkable student. You've got an aptitude for both art and mathematics, which is unusual. Your handwriting needs work and you'd benefit from tutoring in hygiene. The bottom line is that, with an education, you'll have a great future."

The words were thrilling. I tried to smile, but my face was frozen. "We'd like to offer you a scholarship to attend a school for gifted students in Sacramento. I know it's a long way from here, but you're welcome to stay with my family."

"Sacramento?" Great! The farther away, the better.

"My wife and I have a big house and six children. There are always three or four foreign students. You'd fit right in."

I felt dizzy. I struggled to digest this: "Do you have a dog?"

"Two dogs, a cat, a parrot, and two turtles. Sound okay?"

It sounded wonderful, especially if it meant studying to be a doctor instead of a party favor. I relaxed a little. I even felt a bit happy – then he dropped the stink bomb. "Let's set up a meeting with your parents, shall we?"

Shit. I jumped out of my body and hovered at the ceiling, barely listening to him explaining why the Board of Education couldn't speak to me about scholarships or accelerated programs without my parents present – it was the law. My belly hurt – the cramps were back. "I spoke with your mother this morning." *Shit. Shit.* "She hung up on me."

"Sparky, would you please go and ask Miss Fitch to join us?" said Mr. Miller. "Maybe she should be the one to call your parents and set up a meeting."

I barely got outside before breaking apart. My life was being snuffed out and nobody could save me – not even the State of California. I staggered against the wall of the breezeway, unable to breathe. I was locked in a coffin with no air. I'd be a Bluebird until I died. I fell to my knees outside the classroom howling with grief. Miss Fitch came out of the classroom and knelt beside me. "Sparky, honey, what's wrong?"

"Mr. Miller wants to see you," I sputtered.

She helped me to my feet. "Lean on me." She walked me to a chair outside the principal's door. I bawled all the way there. Miss Fitch went into the room and Mrs. Lipsky came to sit with me. The nurse put her arm around my shoulders and offered a hankie. "There now, Miss Sparky, it can't be bad as all that." I bawled louder. "You'd better quiet down and listen to what they're saying about you. It's important." I swallowed my sobs. Mr. Peterson was talking about my parents.

"Why is setting a meeting such a problem? Surely the parents must be pleased with this opportunity for their daughter."

"The problem *is* her parents," Miss Fitch sounded angry. "Just look through that file. Every state that family has ever lived in has documented child abuse and prostitution. As soon as Child Services steps in or the school files a police complaint, they move across state lines and start over. Look at the Illinois file from last summer. Who could do those things to a little girl?"

"That's why we've gone along with her MacGregor fantasy," said Mr. Miller. "This Sparky character is her defense against reality. It's working for now, but her real hope is education."

"I'm aware of how bad the statistics are from this county," said Mr. Peterson. "That's one of the reasons we're taking such an interest in this student."

Miss Fitch snorted. "Imperial Beach is the least of her problems. She disappears from school for days at a time and comes back exhausted. She has obviously been drugged and sexually abused."

"Sounds like a pedophile operation. Have you notified the police?"

"We have. They won't do anything unless we provide proof," said Mr. Miller. "It seems high-powered people are involved."

"Have you asked the girl about it?"

"She just shrugs or says, 'Dunno.' It's possible that she really doesn't know – especially if she's being drugged."

"That, and denial," said Mr. Peterson. "Children can develop selective amnesia following physical trauma. There must be other ways to get proof?"

"You met our PTA president, Mrs. Pendrake – the retired judge? She's gone to their apartment when Sparky's not in school and confirmed that she's not at home either. A few days later Sparky comes back to school with a note from her mother claiming she's been in bed with a weak heart."

"Does she have heart disease?"

"We've had her checked," said Mr. Miller. "Her heart's fine. She's underweight and anemic, but she's out on the playground every recess playing kickball and drawing tunnels to Scotland."

"What is this fascination with Scotland? Aren't most of the students Mexican?"

"These children have no clue where they come from. Most don't know who their fathers are. The girl has some knowledge of family history that's serving her well and it's helping the other students. At this age they're still magical thinkers. Make-believe is more real than reality. That'll change with adolescence."

"Aren't you concerned about playing too far into this child's fantasy by letting her use an imaginary name?"

"I was concerned at first, but it's worked out well," said Mr. Miller. "Besides, it's not unusual for students to attend school under fictitious names."

"Don't you require birth records before registration?"

"It's not always possible in a place like this and we're not denying an education to any child because of some missing paperwork." A drawer scraped open and papers rustled.

Mr. Miller said, "Here's a case in point. Another fifth grader in the same class, Kenny Smith, was born in Tijuana. The orphanage named him Angel Rodriguez after the janitor who found him in a dumpster. The Smiths brought him to California by posing as his parents. Cranston's their real name, and they have police records for trafficking children for prostitution. We suspect they're running a brothel at the Imperial Beach Apartments, but the local police won't investigate. We're powerless unless Kenny talks to us. If he does, I'm afraid the Cranstons will just dump him back in Mexico. He's not adopted so he has no legal rights in California. The best we can do is to educate the boy while we have him."

He shuffled more papers. "Here's another example – Patrick MacDonald. His mother's a prostitute. Her real name is Terry Suarez. She doesn't know who fathered either of her children."

"I heard about the daughter Theresa. Her death was tragic."

"Terry had Patrick when she was thirteen and Theresa when she was fifteen."

"I take it there's no Mr. MacDonald?"

"It's a name taken from the children's song. Terry works in her apartment at night. She's been overdosing Patrick with aspirin to make him sleep since he was a baby. It's nearly killed him a few times. We've warned her of the dangers, but she keeps doing it. There's no doubt that the aspirin contributed to the death of her daughter from a brain hemorrhage. And on it goes with student after student. It's our job to prepare them for life as best we can. Identifying with some historic Scottish clan that fought for honor instead of sex, money, and drugs is something to encourage."

"And the pie plates?"

"Wearing armor makes them feel safer," said Miss Fitch. "Drawing tunnels to Scotland gives them hope."

"The whole school seems caught up with this tunnel thing. I've never seen anything quite like it."

Mr. Miller chuckled. "If they're out on the playground working together instead of fighting or getting mixed up with drugs, then we've accomplished something. I believe in supporting imagination. Sparky's got plenty of that."

"Is the library helping?"

"The library's a big success," said Miss Fitch. "Sparky's one of our most enthusiastic readers. Mrs. Pendrake tells me she's been ordering books from Sacramento. If that child gets the chance for an education, she'll run with it."

Mr. Miller sighed. "Right now, it's her parents we have to deal with – and that won't be easy."

There was a pause. Then Mr. Peterson said, "If I can make an observation, the girl is headed into puberty…."

I gasped. Puberty! Did everybody know? I couldn't listen anymore. I was suffocating. My molecules wouldn't stay glued together. They dissolved and blew away. Mrs. Lipsky pushed my head down between my legs. "Pull yourself together, sweetie. You'll just need to grow up faster than most." I threw up on the floor.

CHAPTER THIRTY-SIX

PSI

I spent the next hour curled under a blanket on Mrs. Lipsky's exam table. I was in no hurry to go back to class and face my friends. They'd seen me on my knees, bawling. I shuddered at the memory of their faces crowded at the door when Miss Fitch came out. They'd want to know what had happened. I had a lot to mull over before I could tell them.

"You'll just need to grow up," Mrs. Lipsky had said. Those were frightening words. Did she mean today? How? I had no money, no rights. My parents owned me. They could sell me, and I couldn't stop them.

I recalled Dr. Green's meeting with Father. He'd said that Mother wanted me to die of a weak heart. Father had said he wanted the NSA to take me away. I cringed and recalled the fear in Father's voice when Dr. Green threatened to cut him off. They'd lose their income if I left for Sacramento. The special school might be free, but my parents would never let me go. I shivered under the blanket, pulling my knees against my chest, rocking quietly like I'd learned to do at Lookout Mountain where children who cried in their beds were beaten into silence. I buried my nose between my knees, breathing the scent of my skin. I smelled nice – like peanut butter.

I picked at the scabs on my shins. Why did my parents hate me? Mother said they took Nicky away because I'd been born. If my big brother came back, would she let me go to Sacramento? Maybe I could find him myself. He must be grown up by now – big enough for high school. What did he look like? I imagined him with the same upturned, freckled nose as Paulie, but with black hair and hazel eyes – like me. He must be brave and smart to be on his own for all these years. Did he fly a plane?

I felt a glimmer of hope, imagining Nicky touching down in the yellow biplane just long enough for me to jump aboard. I saw Mother and Father running after us down Caspian Way, shouting as we took to the air and soared over their heads. They'd be hopping mad that I'd found Nicky and he belonged to me. I'd be his co-pilot for life. I'd never have to see another Nanny Black or spin on that goddamn yin/yang wheel again. We'd fly to Africa like Antoine de Saint-Exupéry, looking down on waves of golden sand that stretched from sunset to daybreak on the starlit Sahara.

I dozed, sweating under the blanket until the bell rang for two o'clock recess. The butcher paper I lay on was wet and torn. I pushed off the blanket and sat up. Across the room Mrs. Lipsky sat writing at her desk. Her black hair shone in a halo of light. Outside, kids ran and shouted in the breezeway. In the office, it was just her and me. I had some pressing questions.

"Mrs. Lipsky?"

She looked up and smiled. "Are you feeling better?"

"Do you think I could be a doctor someday if I work really hard?"

"Yes, honey. I do."

"Do you think I'm strong enough – what with my heart trouble and everything?"

"Your heart is fine. You're a lot stronger than you look." She chewed her pencil like Miss Fitch. "You remind me of a little dandelion poking its head up through the asphalt. You've got a long hard climb, but you'll bloom."

"What's a pedophile?" I asked. "Mr. Peterson said that word. What does it mean?"

She frowned. "A pedophile – " she paused. "A pedophile is someone who does terrible things to children."

I was stunned. "There's really a word for that?"

"I'm afraid so."

Betrayal punched me in the chest. If there was a word for what was happening to me, why didn't the grownups stop it? What was wrong with them? Humiliation burned my cheeks.

Her eyes looked sad. "Is there something you want to tell me?"

There were a thousand somethings, but what good would it do? She wouldn't believe me. I barely believed myself. I tried to smile, but my lips quivered too much. I changed the subject. "What's amnesia?"

"It means forgetting."

That's what I needed right that moment – amnesia. I closed my eyes to conjure up my little vacuum cleaners and brooms. I ordered them to get to work behind my eyeballs, sweeping away every bad memory so I could start over. "Get busy," I shouted in my head, but this time, they didn't respond. They just glared at me as if to say, "We don't work for you anymore."

Cramps struck again, taking my breath. Maybe I should tell Mrs. Lipsky about the pains that were shooting into my back and down my legs, making me want to vomit. Pedro had said that's what typhus does

143

before it kills you. Officer Friendly-Jones told us we'd get typhus from the Tijuana River. If I had typhus, everyone would know I'd been down in the wetlands and I'd be in even more trouble. I lay back down and curled into a sweating ball – trapped in a body I couldn't trust.

"I can't grow up," I groaned. "I don't know how."

"You'll figure it out, honey. That's life. Everybody grows up."

"It's too hard." I wailed.

"Every life is hard. Your life is a little harder than most, that's all. You're plenty smart. You'll grow up and live your own life." Why couldn't she just tell me what to do – or give me a book? I recalled what Mr. Miller said about my friends and how hard their lives were.

I asked, "What'll happen to Kenny if the Smiths dump him in Mexico?"

"I'm afraid they'll sell him to a child brothel in the Zona Norte. That poor boy doesn't even speak Spanish."

"What's a child brothel?"

"That's where pedophiles go to buy sex with children."

I blushed, grateful for her honesty. She frowned and asked me, "Do you know anything about that?"

I pretended not to hear. How could I answer? Should I tell her that Kenny lived in a brothel now? Should I tell her that I knew all about tighty-whities and what the Lobos Locos did to him because I'd heard his screams through my wall. Or that he did speak Spanish? Would that help him – or me? The cramps eased a little.

I pushed myself up, but something else felt terribly wrong, upside-down. Mr. Miller, Mrs. Lipsky, and Miss Fitch were adults. How could they let so many evil things happen? The room spun and I understood that "growing up fast" meant that I was on my own. Nobody was going to fix things for me. I couldn't breathe. My vision narrowed into a funnel of light. "I've got to get to Scotland," I blurted.

Mrs. Lipsky sighed and went back to her file, "Yes, Sparky. Go to Scotland."

I stared at the top of her head and my heart hurt. She'd given me a chance to talk and I'd let her down. She'd spoken to me like a grownup and I'd reacted like a little kid. What a weenie. I had to regain her trust.

"I'm sorry, Mrs. Lipsky. I know there isn't any Scotland. There's no tunnel. I made it all up and lied to my friends because it made them happy. There's no Lady of Loch Tay. Robin Abroch died in 1645."

She looked up. "Oh honey, there's always been a Scotland and you'll get there some day – I know you will."

t/

I was really confused now, but before I could ask her what she meant, a commotion erupted in the hall. Kids shouted, "Punch him. Kick him… asshole deserves it."

The door flew open and Mr. Kerry pushed Gary in, holding him firmly by the scruff of his neck. Gary was all hyped up, swinging wildly. "Get your hands off. He hit me first."

"Goodness. That's some shiner," said Mrs. Lipsky. "I'll get an ice pack."

I made room for Gary on the table. He sat beside me breathing hard. Our legs dangled. "It's not my fault, Mrs. Lipsky. Really! It's that goddamn Albert…." He pressed the ice to his swelling eye.

"Watch your language," said Mr. Kerry, backing out the door. "You've got one detention – you want two?"

"Fuck!" said Gary, pounding his fist on the table. "Shit, shit, shit…" Mrs. Lipsky shot him a look. "…sorry, ma'am," he said and turned his good eye on me. "It's just that Bertie's so damn stuck up – thinks he's so smart. He said The Blob is made of silly putty. He said everything we see in movies is phony."

I shrugged. Albert was right. I'd been in a movie studio and everything *was* phony. The real Blob was probably the size of a baseball and half as scary. I stayed quiet. I wasn't about to confront Gary when he was on a rampage. He was silent for a while. I thought maybe he was going to cry. He and Albert were best friends.

The bell rang and recess was over. Students sorted themselves into their classrooms. When the noise quieted, Mrs. Lipsky handed us hall passes. "Okay, you two – back to class."

We walked alone in the breezeway. Gary wasn't giving it up. "What does that dummy know? He hasn't even seen the movie." He scooped up a pebble and skimmed it into the parking lot. I spotted a bottle cap under the bushes – orange with a black bull. I bent to pick it up just as a black van turned into the drive, passing a few feet from my head.

It can't be. I froze in place, my heart pounding in my open mouth. They wouldn't come for me at school, would they? I kept low, backing deep into the bushes. I peeked out at the van that looked achingly familiar with its dark tinted windows. It didn't park in the lot but idled at the curb near our classroom. My psi tingled. Chip was nearby scanning for my brainwaves. I covered my face, trying to become invisible. If I didn't hide my psi, he'd find me easily. I'd draw him right to me like an antenna.

I forced myself not to think about him. I emptied my brain of thoughts until there was nothing in my skull but fog and the boom… kaboom of exploding tin-can boats. Was he coming to get me because of Mr. Peterson? Chip's silhouette materialized faster than I could mentally erase him. He stood in the imaginary park, trying to pull me to him. "I know you're in that classroom, Suzy Q. We've got you cornered. Come on out so we can beat the traffic back to Oceanside."

I held my breath, shocked by his mistake. I wasn't in the classroom. Chip, the grownup master of psi, was *wrong*. I kept my breathing slow, numbing my emotions while his words ricocheted in my mind. I tried to fathom what this meant without forming ideas that he might detect. The van window rolled open. A man who looked like a Nanny Black flicked ash from his cigarette.

I heard the rumbling of evil and knew that the MPs were in the back. I saw them in spirit, their long tongues flicking as they tasted the air like snakes. Chip's image in my head said, "Come on, Suzy Q. Eat your jelly-beans and dance. We've got a new group called The Freaks. I'll make you a rock 'n' roll star."

I nearly screamed when the bushes parted over my head.

CHAPTER THIRTY-SEVEN

GOD'S HOUSE

"What the hell you doin'?" Gary stared down at me.

"Go away," I hissed.

He didn't move. "You comin' to class or what?" No wonder Albert punched him.

"Get lost." I whisper-screamed. He stepped back, looking hurt.

"Wait," I gasped. Chip would see my empty desk when Gary opened the door. I needed more time. I needed a plan. Static buzzed in my head. I had it: "You're gonna be a U2 pilot, right? Like Francis Gary Powers?" The captured American spy was all over the news. He was Gary's hero. "Go see who's in that black van. Make sure they don't see you. Then sneak around behind the school and report back to me. Stay in the bushes – under the radar."

Gary made airplane noises, spreading his arms like wings. He stopped and pointed. "That van?"

"Shhh! Be quiet. Don't let them see you."

"Why? I've got a hall pass."

"This is a secret mission."

He hesitated. We'd just heard that Powers was being tortured in a Siberian prison. "What if I get caught?"

I rolled my eyes. "You won't – you're the best sneaker I know. You're not scared, are you?"

"Course not." He flew off in a low crouch, disappearing behind the box hedge.

I closed my eyes but regretted it. The park materialized. The jukebox flashed on, music revved up and Chip held out a bowl of jellybeans. I snorted and flattened the scene, slamming it shut like a pop-up book. Chip always said I'd learn to keep him out, and I was doing it. I thickened the fog behind my eyeballs. I didn't need to visualize the park to find Chip. I could locate his energy. He looked like a green radar blip. I could feel his confusion.

He was searching Miss Fitch's classroom with his psi, expecting to find me among all the sparks of life inside. But he still couldn't see me. I pumped up the fog, then pulled back, afraid to overdo it. After all, I was just a kid running on dumb luck and he was a pro. How long could I keep this up? What was keeping Gary? Had they captured him? He'd probably forgotten about me and gone home.

The breath of fear shivered up my spine and the pop-up book burst open again – all daisies and rainbows. "There you are." Chip flashed a white smile. Trapped! My pulse pounded as I churned up more fog. "Come out of that class – now." He was still wrong. Could my psi be working better than his? Could I use it to save myself? First, I had to calm down and mute my fear. I pressed my nose against my knees and focused on a line of red ants that marched across my shoe and up my leg. They were heading for my underpants. I rocked forward into a crouch, lifting my butt off my ankles.

I jumped when Gary crawled next to me. He was sweating, breathing hard. He flashed me a look that revealed the steel of a real fighter pilot. "There're two guys in front – one's bald and one has a ponytail. There're more guys in the back." Then he asked, "Are they the ones that took you away on Christmas?"

"Yeah," I rasped. Up to that second, I'd hoped that the bald guy wasn't Nanny Black – that there was no Chip blip, no MPs with lizard tongues. I'd lied so much already that I didn't know why I should believe myself. I'd lied to my friends, parents, teachers, doctors, police, Chip, and Dr. Green. I'd lied to God, shutting Him out so He wouldn't see how bad I was. If I lied all the time, Chip had to be a lie, too, didn't he? My lip quivered. I was confusing myself. I could not weaken now.

"I've got a plan," said Gary. "Wait for the bell. When the kids come out, hide in the middle of the crowd and run away."

It was a good plan. We were silent for a long time, crouched under the bushes, watching the hall clock take forever to tick down the final minutes of school. Finally, the bell rang. The doors opened and kids shuffled into the breezeway. They looked half-asleep, dragging their feet. "What's wrong with them?" I whispered, then I remembered that it was Monday – half of them had been drugged by their party girl mothers over the weekend. "There isn't enough noise. They'll spot me."

"There's Bertie. I'll start a fight." Gary plunged into the crowd, fists swinging. A brawl erupted in a tumult of punches, shouts, and flying books. I crouched out of sight and watched it in psi – a tangled mass of sparks and lines that roiled into chaos as kids piled into the fracas and teachers tried to pull them apart. "Run!" Gary shouted.

I raced up the driveway, across IB Boulevard and into the shrubbery of St. James Church, where bird of paradise plants and pampas grass grew taller than me. Looking back, I saw the black van speeding away toward Coronado Avenue. It passed the police car of Officer Friendly-Jones pulling into the school. The cruiser blasted its siren, scattering kids in every direction. Mr. Kerry had Gary by the ear. He was waving his arms and crying. Mrs. Lipsky held an ice pack to Albert's face. He was crying, too. The boys were being marched to detention.

The rest of my friends were spread out across Mar Vista playfield on their way to the clubhouse. I could catch them if I hurried. I took a few steps but stopped. Had Miss Fitch told them about my scholarship? Did she tell them that I wanted to go to Sacramento so much it made my bones hurt – even if it meant leaving them behind? It was true and truth was starting to burn a hole in me.

I knew that telling the truth was my one chance to get away from my parents and escape the Annex, but how could I explain Nanny Black, and the yin/yang wheel, or my trips to Disneyland? I'd sound like a crazy person. Everyone would think Sex Magick and psi were stories I'd made up. What if it got back to Dr. Green that I was blabbing? I'd spend the next ten years tied to that damn wheel. I touched the cross on my forehead, recalling the star traced there in Minerva's blood. I might be the next sacrifice.

The pampas grass shimmered in a hot wind. Beyond the swaying fronds, I saw an old man on a bench. My heart skipped two beats – Mepa? No, it was just old Mr. Cortez, the gardener. He smiled and waved. I waved back. My eyes followed the church steeple rising behind him like a really big antenna – all the way up to the cross on top. I remembered how the John Muir flagpole had buzzed against my ear, sucking out my thoughts and sending them to God. If I pressed my forehead against this cross, maybe He would hear me and know that I wasn't lying. But what if He struck me dead, or sent me straight to Hell for the things they'd made me do?

In my favor, Mr. Peterson had called me a remarkable student. He'd even offered to let me live with his family. Miss Fitch said I was the best reader in school. Mrs. Pendrake told me I was a wonderful artist. Mrs. Lipsky said I could be a doctor. They were grownups, their opinions should count with God.

I paused on the stone steps of St. James. Should I risk it? Yes – these were desperate times. I climbed up, but hesitated again at the church door, afraid to try the latch. I'd already turned to go when the door swung open.

I jumped and let out a shriek. Pastor John jumped too. He smiled. "Sparky, what a nice surprise. Come in. We're boxing up the Bluebells' blanket donations for Tijuana."

Blankets? I'd forgotten all about them. The chapel was bustling. Ladies sorted piles of clothing and folded the heavy blankets, packing them into three large boxes. I ran my hands over the rough green wool, stamped with USAAF in black letters.

"Thirty-three dollars bought ten blankets at the PX. The base auxiliary donated ten more," said Mrs. Pastor John, offering a plate of oatmeal raisin cookies. I took one. "Would you like to write a note from the Bluebells before we close the boxes?"

"Yes." Here was something else that I could do to impress God. The blankets, the medicine deliveries, my quest to help the sick – these were all positive things. So were the murals, the fawn, and hiding the angels in library books. Surely God would see that I wasn't all bad. "Can I draw pictures, too?"

"We've got crayons and paper in the Sunday School."

Mrs. Pastor John showed me to a classroom. I sat at a table and folded sheets of foolscap into cards. I drew a picture of little Conchita in a cute outfit, surrounded by angels and stars. I drew her in a different dress for each of the three boxes and signed the cards with hearts from the Bluebells of Scotland. It wasn't my best work, but the ladies were in a hurry. They wanted to be back from Tijuana before dark. They thanked me, saying that I sure could draw. I stood with the pastor and his wife waving as the old woody station wagon drove off toward Tijuana.

I felt braver. "Pastor John, can I speak to you?"

"Come, sit." We sat in a pew.

"Would you like another cookie?" Mrs. Pastor John passed the plate. I put one in my pocket.

"I want to confess," I said.

Pastor John looked surprised. "We're not Catholic, honey. We're Lutheran. We don't do confession."

My face flushed. He was speaking to me like a child. "This is God's house, isn't it?"

"Yes, it is."

"Is He here?"

"He's always present."

"Then I need to tell Him the truth about the terrible things I've done. I need to know if he's mad at me."

"There's no need, Sparky. God grants you absolution, no matter how you've sinned."

"What's absolution?"

"It means that He forgives you without judgment. God's grace is a gift. There are no conditions."

I shook my head. "No, no, no." Did he think I was an idiot? God didn't just give things away for free. That's not how it worked on the *Rosicrucian Bible Hour*. "I want Him to punish me and get it over with. If He wants to feed me to giant spiders and turn me into a human husk, then fine. I'm ready. If He wants to put me on the yin/yang wheel for the rest of my life, that's okay because I've been bad. I've been very bad."

I burst into tears, raising my eyes to heaven, prepared for death – or spiders. Mrs. Pastor John put her arm around my shoulders. I leaned against her and bawled. "I want to tell the truth, but I don't think He'll believe me."

She rubbed my back. "Poor sweetheart. I've called someone for you," she said. "She's coming to take you home." I heard footsteps. Please, God – not Mother.

"What's wrong, child?" It was Mrs. Pendrake. She slid onto the pew next to me. "I just heard about your scholarship to the Brookfield School in Sacramento. You should be over the moon."

Mrs. Pastor John stroked my hair. "Congratulations, dear – that's wonderful news."

"No – it's terrible news," I sobbed. "My parents won't let me go. And God won't help me because I deserve to go to Hell. They make me do terrible things and I'm so sorry...."

"What are you saying? Who makes you do things?"

"Dr. Green, Dr. White, Dr. Brown, Nanny Black, Mepa...Vito...Father..."

"I don't understand," said Pastor John.

"I'm afraid that I do," said Mrs. Pendrake, who used to be a judge. She took my hand. "Where do they take you, Sparky? Do you remember? Can you tell us?"

"A lot of different Annexes. This month it's a place in Oceanside called Camp Ecclesia."

"I've heard of that place." Pastor John shook his head. "Are you sure?"

I nodded. The truth was bubbling up – unstoppable. "I take the bus from San Ysidro to the Oceanside Pie Shoppe. Nanny Black drives me and other kids to Sex Magick in a van with dark windows. We go through a barbed-wire gate. There are guards with dogs and a sign that says 'Camp

Ecclesia.' I just saw their van at the school. They were coming for me. I don't want to go back there – ever."

"Good Lord," Pastor John lowered his voice. "I've heard the accusations of pedophilia...."

"Wait a minute," Mrs. Pendrake tensed. "You said the black van was at the school? Today?"

"They tried to get me, but Gary started a fight. I ran away."

"I'm calling the police," said Pastor John.

"Hold on," said Mrs. Pendrake. "We've got to think this through. I'm afraid we're dealing with something more powerful than local cops."

"It's called the NSA," I said. They gave me puzzled looks. "It's the government."

"I've never heard of the NSA," said Mrs. Pastor John.

"I haven't either." Pastor John shrugged. "It must be one of those new agencies that sprouted up since the war."

"It's like the CIA," I said, but they still looked confused. How could they not know? I'd known about it all my life. "My uncle Wally works for them. He's a spy."

"Good Lord," said Pastor John. "This is terrible. Why would a federal agency support pedophilia?"

"They want my psi – that's P-S-I. They want me to be a Vril girl."

"What's psi? What's a Vril girl?" asked Mrs. Pastor John.

"I've read about this," said Mrs. Pendrake. "Hitler had beautiful spies called Vril girls. They were tall women with psychic abilities who were experts in seduction, science and blackmail."

I recalled my trips to Disneyland. "That's right...and Dr. Green talked about Hitler."

"This sounds like science fiction," said Pastor John.

"I wish it was," said Mrs. Pendrake.

Mrs. Pastor John drew me closer. "You poor child."

I spoke faster: "They dress up like goats. They drug me and have sex with me." My words slurred in my rush to get it all out before they stopped listening – or God struck me dead. "They killed Minerva and Elfin at the Saturnalia. They cut out their hearts and drank the blood. I'm so sorry."

Mrs. Pastor John gagged. "I'm going to be sick...."

"Look." I lifted my bangs and pointed to the cross on my forehead. "It's the mark of Satan. My grandfather cut me with a knife when I was three. He promised me to the Prince of the Air. He sacrificed my cat PooPoo. He killed PooPoo because I loved him."

Mrs. Pendrake squeezed my hand too hard. "Poor little Sparky."

"They sent me to Annexes in Seattle, San Luis Obispo, Lookout Mountain, Laurel Canyon…lots of places. I don't want to go there anymore. You've got to help me get away. I want to go to Sacramento. I want to grow up and be a doctor…please." I paused, breathless. The room spun. The grownups were silent, staring at the ground. I sensed their fear and confusion. I lost my nerve. I had to get out of there. I pulled my hand away and jumped up. "Gotta go." I backed away.

Pastor John patted the seat. "Sit down, Sparky. Please, give us a minute. This is a lot to take in. It's all so shocking." His voice quavered and he wouldn't look me in the eye. I'd risked everything to tell the truth and all I'd done was scare him. Grownups weren't supposed to be afraid. Was it possible that they didn't even know how to help me? Maybe they all hated me now that they knew I was damaged goods.

We were in God's house but where was He? I looked at the stained-glass window over the altar. Sunlight slanted through the colored glass. I was looking for Jesus, but what I saw was a jukebox. Horror crashed over me in a cold wave. I had to escape. I backed up the aisle shaking my head, "No…no…"

Mrs. Pendrake reached out to me from far away, "Sparky, wait. Please let us help you." Behind her, the jukebox in the window whirred, lights bubbled and danced. A record snapped into place. I didn't wait. I ran from the church and through the garden, darting into traffic. Horns honked, tires squealed, drivers shouted in Spanish, but I kept running.

I'd barely reached the IB Apartments when I was doubled over by cramps that split my body in two. I bent over, gasping for breath, certain the typhus was killing me. I staggered across the lawn. The door to Apartment C was open wide. I wanted to run upstairs, climb into bed, and shut out the world with Miracle Sword. I was nearly at the porch when the upstairs blinds tilted open. I froze.

Chip stood at my bedroom window. I backed deep into shadow, surrounding myself with white static. Did he see me? No – not yet. I was really getting good at disappearing. He knew I was close, though. I watched his psi scanning the yard with regular sweeps. He'd find me soon. I thought about running back to the church, but the van with Nanny Black was waiting somewhere on IB Boulevard – I felt it. I also sensed the MPs closing in, tasting the air for my breath. I was surrounded. My static shield broke and my psi weakened. Chip's psi swept closer – I was as good as dead.

Suddenly jagged energy spikes shredded the air into smoking crags and volcanos. "The fuck, you say." Mother's anger disrupted Chip's radar. It was the break I needed. I hummed to shut them both out while I concentrated on whipping up my fog cover.

"Back off, Weezie," Chip threatened. "You screwed up. I'm taking the girl." Chip started a fresh sweep of the courtyard, but Mother intruded again – emitting chaos and fragmenting his psi.

"If you think you're just going to waltz in here and take my daughter for free, you better think again. I have rights."

"You and Jimmy had your chance."

"Is that so?" She lit a cigarette and blew smoke. "I'll have you know that I've got other options. In fact, we've had another offer."

"What the hell are you talking about?"

"That big shot from the Board of Education – Mr. Peterson. He wants to take her."

"Take her where?"

"He says it's for a scholarship to some fancy school – Brookside or something. But I'm not naïve. There's only one thing he wants. He's coming tonight to make us an offer. You want her? It'll cost you plenty. . . ."

Mother had it wrong. Or was I the one who'd gone crazy? Mr. Peterson was a good guy, wasn't he? The cramps came back so bad that I curled up in a bed of geraniums. I must be dying. I hoped so. I stared at the red petals and saw God in them. "Turn on your color," Mrs. Roberts had said in art class. I turned it on now. I breathed in their sweet, metallic scent.

A breeze rustled the shrubbery. Through the dappled green leaves with their purple underbellies, I saw the brown eyes and wet black nose of my fawn. She sniffed the air, flicking her ears. "You've drawn God," Mrs. Pendrake had said. Now here she was. I embraced the little deer, spooning against her. She was soft and warm against my belly. Her heart beat in synch with mine. We looked up through palm fronds together. White clouds buzzed and scudded across the sky. She licked my cheek. It tickled.

CHAPTER THIRTY-EIGHT

TUNNEL TO SCOTLAND

"Sparky, wake up."

My eyelids flickered. I was lying in the dirt, hot and sweaty – my arms flung wide. Angels on bicycles hovered over me. Their faces were dark silhouettes against the too-bright sky. Red ants marched up my arm. I wasn't dead. I sat up and brushed them away, shaking bark and leaves from my hair.

"Pedro's waiting," said Patrick. He pulled me to my feet, but I stayed low, crouching behind the bicycles – out of sight of Apartment C. He wrinkled his nose at me. "What's wrong with you?"

"Is there anyone in my window?"

"Just your mom smoking a ciggie."

"No guy with a ponytail?"

"Nope."

"Get your bike," said Rock. "There's lots of cool new gear."

I balked. "No, wait!" The black van might be idling in the carport. I looked for Gary, but he was probably still in detention with Albert. Rock was our second-best sneaker. "Go scout the carport," I told him. "And check out Caspian all the way to IB Boulevard."

"What for?"

"A black van or a guy with a pony tail, or MPs, or a big bald guy with a mustache."

"Why?" He glanced at Patrick. Patrick was in command of military operations. I hoped he wasn't mad at me.

"Just do it," said Patrick. "We'll wait here." Rock was back in less than a minute.

"Nobody there," he said. "Gary's at the clubhouse with Bertie."

I moved with the herd, well hidden behind the bikes. My psi was surrounded by blips of kid energy. I didn't look at my window or scan for Chip – I couldn't do that on the run. The rest of the warriors waited in the clubhouse. Gary and Albert were showing off their matching black eyes. They were best friends again. Albert was excited. "They're wiring the searchlights. Each of those suckers has the power of eight million candles...."

"Mount up," Patrick shouted. I jumped on Blue Balloon and followed him to the rim of Caspian. At his signal, we formed our recon line along the crest of the hill.

Rock wasn't kidding. Piles of equipment stamped USAAF were stacked from the settling ponds all the way to the border. I'd never seen so many men in camouflage. Pedro's jeep was parked on the far side of the river. He would never cross to our side with all those American soldiers in the way. We'd have to sneak around soldiers, boxes, electrical wires, and all kinds of strange stuff. Meanwhile, trucks unloaded huge wooden spools of black cable.

An engine roared to life and I jumped, my heart pounding – the van. But it wasn't. The mechanics had fired up the diesel generator which raised a cloud of dust and exhaust. "Cool," said Albert. "It works."

"Ardchoille! Ardchoille!" Patrick screamed, plunging downhill. I followed, safe in the middle of the pack. We flew across the earthen dikes and onto the marshy sand where the van couldn't catch me. Blue Balloon galloped so fast that I became invisible. No one tried to stop us – the USAAF guys were too busy looking for smugglers. We stopped to stare at a shiny silver half-sphere with a glass face and innards like a giant light bulb.

"Hey Sparky, let's see you steal one of those," Linda teased. It was about five feet in diameter and mounted on a metal trailer. It was one of a row of spheres attached by cables to the diesel generator that rattled and spewed fumes.

"These are mobile arc lights," shouted Albert over the racket. "One generator like this can run all four lights on the battlefield...."

"Stuff it, Bertie. Let's roll," shouted Patrick, leading us to the river. It was too deep to cross. Pedro drove over to our side.

"That's one of them searchlights," he said, handing out parcels and dimes. "They'll test it tonight – gonna catch them Cubans smugglin' bricks of coke in airplanes." He gave us a salute. "Better get goin', bambinos. You runnin' late."

It was dark when we finished deliveries and the kids headed home for dinner. Down in the wetlands with my friends, I'd been free from the nightmare at home. But now I was up against it. I crawled into the space behind the dumpster, curling into a ball against the cool of the concrete floor. I needed time to think.

I scanned for Chip, the van, the MPs – nothing. I kept myself hidden in mental fog just in case. The cramps were back, worse than ever. I vomited in the dumpster just as the first of the Lobos Locos rolled into the carport.

He looked me over and whistled. The rest were roaring across Caspian. I had nowhere to go but home.

I pushed open the kitchen door with an aching sense of doom. It was too quiet. There was no smell of TV dinners, no television blaring, and no sign of Father, Mother, or my brother. They should have been sitting on the couch watching television. I climbed the stairs, planning to sneak into my room unseen. My arms and legs were lead weights and my back ached. I had to lie down. Water was running in the bathroom. Father and Mother were in there – speaking in low tones. I listened at the door.

Father grunted, "Who does that asshole think he is? If he wants the kid, he'll have to pay like everybody else."

"Don't worry, Jimmy. He'll pay."

"What should we charge? What do you think she's worth?"

"He's a big shot. The question is what do we think he's worth?"

I drew back in horror. They were talking about Mr. Peterson … and me. A thousand thoughts and emotions raced through my head in a jumble. I fought for enough control to keep from screaming and giving myself away.

"I'm gonna go for cigs. Get the kid ready." Father opened the bathroom door and I slipped into their bedroom to hide. The red baby-doll pajamas were spread out on their bed. "I'll be back before seven."

"You better be. He'll be here at 7:30."

He clumped down the stairs and out the back door. My heart pounded in my ears. I was numb from head to foot. This was worse than anything I could have imagined. I wished that Mr. Peterson wasn't coming. A cramp doubled me over and I wished that my body would stop turning on me. I wished that I had been born in Scotland to different parents. I stared through the open window and wished that I would die of typhus right now.

A light shot straight up from the wetlands, piercing the sky in a perfect tube of illumination. It was beautiful. I picked up Father's binoculars. No doubt about it – the tunnel to Scotland was open. It was time to jump.

"It worked," I shouted, raising my arms in victory. I ran onto the landing, straight into Mother.

"Bath. Now!" She pointed to the steaming water. "Give me your clothes." She grabbed me and started to yank off my pink tee shirt. She got it high enough to see the black bra. "Is that from your boyfriend?" She slapped my face. "Is that from the big shot from Sacramento? He's been getting it from you for free, hasn't he?"

"You've got it all wrong." I struggled to pull away. She pummeled me with her fists. Mother was a big woman. She'd always been able to overpower me, even when she had to sit on me to do it. But something had changed. I'd grown six inches. She outweighed me by a ton, but I was wiry and fast. She tried to grab my hair. I ducked and pushed her – hard. She slipped on the wet floor and splashed into the tub. I sprinted down the stairs and out the back. "Ungrateful little whore. Come back here," she screamed.

I ran to the carport. It was filling with more Lobos Locos on their motorcycles. They grabbed at me, but I darted between them and kept running. In the time it took them to dismount, I leapt onto Blue Balloon and raced across Caspian, plunging blindly down the hill, across the settling ponds, and into the wetlands. I was riding on instinct with my eyes fixed on the tunnel of light. I had to get through before it closed. I dodged around the trucks and gear and men in camouflage. I heard the generator and smelled diesel. They'd moved the motor across the river, closer to the border fence. The tunnel was on the other side of the river, too. Wetbacks were moving north and I was surrounded on all sides, riding against the human tide.

I pedaled across the river at the shallowest point, where people crossed on foot. The river was flowing faster than usual, eroding its banks. On the far side, I pedaled too close to the edge of a soft shoulder and the sand gave way. I toppled over, sliding head first down the muddy bank toward the typhus-ridden sludge. I would have plunged into the deadly water, except that the crowd scrambled down after me. Men grabbed my legs before I went in. They were kind and concerned, brushing away the foul-smelling dirt and helping me to my feet. My bike! I couldn't see Blue Balloon anywhere. A woman pointed – it was being swept to the Pacific Ocean in a torrent of muck.

I wanted to cry, but I had no time. I had to be far away in Scotland when Mr. Miller and Mr. Peterson arrived at our apartment. I could still see the light and ran toward it on my new long legs. I had no idea that I could run that fast, like a powerful animal – a leopard or a gazelle. I ran with broad, easy strides, drawing closer to the brilliant tube. The sound of my breathing and the slap of my feet on the hardened sand was all I heard.

I was running away from my parents, Mr. Peterson, Chip, the MPs, and all the grunts in the Navy. I was almost there when I was seized by belly pains so severe that I was paralyzed. I stumbled to my knees. The tide of humanity split and walked around me as I crawled into a copse of reeds, betrayed again by my body. I lay there sobbing and retching. Surely this was the end. I was dying. I tried to stand and see the light, but it was gone.

Even the generator was silent. I was swallowed by darkness. I stopped breathing, awaiting death.

"Sparky, muchacha, that you?" Pedro shined his flashlight on my face.

"Go away," I groaned, covering my head. "I'm dying of typhus."

"This ain't no place for a little white chica. Come on." I didn't move so he grabbed my arm and pulled me to my feet. "Get in the jeep, chica. I gonna drive you home." Home was the last place I wanted to go, but Pedro was insistent. I followed him to the mud-spattered jeep and climbed onto the passenger's seat. Maybe I'd be dead before we reached the IB apartments. That would solve everything.

I was still alive when he pulled onto Caspian. There were police cars in our carport. Red lights flashed and radios squawked. I could see Mr. Peterson and Mr. Miller standing by our back door with Officer Friendly-Jones and Mrs. Pendrake. "This is as far as I go," said Pedro. "Looks like police at your place. Shit's hittin' the fan."

The worst must have happened and they'd come to arrest my parents. Mr. Miller and Mr. Peterson knew everything. I should never have confided in Mrs. Pendrake. Now I could never go back to that school. I saw Kenny watching out his back door and my humiliation was unbearable. I broke apart, flying into pieces. My breathing slowed to practically nothing. I tried to dissolve. I wanted to disappear.

"Outta the jeep, chica." Pedro nudged my shoulder. "I gotta get outta here."

I gave him the evil eye and climbed out. I didn't thank him for rescuing me or bringing me back. I was furious at him and the world around me, which continually forced me back to my parents. I had no intention of going home. As soon as Pedro pulled away, I started to run in the opposite direction.

I didn't see the yellow Mercury until the door flew open and I ran smack into Father. He grabbed my arms, pinning them. Then Mother came up behind me, grabbing my waist and holding me tightly. When I tried to cry out, Father punched me in the stomach so hard that I collapsed. My parents threw me onto the backseat while I struggled for breath. Father gunned the engine, burning rubber onto IB Boulevard.

"Your lover boy called the cops," he shouted over his shoulder. "And that bitch Pendrake tried to have us arrested for pedophilia. Who does she think she is – calling Child Services? Telling them we're a bunch of pedophiles. Now it's Mexico or prison. I hope you're happy."

"I'm not going to Mexico," Mother dug in. "No way – it's full of Mexicans."

"We can't stay in this country. Pedophilia is a federal crime."

"Then you better get us to Canada because I'm not going to Mexico."

As soon as I could breathe, I was screaming at the top of my lungs, smashing my feet against the window glass, trying to break free.

"Shut up." Mother smacked me in the head so hard that I saw stars. "We found that stash under your mattress, you cheating bitch. He gave you those bras and the fancy pants, didn't he? You think I'm stupid? Men don't give pretty things to a woman unless she's putting out."

"You've been cheatin' on us, Fatso." Father slurred his speech. "We're gonna beat that out of you once and for all."

"My book," I sobbed. "What did you do with *Miracle Sword*?"

"It's in the trash with the rest of your stuff," Mother snapped. "It's in the trash where you belong. You're a worthless nobody, a piece of shit. We give you a home and food and this is what we get in return. You owe us. Get that through your thick head and stop your tantrums."

"Your mother's right. You owe us big-time, Fatso."

"It's my mother's fault," Mother snorted. "Mema's filled the kid's head with MacGregor crap. And now the little bitch goes and turns on us."

"You're such a failure," said Father. "All those opportunities at the Annex and you just couldn't make the grade."

"I hate the Annex," I screamed. "I never wanted to go and I'll never go back."

Mother gave me a withering look. "You'll go back when I say so. They want your psych and they'll pay to get it."

"Do you think they'll deal?" asked Father, concerned. "You think they'll get us back into the country?"

"Sure they will. Don't you ever forget who my brother is. One phone call and they'll make this federal pedophilia crap disappear."

They went on and on, but something had snapped in my head and I didn't hear them anymore. I stopped listening. My ears were ringing from the blows, but beyond that, I'd begun to forget their words as soon as they were uttered. They would beat me later – I had no doubt about that – but their words had lost all power.

The car roared across the desert and the road filled with jackrabbits. They froze in the headlights, and Father mowed them down. Bump… bump…bump… I turned away from the slaughter. The worst pain yet surged through my belly. It threatened to paralyze my lower half again. I drew up my legs, wrapping my arms around my knees. My fingers felt wet. I looked at my hands. They were dark with blood.

"I'm dying," I shrieked, gawking at my gory fingers. No one had ever explained to me that little girls became women in this way. I was dizzy, nauseous. The car receded in a cloud of stars. When they cleared, Sparky sat beside me. I felt like she'd just been ripped from my insides, but she looked neat in her kilt, unchanged since I'd first met her on the train in Peoria.

"Relax – you aren't dying," she said. "You've got your period, that's all. It's in that book *Here's To You, Miss Teen!* We read about it, remember?"

"Yeah, I guess..." I vaguely recalled the chapter on menstruation. I hadn't paid much attention.

"This is a good thing," Sparky winked. "Getting your period means that you're turning into a grownup. In a few years you'll be big enough to do whatever you want to."

"Years?" I sobbed. "I can't wait years."

"The bigger you get, the better it will be. You're the smartest kid in California, remember? Quit your whining and use that great big brain."

"But what can I do? How can I make all this right?"

"You can't. Nothing can make this right, but when you grow up, you can make it beautiful."

I rolled my eyes. "How?"

"You must be a kind and good person. Be everything these people are not." She flashed her crooked smile. "Then write your story."

"Okay – but years? That's too long."

"You've got no choice, so get over it. Now climb up on the seat. I've got something to show you." We knelt side by side and she pointed out the back window. Four tubes of brilliant white light shot into the sky. Four tunnels were open.

I lost it – screaming, "Let me out.... Let me go...." I pounded on the window. It was my last chance to jump and we were driving in the wrong direction. Mother swung her hands around and hit me in the head. I quieted down, dizzy.

"Look," Sparky pointed again. Something was in the lights. The warriors were making the jump, flying upwards, tumbling in somersaults, arms spread wide. They'd seen the tunnels open and were on their way to Scotland. I saw Patrick go, then Kenny, Linda, Cookie, Rock, and Albert.

I saw Theresa, carrying Conchita. They were followed by Elfin and Minerva and all the other little stars and angels. Mrs. MacDonald was jumping too. They soared upwards into the night where the light beams illuminated a cluster of low clouds that glowed green like the Scottish

161

SPARKY: Surviving Sex Magick

Highlands. The lights caught the edge of a yellow wing and the underbelly of Paulie's plane.

"You gotta go," I whispered. "They'll need your help in Scotland."

"I know," Sparky said. "But first, take my hand. I have something to give you."

I closed my eyes and reached out. Sparky's touch felt electric. Her life force and determination flowed into me, strengthening all my empty places with her refiner's fire. I was suddenly calm even though I was losing everything that mattered to me. My bicycle was gone. My book was gone. The charm bracelet, my underwear and clothes were gone...and everyone I cared about was leaping through the tunnels without me.

I was hurtling toward a strange new country in a car with crazy people who were going to beat the daylights out of me, then sell me back to the Annex, but I was no longer afraid. It might take a long time, but I was going to grow up. As of that moment, I wasn't a child any more. I would get away from my family by being stronger and smarter than they were. I was going to survive and become a good person. I would become a doctor, despite them.

Sparky squeezed my hand: "Now give me your most solemn promise that, when you write our story, you'll make it a beautiful story. No crybaby crap. You're a warrior. Remember that."

"I promise." I coughed, choking on tears.

"I'm gonna jump now," she said, letting go. I nodded, keeping my eyes shut tight.

"Be yourself from now on. You don't need me anymore," she whispered.

When I opened my eyes, she was gone.

CHAPTER THIRTY-NINE

CANADA

"Big deal. You have the curse." Mother pulled a white pad from her purse. She pinned it to my underpants in a Union 76 toilet when we stopped for gas in Victorville. The cramps had eased, but I ached inside and out from the losses that had stripped me raw. "You'll get the curse every month from now on," she said. "It's your punishment for being a woman. You can have babies now." I was shocked to learn that Mother had periods, too. Back in the car, I curled up on the backseat, feeling gutted and confused – babies?

We crossed the California state line about midnight and stopped at a Nevada visitors' center. Father got us Cokes and Mother bought a Rand McNally Road Atlas. My brother spent a nickel on a slot machine and won twenty-five cents. He bought a fossil fish in sandstone with his profits.

We drove back onto Route 18, and I watched my reflection in the rear-view mirror. I looked disheveled and messy like a half-hatched chick with wings that couldn't lift off. Sparky was gone. She'd taken her shiny hair and cute Scottish outfits with her. She'd left behind a tall, skinny girl with sad eyes and long scabby legs. I looked over my sinewy arms and dirty fingernails – not much to work with, but it was all I had left. It was time to close the memories of Sparky in a sealed box along with the rest of Imperial Beach. It was time to forget and move on.

I should have slept, but I had pressing questions. What happened next? Where were we going? What did Mother mean by saying, "You can have babies now"? When would that happen? I knew better than to ask. I kept silent, dozing on and off until we reached Las Vegas.

We stopped at an air-conditioned motel. The morning sky was brightening and it was already over one hundred degrees. We'd wait out the worst heat of day there, driving again at night. Father wanted flapjacks so we crossed the parking lot to an all-night pancake house and slid into a booth with red vinyl seats.

Mother opened her road atlas, spreading maps on the table. She had her head down, marking our route in pencil. I noticed streaks of gray in her black hair. Her hands trembled. Her eyes were wide and bright. She chattered about road trips she'd taken as a child with her parents, Mepa and Mema. I hated it when Mother talked with a lisp, trying to sound like a little girl. She did it whenever she talked about her daddy.

Father grunted as if he was listening – I knew he wasn't. He drank black coffee and smoked a Lucky Strike. I noticed deep circles under his red-rimmed eyes. He was sitting next to me with an invisible ocean between us. The smell of his Old Spice awakened old longings for safety in his arms. I wanted to curl up against him with my head on his shoulder. I wanted him to stroke my hair and tell me that everything would be okay. My throat ached with longing, choking on what could have been, but wasn't.

I shook it off. The past was over – lost forever. Just like the smart girl with a scholarship to Sacramento, a life of safety in my father's arms would never be mine. It was best forgotten. I shrugged, steeling myself. Something had changed in me. Scholarship or not, I had glimpsed my future as a scientist. I had outsmarted Chip, at least for a little while, and Mrs. Lipsky had said that I was smart enough to be a doctor. I would focus all my energy on that. I would live for the promise of the day when I could fly away. Hard work and patience were necessary – I could do that. I smiled at the waitress, thanking her politely when she brought my blueberry pancakes with extra syrup and butter.

Father ate his short stack and lit another cigarette. He snapped open a newspaper. Niagara Falls was all over the headlines. A boy named Bobby had gone over the top in a wooden boat, plunging one hundred and sixty-seven feet. He was seven years old and he survived. His picture was on the front page. They called him "miracle boy." Mother decided that we'd cross the international border in Buffalo and visit Niagara Falls on the Canadian side. I half-listened to her stories about her family trip in the 1930s – how she'd sailed under the falls in a boat called the *Maid of the Mist* and climbed into a rocky cave behind the waterfall wearing a rain slicker.

For the next few weeks we drove across the continent, visiting places like the Grand Canyon and the Petrified Forest, spending hot nights in motels with neon signs and swimming pools. We bought a new car in Arizona, trading in the big yellow Mercury convertible for a '57 Chevy with air conditioning and Texas plates. Eventually we drove across the Niagara River on the Peace Bridge and entered Canada.

Father parked the Chevy under a sign that said, "Journey Behind the Falls." It sounded exciting and dangerous. My brother and I ran across a grassy park to lean over the iron railing. Beneath us roiled a cauldron of cold water, churning up mist so thick that we disappeared in it. Mother found us. "Where are your shoes?" She pointed at my bare feet.

"I lost them in Kansas," I shrugged. I'd been barefoot for days. "They were too small anyway."

She turned to Father. "Can she go in like that? Shouldn't we leave her in the car?"

"Please, please, please," I begged, whining like a six-year-old. "I'll hide my feet. No one will know." My fussing earned me odd looks from the crowd. I was as tall as some of the adults. I blushed – I was too big to act like this. Father was already in line buying tickets. I shut up and hurried behind him into the visitors' center. Once inside, I forgot my embarrassment, mesmerized by the roar of water vibrating the stone floor.

We were given black welly boots and heavy yellow slickers with hoods. We clomped down wet stairs hewn from the granite cliff. In a mist-filled stone chamber, the rest of the tour group faded from my sight, and I stood alone, staring open-mouthed into a thundering wall of water. We really were behind Niagara Falls. I leaned over the rail, looking up until my face and hair were soaked under the hood of the slicker. Water trickled into my boots.

I imagined jumping – tumbling through that screaming curtain like Bobby the "miracle boy" in his wooden boat. I was a miracle girl myself. Here I stood in Canada – on the other side of the world from Imperial Beach. I'd made it through the torrent alive. I watched as the terrors of my childhood were swept up and drowned in the white water, washing away in the roar of the falls. I felt clean, and cleanliness was suddenly important to me. I was starting over in a new country in my new grownup body. No more whining.

The tour guide herded us back up the steps to the changing room. We turned in our slickers and boots. I noticed the shelves where tourists had left dozens of pairs of shoes when they put on their wellies. I grabbed a pair of white sneakers and crammed my feet into them. They were too tight, but I wasn't picky. I followed my parents, hobbling back to the car.

We spent a week at the Happy Canuck Motel. It had a pool, and my brother and I passed our days playing in the water or sitting on the diving board, our legs dangling, watching the cars rush past on the freeway. At night, Mother and Father would lie in their bed and discuss "options."

"There's a one-year project in Toronto," said Father. "Or we can go to Haiti or Siam. The pay is better overseas, but we'd be stuck there for at least three years. Where should we go?"

I willed Mother to say, "Siam." I'd seen the posters for *The King and I* with Yul Brenner. There wouldn't be an Annex in Siam.

"I want to go back to California," said Mother with a trembling sigh.

Father gave her a kiss and a squeeze. "I know you do, Weezie. I'll take Toronto."

We settled into an old brick apartment building in the Toronto suburb of Don Mills. I started sixth grade at Don Mills Elementary, showing up for class as myself.

In a few weeks the weather turned cold. I didn't have a sweater or a coat. I walked several blocks to my new school on a blustery day wearing a cotton dress and the white sneakers with my toes poking through. I told everyone that people from Southern California never got cold. I couldn't tell them that Mother hated Canada and as far as she was concerned, we didn't need to waste money on warm clothes since we'd be back in California before the school year was over.

Mrs. Stewart from the apartment upstairs saw me come home from school shivering. "Oh, honey," she rubbed my arms. "Your lips are blue." She gave me hot chocolate and rummaged in her closet. She found a green sweater with holes in it and a plaid wool skirt with a big safety pin. It was red and green Stewart tartan and it smelled of moth balls. I was thrilled – I finally had a kilt. I wore the kilt and sweater every day and grew to love the smell of camphor. When it snowed, Father brought home an old Navy pea jacket with a hole over the heart. It smelled like sweat.

I told my new friends at school that it was from a military academy and that all Americans went there. I told them that the coat smelled bad because someone had been shot and died in it. I stuck my finger through the bullet hole to prove it. After school, I would join the swarm of neighborhood girls who attended Don Mills Elementary or the Catholic academy. We didn't play with boys any more. A number of us lived in apartments on Overton Crescent and the rest lived in houses. We'd roam in a hungry pack from home to home, eating and playing games that we took turns inventing. My new friends were as good at imagining as I was.

On sunny days, we'd go down to the ravine and put pennies on the railroad tracks or search for fossil trilobites in the quarry. When it snowed, we built igloos and snow animals. My specialty was the snow lion. When the wind howled and ice slivers stung our cheeks, we'd stay inside, climbing up the walls of the narrow apartment stairwells like spiders, to hover at the third floor ceiling. From there we did recon, spying on the neighbors and dropping spitballs on their heads as they came and went.

The basement storage locker became our warm, dry clubhouse where we staged plays, listened to records, sang, and danced. Valri and Lois Bromfield did comedy acts that sent us into stitches. The Oscar Peterson Trio rehearsed in one of the apartments. Conrad, the drummer's son, let us in to see the instruments when no adults were around and as long as we didn't touch anything. On Christmas break, the older kids flooded the lawn between buildings with water and made a skating rink. I badgered my parents for a pair of skates until they relented.

At school, I was the strange new girl from California. I was a head taller and much more mature than the other sixth graders. My teacher, Mr. Peganaugh, didn't like Americans and picked on me for my terrible handwriting until he discovered that I could draw and sing. In October, when Don Mills Elementary administered IQ tests, I came out as one of the smartest kids in Ontario. From that point on, Mr. Peganaugh was my friend. He taught me how to write in neat cursive and to organize my time. He taught me the concept of efficiency, "to do" lists, and appointment books. He impressed on me that stealing was bad and gave me a book about Moses and the Ten Commandments. He told me how to decide when my hair needed washing – it got stringy.

He called my parents to the school and told them to buy me a coat that didn't stink, which they did. They seemed grateful to Mr. Peganaugh for my high IQ scores. Father called them "our ace in the hole to get back to California." Mother was soon making long distance calls to discuss them with her brother. Apparently the Annex wanted me back enough to keep Child Protective Services from sending Father to prison. It would take some time to sort some things out – the longer, the better. I had most of a year without Nanny Blacks or psychedelic drugs. I got to spend Christmas at home with my friends instead of as a party favor at another Saturnalia.

Santa brought me mittens and a red and white striped stocking hat that wrapped around my neck like a scarf. Being eleven and turning twelve, working hard at school, and playing with my friends were all that I had to do. The Board of Education of Ontario wanted to advance me directly to high school. I looked like a high school girl and I was smart enough, but before the school year ended, Mother got her wish. We were back in California and I was registered at La Vista Junior High School in Hayward. We moved into a small tract house on the east side of San Francisco Bay and I woke up to the sting of a needle in my arm.

CHAPTER FORTY

MOSCOW DREAMING

I struggled, but my wrists and ankles were strapped down, buckled into leather restraints. I was on my back, stretched out in my nightie on a wheel like I'd never seen before. It was a wheel within a wheel, each one engraved with strange symbols. Pinhole lights in the ceiling mapped out constellations. "There's no point in fighting it, sweetie," said the new Nanny Black, sucking my blood into his syringe. "We've missed you." He forced down the plunger, burning my vein in the rush of heat up my arm. The drugs kicked in. My vision blurred. Click…click…click…The wheel started to spin and the room was smeared with colors. I spun faster, the clicking merging into a hum. I recognized the scratch of a phonograph needle and I fell into the familiar music of the Don Cossacks – the wild Russian music from Mepa's record album. "*Dosvidanya*," said Nanny Black. "You're going to Moscow."

I saw Cossacks on galloping horses and the onion domes of Russian churches. I knew them from the colorful picture that I'd seen on Mepa's album. My eyes snapped open and I heard myself breathing. Everything had stopped except the falling snow, the silence, and the cold. A clock chimed. I was in the center of a vast, snow covered square. The tower clock on a massive red brick gate was striking midnight. I turned around, staring at dark, unfamiliar buildings, sensing danger from all directions. "This is Red Square." Nanny Black whispered in my ear, "Run!"

I hesitated too long. Men with guns surrounded me. Bullets pierced my legs and chest. I died, my blood running red on the snowy cobblestones. Click…click…click…The dream re-wound. The music started again. The clock chimed. My eyes snapped open. I didn't wait for the whispered warning. I leapt over the cobblestones and ran until I was gunned down in an alley. Click…click…click…The dream rewound and started again and again. Each time I made it further. When the drugs wore off, I'd wake up at home. The next morning, I'd go back to school on the bus with my friends and a note from Mother apologizing for my latest absence due to a weak heart.

I looked up Moscow in *Encyclopedia Britannica* in the school library. There was Red Square on the map. I located the Kremlin, the clock tower,

Spassky Gate, Lenin's Tomb. My best chance of escape looked to be past St. Basil's Cathedral and into the maze of alleys and old churches along the Moscow River. My next turn on the wheel, I tried the new route and made it a little further.

Click…click…click…Night after night I ran through the darkened maze of cobbled streets outside the Kremlin walls until I knew each turn, each shop, church, and bus stop. If I tried to get on a bus, the dream reset and started over. Some nights the air was warm and I sprinted in high heels. Other nights, I ran through snow, slipping over icy cobbles in heavy boots.

The dreams went on throughout seventh and into eighth grade. I learned my way by trial and error around every alley between the Kremlin and Taganskaya Square. Men always chased me – some wore uniforms and some didn't. I never knew who they were or when they'd appear, but they'd shoot me if they could. I wore a cyanide pill like a pearl on a gold chain around my neck. When I was winded, my sides aching from gasping air, I'd fall against an ancient brick wall and hear Nanny Black whispering, "If they catch you, they'll skin you alive. Better take the pill."

"No!" I'd shout and run again. I never took the cyanide. I'd run until they shot me. When I could finally run the distance undetected, Nanny Black gave me a new mission. I was to find an entrance into the top-secret USSR communications center beneath the Rostelekom building between the Kremlin and Taganskaya Square. Soviet intelligence operations were a secret that no American spy had ever penetrated.

Every day and night, hundreds of workers went into tunnels that formed a web under the city, but no one on the American side knew how they entered or where. My job was to find the way in. The game had changed and so had my costumes.

Now I strolled the night streets dressed like a factory worker from MosEnergo. I spoke Russian. I had identity papers. I began to recognize people in the street and follow them. Eventually, I trailed two women in black wool coats and fur hats into a huge new gothic apartment complex called the Vysotka, next door to Rostelekom. There was nothing unusual about women entering an apartment building – hundreds of people lived there – but on a hunch, I followed until they stepped into a lift. I nearly turned away until I saw the lift start down instead of up.

This was it – the way in. I was so excited that I gave a whoop and broke out of my trance, fighting the restraints, disoriented. "I know where it is! I've found the way in!" Why was I tied up? Had the Russians captured me? I tried to find the suicide pill, but it wasn't there. I fought the effects of the hypnotic drugs until I realized that I was in the Annex. The wheel continued to turn slowly until it clicked on the symbol IO and the restraints released.

Nanny Black helped me sit up, "Come on, honey. That's a good girl." He gave me a bathrobe and led me barefoot to Chip's office.

Vito sat behind the desk, tapping his pencil impatiently. His nametag said "Dr. White." I'd known several Dr. Whites in the various Annexes, but there was only one Vito. The sight of him made me shiver. Chip handed me a mug of coffee and said, "Here, warm yourself up." He rubbed my shoulders. I shivered again, still cold from the transition from the winter snows of Moscow. I wrapped my fingers around the cup, taking in the warmth, trying to clear away the fog between my two unreal realities.

"Nanny Black says that you found the way into Rostelekom. So where is it?" demanded Vito. His voice was amplified in my drugged-up head. I cringed, leaning away from him, trying to hold onto my vision of Moscow that had seemed real, but it was breaking apart.

"Don't push her," Chip admonished. "She's still in the interzone. Give her a chance to come back or you'll trigger her amnesia and we won't get anything."

"Damn it, McNab. How long is this remote viewing program of yours going to take? It's been over a year and we haven't got squat."

"This Soviet operation has been going on for years and no agent has made it underground yet, have they? They've all died trying and we've wasted millions of dollars. How many of our agents have you lost? Five... six, dead and floating face down in the Moscow River? Let's give Sex Magick a try, shall we?" Chip stood over me protectively. "Take your time."

I stared at my hands, seeing every blood vessel and pore, fighting to regain my senses. I pinched myself. My skin still felt numb, but my brain had started working. I was shocked by the discord between Chip and Vito. I wondered if it was something I might exploit. I'd also sensed urgency in Vito's question. It was the first time I'd seen him distressed. Why should he care what I saw in my dreams? I never thought they were real – did he? And why did he have to ask anyway? I'd always imagined that my spirit travels and my remote visions were projected onto a television set that the whole Annex could see.

Cybernetics was a big topic at the Annex – combining the human mind and machines to create superspies who could transmit images. Was it possible that my thoughts and dreams were still my own? Too much thinking. My head lolled forward and I drifted off toward sleep.

"Well?" Vito demanded again. "Speak up. What did you see?"

"I ... I've lost it," I lied, shaking my head to chase away the bluebirds and stars that lingered with the drugs. "Stop pushing me."

"Fuck it, McNab," Vito snapped, slamming his fist on the desk. "This one's chock-full of crap. She always has been – just like her mother."

I started to cry – grief poured from my core and heated my blood. Stop it! Use your brain! Wailing like a child just turns this pedophile on. I slammed the lid on my well of tears. I was a warrior with a spirit annealed into steel. I sat up ramrod straight and calmly met his gaze. "I can do it," I said.

"Oh yeah? Do what?" Vito eyed me through the yellow reptilian slits that passed for his eyes. I saw his tongue flick like a snake's. He repulsed me, but I was jubilant. He'd given me a tiny opening through his sliver of doubt. I flowed into the space like light and filled the darkness. Speaking from a universe that wasn't my own, I set my critical mind aside, and let the uncensored words from my psi through.

"Bugging Rostelekom – that mission has you stumped, right?" I leaned forward.

He flinched. "What of it?"

"There's a secret stairwell in the Vysotka. I can see it in my mind," I pushed ahead. "I can go underground into the tunnels with a flashlight, identify the cables that link Russian Military Intelligence to every Soviet embassy in the world, and insert devices to bug those lines. The conduits are massive and it will take me multiple trips into the tunnels to tap them all. But I'll get it done."

Vito blustered, "Dammit, McNab! How does she know all this? Pillow-talk? You blab in your sleep, asshole?"

"I told you, she's psi," Chip gloated. "She gets it right out of her head and I can communicate and control her using sex, LSD, and psi. That's how she learned the streets of Moscow and found the way into Rostele-kom when no one else could." He pointed to his head. "She got it from here."

"So, what about this secret staircase in the Vysotka?" Vito asked. "Where'd she get that?"

"I don't know yet. We'll have to keep running her and find out. You just fund Sex Magick and I'll deliver you your team of super spies. Until then, keep your filthy paws off my trainees."

From then on, my life improved. Eventually, the Moscow dreams stopped and I never knew their significance. To me, dreams were nothing more than dreams, but others were impressed. I was sent to classes at the Hoover Institution of Soviet Studies at Stanford and my family was moved to Palo Alto into a much nicer house.

I started Palo Alto High School across the El Camino Real from the Stanford University campus. I attended public high school exactly ninety-one days that year – just enough to advance to the next grade. Once again, teachers questioned me about my absences and my exhaustion at school. I had physical examinations and blood studies done at Stanford University Hospital. I knew what they would show – anemia, but good health otherwise. I was sent home with pamphlets on nutrition.

My faculty advisor Mrs. Wolfsohn was constantly probing. She knew something was wrong, but I kept quiet. I was a short timer. Every day brought me closer to independence. I just had to survive and keep everyone happy until I was seventeen and could get a job and take control of my own life.

I had become expert at living a dual existence. At home and school, I acted the part of a normal teenager – listening to the Beatles, curling my hair on rollers made from orange juice cans, then teasing it into a stylish bouffant, lacquered with hairspray and topped with a clip-on bow. I learned to sew and made wrap-around skirts with matching headscarves from scraps of fabric I found in Home Ec. My friends were all girls. We floated from house to house in a cloud of hairspray. Boys like the ones I used to play with were endowed with mysterious heroic powers that made me giggle and blush. At school, we played records and danced at recess. I could do the Monster Mash and the Wa-wa-tutsi. I learned to flirt. I had boyfriends who wanted to kiss my cheek and take me to the movies.

The rest of the time, during my many absences from school, I spent at the Annex in the Stanford Research Institute or the Hoover Institution on the Stanford Campus. There, my body and mind were broken on the wheel into multiple disconnected pieces and locked behind impenetrable barriers. Each isolated chamber could only be accessed through symbols spun on the wheel within a wheel.

The wheels became more elaborate over time as my memory was divided into dozens of fragments. Chip was my handler, the Dr. Whites and Dr. Greens my masterminds. The Nanny Blacks injected the drugs that sent me into fractured spirals of colored lights and rendered me helpless against their sexual assaults. I fought them, but they could do what they wanted with my body once they had me strapped down with the needle in my arm.

My spirit they could not have – it never broke. I had found grace. I knew who I was and what I believed. I knew right from wrong. I kept my essence and my dignity secure in a walled off room at the end of a maze where only I could find them and no mastermind could touch them.

Music had become a major part of Sex Magick, which meant I spent time in studios at Laurel Canyon and the Hot Springs in Big Sur. They were training musicians to sing and play at certain new mind-bending frequencies, then promoting them onto the pop charts. Most of the new performers were children of intelligence assets from spook families like me.

I was tall, slender, pretty, and I could dance. I was driven to parties around Laurel Canyon and Hollywood Hills with a dozen other tall girls, dressed in psychedelic mini-dresses, hyped up on amphetamines, with our pockets full of LSD and ecstasy. We were called the Freaks, and we were notorious for showing up in an old troop transport truck painted pink with daisies and peace symbols.

We'd take over outdoor parties with our drugs and wild dancing – jumping from the back of the truck and skipping through the crowd, handing out neon-colored blotters of LSD, and dropping ecstasy into drinks. We'd go-go dance, screaming and shimmying until party-goers were hallucinating, naked, having sex, and being photographed by the Sex Magick technicians.

I'd close my eyes to the poor fools rolling on the floor. Their lives were about to be ruined by blackmail. Maybe they deserved it, but probably not. They were just record executives, producers, performers, and DJs. I was helping to entrap them in the same web that held me in bondage. I was repulsed by what I was doing, but it was that or death at the Saturnalia. I chose to live.

The music was cranked up louder and faster as the debauchery ground on, mulching into a screeching blur in my brain. I set myself loose and danced alone in a universe where I was free – taking flight over oceans and deserts, reminding myself that the Annex wasn't my life. I danced until I collapsed – finding peace amidst the pile of sweating bodies.

CHAPTER FORTY-ONE

THE MASTERMINDS

Despite missing half of my classes, the high school moved me into advanced placement math and English programs that could lead to early graduation. I needed to get to college as soon as I could. I'd seen the world beyond my prison and every day that I couldn't reach it was torture.

My parents refused to talk about college with me. I'd overheard them discussing some kind of final payoff from the Annex. As far as they were concerned, I had one more year left and then I wouldn't be their problem anymore.

Click...click...click...The wheel turned and I began dreaming of a rambling psychedelic locomotive called the Freedom Train. It had old-fashioned wagons painted bright colors and decorated with neon peace symbols, rainbows, and flowers. Colored lights twinkled in the windows and the wheels pounded out cartoon stars. Pop stars and beautiful people on board played rock music, dropped acid, and made love on over-stuffed pillows scattered over the floor. When the music reached an ecstatic climax, the beautiful people reached collective orgasm and jumped naked from the open doors into a brilliant vanilla sky.

I never jumped. I woke up on the wheel screaming, "It's a trick! They're killing you!" Click...click...click...The dream would reset and the train would take to the sky with me aboard again. I tried to keep the others from jumping, but I couldn't stop them. I didn't want to die and I didn't want them to die either. I'd seen life and was determined to have it. They should have it, too.

I knew that Chip was doing this to me – putting thoughts of death in my brain to scare me. What was he up to? There was only one way to find out. I waited until my psi was enhanced enough on the turning wheel to penetrate Chip's mind. That was always dangerous because, as soon as I saw him, he saw me. I knew that I would be punished, but I'd glimpsed the future and something terrible was coming that ended in my death. I wanted to know what it was. I fell into a trance and worked fast. I visualized a cabinet in his head and opened the drawer with my file in it. He caught me and grabbed my hand, but not before I'd seen the words "helter skelter."

As punishment for my intrusion, he force-fed me LSD. Click…click… click…The wheel turned and the Freedom Train rattled to life with both of us aboard. He grabbed me by the hair and pushed me nearly through the open door. I held onto him to keep from falling into the swirling pit of primary colors and the growling whine of electric guitars that engulfed the train, swallowing it whole. "Open your eyes," he screamed, pushing me farther out the door. "It's beautiful. It's the rapture. This is where the Freedom Train is taking you. This is the face of God." The enormous face crystallizing in the psychedelic vision was his.

"What's 'helter skelter'?" I shouted at the monstrosity.

"You know what it is," Chip said as he pushed me from behind. I fell, tumbling head over heels into his giant mouth, sliding on his purple, pulsing tongue into the yellow sea that sloshed in his rib cage. "Helter Skelter is a dance. One, two, three, four…" He sang to the beat of drums and guitars, with the notes blowing into spirals and striped, spinning cones like barber poles

I screamed. I burned. I froze. I sweated. And then I vomited. The wheel stopped and Nanny Black wiped my face and led me back to my bed. The key in the lock clanged with a chime like Big Ben. He'd locked me into Hell. I screamed, banging on the door, pacing the room. I couldn't stop moving. The walls were crawling with buzzing flies. I slapped at them, trying to kill them all. They closed in on me, then burst – propelling me into the vanilla sky. The words, "Don't let me break you," screamed over and over in my mind until I slept.

A few days later, I was back in high school sitting in Mrs. Griffin's history class, staring out the window at the Hoover Institution Tower across the street. The Annex was so close to Palo Alto High that my two lives seemed to cross the highway and merge in the middle of El Camino Real. Maybe I could use this proximity to my advantage. The lessons I learned at the Annex might help move me closer to graduation from high school – and my escape. I had taken an oath never to reveal anything I'd seen or learned at the Annex, but now I'd seen death coming on the Freedom Train. I had nothing to lose.

I started bringing the two worlds together by writing a poem about geopolitics in the nineteen sixties for my English class. I called it, "The Masterminds," and illustrated it with ink drawings of Chip and Dr. Green. Chip had grown a beard by then and wore a gold earring. The new Dr. Green had a thin face, a beard, and long, greasy hair. I wrote:

They'll be working late tonight
Molding hatred, love, and spite
In an old brick building with a bare bulb light.
Underground! The masterminds.

They guide our hopes, control our fate,
They shape our flaws and stay up late.
"No lagging men. We are the great."
Underground! The masterminds.

They make us dream; they write our laws
They listen through enchanted walls
They lead us where our destiny calls
Underground! The masterminds.

I earned an *A* for my effort and the poem was published in the school magazine. Emboldened, I wrote an essay for social studies on eugenics and why there would be no black people living in America after 1982. I was parroting lectures on ariosophy from the Hoover Institution. That raised some eyebrows. Palo Alto High School had just started integration, busing in black students from Menlo Park. I also wrote a paper about the destruction of world religion that was scheduled to occur by the year 2000, giving references impossible for my level of education.

I was invited to attend summer school at Stanford University, but my parents nixed the idea. They were sending me to the Hot Springs at Big Sur, where top artists in the music business went to record. Mother thought I should be grateful that I was getting to rub elbows with such big names. I didn't bother trying to tell her that it was Hell on Earth for me – and for the artists that I'd seen on the Freedom Train. I knew that many of the stars were slated for an early death.

I kept up the pressure at school by writing a report on cybernetics, detailing work on combining humans and Turing-based machines called computers. The faculty of Palo Alto High School had never heard of cybernetics or computers. They thought I'd made them up, writing science fiction – but they weren't certain, especially when the references I quoted from Dr. von Neumann's lectures checked out. They showed the paper to Dr. Hewlett – the inventor of the oscilloscope – whose son was in my class.

After that and after they saw my scores on the next round of California IQ tests, the school district wanted to advance me with a scholarship to the University of California at Berkeley. I knew that my parents wouldn't allow me to go and there was no point suffering about it. Still, I needed an outlet – a pressure release valve to keep me from losing my mind. The stress was unbearable.

Fortunately, I discovered the piano, playing by ear at the Annex in Laurel Canyon. Pretty soon, I knew enough to make it sound like music. Chip decided to have me trained in the classics. I took lessons at the Annex, but it wasn't enough. I needed a piano with lessons at home. What leverage did I have? What could I give my parents in trade?

I'd discovered that I could hear them talking in their bed by opening the medicine chest in my bathroom. It was barely separated from theirs by a thin layer of tin. Mother sounded stressed. "It's that damn Howard K. Smith on the news," she hissed. "He's at it again."

Father grunted.

"Damn it, Jimmy – this is serious. He's an alien, I tell you. He's threatening to kill me right there on ABC."

I could hear Father's mental gears grinding, looking for a way to change the topic. "We've got to do something about Fatso," he said. "That teacher has been snooping around."

"You mean Mrs. Wolfsohn?" Mother asked. "She called today. She wants a parent-teacher conference."

"That damn kid has a big mouth."

"Chip wants us to buy her a piano and pay for lessons," said Mother. "I told him it's a waste of money."

"But … it might keep her too busy to make trouble for us all the time." I stopped listening. Father had told me how to get what I wanted.

"If you get me a piano," I said at breakfast the next morning, "I'll be too busy practicing to talk to Mrs. Wolfsohn. Otherwise, who knows what'll slip out when I open my big mouth?"

Mother eyed me suspiciously and Father blew a smoke ring. Fear hung over their heads in thought bubbles. I knew I'd won.

A week later, I came home from school to find a piano in the living room. I poked a few keys. It was out of tune, but I could live with that. From then on, I practiced four hours a day, pouring my frustration, angst, terror, and longing into the music. I had long, strong fingers that moved speedily through beginner and intermediate classes. In tenth grade, I was invited by Mr. Peters, the assistant conductor of the California Youth Symphony, to debut a new piano concerto by Alec Rowley on their tour to Japan.

I began rehearsing with the symphony. Chip and Dr. Green were all for it but I had to bring a permission letter home to be signed by my parents.

I would have signed it myself, but the tour cost $700. I didn't have any money, and the Annex wasn't paying.

"You little whore," Mother screamed, ripping the paper to shreds and slapping my cheek. "What did you do to get this?"

Mr. Peters came to our house the next day for my piano lesson. He was all smiles as he spread the orchestral score for "Concerto in D" on his music stand. He was teaching me how to follow the conductor. I sat at the piano, trembling, knowing what was coming. He tapped his baton on the music stand, but I couldn't meet his eyes. "What's wrong?" he frowned.

"I can't go to Japan," I rasped, feeling worthless and broken. "My parents won't let me." I'd cried all night, drowning in a sea of grief. Mother had torn apart my room, looking for evidence that I was sleeping with Mr. Peters. I knew that she was perched like a cat in the kitchen, watching us – waiting to pounce. I should have warned Mr. Peters, but I choked.

"What is it? What happened?" He put his hand on my arm in a gesture of kindness.

The kitchen door burst open. "Gotcha!" Mother rampaged into the living room. She accused him of sleeping with me and demanded money.

I fled from the room and crawled to the back of my closet, sobbing, hating myself for not defending him and for being stupid and weak. This was my fault. I'd reached too high and been shot down, taking an innocent man with me. I should have known better than to try for Japan while I was still helpless. I could never face Mr. Peters again.

He called the school and wanted to talk to me, but I was too humiliated. I quit the piano. My parents demanded that I keep practicing, but I refused. Chip was furious. Mother had a screaming showdown with him over it while I moped around the house, hating every inch of it and them, slamming doors and leaving faucets running.

A few months later when Father's boss came to our house for dinner, I saw another chance. I knew he was an important man in Seattle and a graduate of the University of Washington. If I could persuade him that I should apply to the university a year early, how could Father disagree? I borrowed a pink mini-dress and big hoop earrings. I washed and curled my hair. I dabbed Chantilly Lace behind my ears.

I wasn't allowed to wear makeup at home, but I brushed my lips with pale pink gloss that tasted like strawberries. I used an eyebrow pencil to accentuate the spray of freckles across my nose. I looked good, smelled delicious, and I was ready to give the performance of my life.

I used my psi and Sex Magick techniques to project sex into that old man's body until he was so distracted that he started agreeing with everything I said. I sat on the sofa next to him and gave him my best Bette Davis eyes. "I think girls should go to college. Don't you think so, sir?"

"Yes, of course," the poor man fidgeted and stared at my thighs, willing my miniskirt to creep higher.

I crossed my hands demurely on my lap, palms up, the way I'd learned at the Annex. "I'm just a junior, but I'm applying for the University of Washington a year early. Isn't that your alma mater? I bet you're a very important alumnus."

Mother spotted us from the dining room and nearly dropped the pot roast. "Jimmy…in the kitchen," she hissed at Father. "Now!" As the door closed, I heard Mother whispering, "What in Hell is she up to? Stop her…"

The boss wasn't listening to anyone but me. His eyes were on my slightly parted knees. "Why yes. I do contribute generously to the College of Arts and Sciences."

"Wow! That's where I want to go! I'm going to be a doctor."

"That's splendid. A beautiful girl like you will make a fine doctor. What can I do to help?"

"You're a very kind man. Maybe I can come to see you sometimes in Seattle?"

"Come to my office…anytime." He patted my knee.

By the time Mother and Father returned, I had his business card, private phone number, secretary's name, and the promise of a letter of recommendation. For the benefit of my parents, I pouted, "I really don't stand much of a chance, do I, sir? I'll probably be terribly disappointed."

"It's tough getting in from out of state. And early, too…that hardly ever happens…and you're a girl."

"Still, I've got to try," I rallied. "I want to make my parents proud of me."

Mother scorched me with her eyes. The old man patted my knee again and I gave him a chaste peck on the cheek. He blushed and said to Father, "Quite a girl you have here. I expect you to keep me briefed personally on how her application is progressing. Anything I can do to help, just let me know."

"She'll never get in," said Mother, but she was wrong. I mounted a clandestine campaign, keeping it secret from the Annex and my parents. I got a letter of recommendation from Dr. Hewlett, who had reviewed my cybernetics paper. Alexander Kerensky, the exiled former Chairman of Soviet

Russia, who taught me Russian history at the Hoover Institution, wrote me a letter, as did Dr. Robert Schusterman, the head of sonar research at the Stanford Research Institute for whom I did biological illustrations.

I finally called Mr. Peters, apologized tearfully, and received a letter from the California Youth Symphony. I had the correspondence from the University of Washington Admissions sent to Mrs. Wolfsohn at school. My parents never saw it. I forged Father's and Mother's signatures on my application and financial affidavit, pledging to cover all my costs. I packaged everything together with a copy of Father's bank statement that I'd taken from his dresser drawer and mailed them at school. It was this or the Freedom Train.

A few weeks later, a letter came to me at school. Trembling, I took it to the girls' toilet and opened it in a stall, so no one could see me. I'd been accepted to the University of Washington.

I wanted to jump into the air, and run down the hall screaming victory – but I knew better. No one could know but me.

CHAPTER FORTY-TWO

THE COAST HIGHWAY

I spent the first half of the summer of 1966 at Stanford Research Institute's Biological Sonar Laboratory at Coyote Hills. Then I was transferred to the Hot Springs in Big Sur. I was scheduled to stay for two more weeks until the first day of my senior year of high school. I had no intention of staying that long.

Registration for my freshman classes began in two days in Seattle, but I was locked inside a compound, surrounded by a ten-foot-high electrified fence, topped with three feet of razor wire and encircled by corn fields that dropped off cliffs into the ocean. Staff, celebrities, and musicians flew in by helicopter from Laurel Canyon for events like record launch sex-and-drug parties. but I couldn't escape that way. The only other access that I knew of was a narrow dirt track that ran for miles through pine forest to a rural road. It had taken two hours for Nanny Black to drive me to the compound once we turned off the Coast Highway. Even if I could manage to climb over the electrified fence and run away on foot, how far would I get?

I had been searching every day for an escape, hiding my frantic thoughts behind clouds of static with my mind on high alert, watchful for opportunities. I might have looked stoned like everybody else, but I wasn't taking the drugs. My half-closed eyes and dreamy smile were disguises. I was determined to get to Seattle or die trying. I would never be a party favor again.

Chip was still my handler, but he'd grown lax. He was sharp enough to intrude on my mind when he was sober, but he was drinking and tripping on LSD. I did my best to make him look good because he kept people like Vito away from me. He wasn't around on the night of the Magick Top Ten record party. He was out selling blotters of LSD in Monterey for twenty bucks a spot.

The helicopters had been ferrying in record execs and promoters all day. That night they were celebrating the Prince of the Air – or "Prince of the Airwaves," which is what the banner across the stage said. I shimmied and sang backup with the rock stars, banging on a red tambourine that I'd woven with ribbons and flowers.

The air in the candlelit barn was thick with hashish and pot. The audience sat on the floor and rolled joints, puffed on hookahs, and snorted lines. I was barefoot, with daisies braided in my long hair. I wore earplugs because the static pulse of electric guitars and drums gave me a headache. The techies always cranked the volume up too high. The pill-popping politicians and record execs who lounged on pillows liked the music loud and their girls young. Some already had their pants down, screwing the new little party favors.

The musicians finally stopped to take a hookah break. While they got higher, I slipped outside alone. If I was ever going to escape, it had to be while Chip wasn't observing me. I climbed the low stone wall surrounding the fountain and watched the stars tracing arcs of light on the Pacific Ocean. I heard the crashing surf. I knew that I couldn't go that way – I'd already tried.

I scanned the horizon in all directions. There were no lights except the candles surrounding the barn complex where we lived and worked. I stared at the iron entry gate, praying for it to open. I jumped when headlights flashed, locks clicked, and the gate slid open. Chip's beat-up red Triumph convertible sped through, spinning into the drive and churning gravel. He jumped the curb and rolled across the lawn, stopping when he bumped into the fountain at my feet.

I leapt down and ran around the idling car. Chip was slumped forward on the wheel, unconscious. I shook him. Nothing. I didn't see any blood, just syringes, pills and blotters of LSD. He was stoned senseless. "Thank you, God," I said aloud. The car kept purring. A buzzer sounded and the gate started to close. I yanked on the driver-side door but it wouldn't open. Chip was a big guy. I'd never get him out with the door closed.

I sat on the door and shoved him onto the passenger seat with my feet. He slid halfway onto the floor. I climbed in and ground the gears until I figured out how to shift into reverse. I gunned the gas, spinning the wheels, ripping up lawn until I was back on the driveway. Too late! The gate had closed. Shit! I revved the engine, ready to ram it and noticed a remote control clipped to the sun visor. I pushed the button.

The gate rolled open and I raced through the portal into the blackness of night. The car bottomed out on the bumpy road and the dirt track zigzagged around trees. I skidded into a cornfield, but regained control and kept going. I checked the gas tank – 3/4 full. Was it enough to drive to Seattle? Who cared? I was out! But would I get away with it? Were they coming after me? What if there were roadblocks? What if they called the police?

I was driving barefoot – that was probably illegal, and I didn't have my license. My purse and shoes were back at the barn. All I had was the red tambourine and a stoned guy who looked dead in the front seat. There were drugs all over the car – I could be arrested for that.

Without slowing, I pitched them by the fistful onto the road. Finally, I saw the highway – no roadblock, no black vans, just open road. I slammed down the pedal and sped onto the Coast Highway. I turned up the radio and belted out "Stewball" with Joan Baez. I had just been doing backup vocals for her, shaking my tambourine and swinging my hair while record exec wannabes looked up my miniskirt. "Never… again," I shouted.

A few hours later, I sailed across the Golden Gate Bridge with my hair streaming behind me, whipping it into a hopeless tangle. I was already erasing memories, scrubbing out the bloody stains of my teen years – flushing my brain of the parties, experiments, drugs, freaks, Nanny Blacks, Dr. Greens, my parents, and my pedophile "uncles."

Freedom was a heady thing and I was drunk on it. I was done with Sex Magick. No more short skirts and tight clothes – no more drugs or booze. I was starting over as my own person. I wanted to wear horn-rimmed glasses and a white lab coat.

By Eureka, I was low on gas. I pulled into a Texaco and found Chip's wallet in his pocket. I raided it to fill the tank and buy candy bars. I paid ninety-nine cents for a pair of flip flops. When I started the engine again, Chip moaned – the drugs were wearing thin.

I looked into his mind. His blue eyes glared back at me. I gasped and withdrew. He was dreaming about me. He groaned again and shifted in the seat, his head rolling back. I had to get him out of the car before his coordination returned. I probably had ten more minutes.

I drove into the woods behind the gas station, keeping him quiet by projecting visions of his comfortable bed at the Hot Springs. To get him out of the car, I projected myself naked, beckoning him from under the covers. "Come on," I whispered. "Let's get it on."

I helped him stand up. He peed on a tree and I tried to get him to lie down on a bench, but he pulled away and staggered into the road. I should have jumped in the Triumph and left him there to get hit by a car, but I couldn't. I wasn't a killer. I pulled him to safety.

He lunged at me, his psi spiking around his head, projecting wild, psychedelic swirls. He was struggling to focus his addled brain – furious to find himself at my mercy. The surge of power intoxicated me. Once again I should have fled, but I couldn't resist looking into the heart of this man who had controlled so much of my life. I wanted to know who he really was.

I centered my energies and drew on the power of the earth. I felt it flowing up through me from the forest floor. I mentally tied his arms and legs to the wheel and started the inner wheel turning. Click…click…click… the symbols blurred and he struggled against the mental restraints. He knew what I was doing, but was helpless under the drugs. The wheel spun faster and an ocean of hate roiled from his soul like a black tsunami that swallowed the forest and darkened the stars.

I staggered backwards, stunned. This monster was more dangerous than I'd realized. The wave of evil sucked the oxygen from my lungs. I nearly lost consciousness. Gasping for air, I saw myself through Chip's eyes – a piece of flesh to be despised, tortured, and devoured – body and soul. "Helter-skelter…helter-skelter…" The words roared in my ears. I saw murder, violence, sacrifice, and death.

The force of his hatred weakened me. My hold on him was failing. Now he was screaming in my head, "You're pathetic. You think you can get away from me? I can find you wherever you go. I own you." He was sobering fast, his will-power growing.

I rallied, grounding myself again by sucking in a fresh burst of energy from the forest, sending it rushing from my feet up through my body and out my arms. I still held him back, but not for long. He broke free of my spell and staggered toward me, intent on killing me. I backed toward the car, ready to run.

"Stupid bitch – you'll never get away!" I saw a half-empty syringe on the passenger seat. He must have been lying on top of it. I grabbed it. He lunged at me and I buried the needle in his neck and pushed the plunger.

He choked, grabbing his throat. His psi shattered into jagged spikes and sparks. I sensed his nausea and racing pulse. He pulled out the syringe and staggered into the roadside ditch. I left him kneeling in a foot of muddy water.

I jumped into the car and sped back to Highway 299. I turned east and revved the Triumph through miles of treacherous hairpin turns, dodging lumber trucks. By the time I reached Redding, I was exhausted, drained. I kept expecting Chip to intrude in my mind, but there was nothing. Was he dead? Had I killed him?

The night grew colder when I gained elevation in the Siskiyou Mountains and the enormity of my situation crept up on me. I had just defied Satan himself. Could I do that and get away with it? I stopped at an all-night truck stop and searched for Chip's psi in my mind. I spotted it as a distant blip glowing red hot. He was conscious and livid. I conjured static and disappeared before he could see me. I turned up the radio. Odetta was singing, "Down on Me."

Because it looks like everybody in this whole round world
Is down on me…

Her words clutched at my heart. I had no food, no money, no clothes, my university admission documents were forged. My parents would be furious when they found out. They'd never pay. I'd be kicked out of college and sent back to the Annex where Chip would torture and kill me.

I needed a miracle to survive until I could get a job and pay for school myself. My stomach growled. I was hungry, cold, and not so high on freedom. I prayed to God for a sign that I was doing the right thing in my crazy run for freedom. God was silent, so I turned my attention to the long-haul drivers in the brightly lit diner. They were eating burgers and drinking hot coffee.

The door to the diner opened and the smell of French fries made my mouth water. I decided to use the only tools I had at hand. I watched a trucker going in. He was big, old, and bald. He had a nice rig and looked like a good daddy candidate to buy me dinner. I looked at myself in the rearview mirror. My hair was a wild tangle – I looked like a banshee.

Hoping to find a comb, I popped open the glove box. A fat roll of twenty dollar bills fell on the floor. There were dozens of them tightly bound by a rubber band – Chip's drug money from a profitable night in Monterey. I gave the glove box another look. It was stuffed with S & H Green Stamps. I searched the car and found sheets of Green Stamps in the back compartment, under the seats, and in the trunk. There must have been years' worth from gas purchases. I was rich!

I rolled my eyes to heaven, "Thank you!" I went into the convenience store and bought a hairbrush, a University of Oregon sweatshirt and pants, some tennis shoes, and socks. In the diner, I ordered a blue plate special with a slice of apple pie ala mode. I sat in a warm booth enjoying my second cup of coffee and counting the Green Stamps. I had enough for thirty books. With the stamps and cash, I'd have everything I needed to start college. No more daddies – ever.

I drove into Grants Pass and ditched the car at a Greyhound Bus Terminal. I bought a ticket to Seattle and slept the rest of the way, safe in the belly of the bus.

CHAPTER FORTY-THREE

THE SMART BOY

I arrived at the University of Washington the next afternoon with enough money to register for classes. I signed up for housing and was assigned to McCarty Hall. I took the bus downtown to the international head-quarters of Father's company. I wanted his boss on my side before my parents found out what I'd done. To my relief, he was delighted to see me.

"Miss Proudfoot," he buzzed his secretary on the intercom. "Get Jimmy on the line." I sat in the big leather desk chair, my heart pounding, and listened to the boss tell Father how thrilled he was to see me in Seattle. "I'm giving my secretary a hundred dollars to buy the girl some clothes. She's got to look sharp if she's going to get into medical school." I couldn't hear Father's reply, but I could imagine his shocked surprise. There was nothing he could do but agree. "Oh no, it's no trouble at all. We'll deduct it from your Christmas bonus."

Miss Proudfoot took me shopping for clothes at Frederick & Nelson and for shoes at Nordstrom. The bill for skirts, jumpers, sweaters, trench coat, underwear, loafers, and boots topped two hundred dollars. She assured me that Father wouldn't mind.

Then she took me to Jafco, where I redeemed my Green Stamps. I arrived at McCarty Hall in a taxicab with luggage filled with clothes, towels, pajamas, hair dryer, stockings, make-up, Yardley soap and shampoo, and all the other items I needed for life as a co-ed at the University of Washington. I had enough cash left to buy a meal ticket, my books, a green vinyl book bag, and an umbrella.

I passed a rough first night in the dorm room, half expecting to wake up on the yin/yang wheel, but nothing happened. For my first day of class, I dressed in a pink and purple plaid skirt with a pink blouse, purple cable-knit sweater and pink knee socks. I smelled like a gardenia. My hair was clean and brushed to a shine, pulled back into a ponytail with a black velvet ribbon. My book bag was stocked with textbooks, notebooks, pens, and pencils.

I walked across the Quad looking like every other freshman co-ed as I bumped my way through crowds of students, feeling safe in my anonymity. My first class was Chemistry 101 in Bagley Hall.

I walked downhill, following the path I'd marked on my campus map. The crowd parted when I reached Drumheller Fountain. Students sat on the rim of the circular pond, talking, reading, waiting for the first bell to ring. Beyond the expanse of flat water, the campus dropped downhill to the shores of Lake Washington. In the distance, the white peak of Mount Rainier floated above the clouds like a party hat. Beyond it, a second peak stood like a sentinel between me and California – Mount Saint Helens.

The view felt vaguely familiar. I saw the floating bridge and knew that beyond it was Seward Park. I remembered that I used to live down there somewhere. A memory of pink rose wallpaper flickered, or was it yellow? I wiped it clean. I was starting over as a new girl from nowhere and this time things *were* different. I was one young face in a crowd of thousands of young faces. No one cared about home towns, kid brothers, or high schools. College was about the future. This was where life as an adult began.

"So you took my advice." I was startled by the familiar voice. I couldn't place it. A co-ed with a shiny black pageboy sat on the edge of the fountain. She patted the place next to her. I sat down on the rim, captivated by her bright blue eyes and turned-up nose. She wore a Scottish kilt in a familiar red-and-green tartan. "You used your big brain and now you're all grown up. I'm proud of you."

"Who are you?" I asked, struggling to find her in my memory.

"It doesn't matter anymore." She patted my hand. "That's the whole point. But you must remember what you promised me."

"That I'd grow up to be a kind and generous person," I said without hesitation.

"That's right. You'll be a doctor in a few years. You will save children. What else?" She smiled a crooked smile that brought a lump to my throat.

"I promised that I would write my story and make it beautiful." The bell rang for class. I jumped to my feet and started up the steps of Bagley Hall. "But how can I do that when I don't remember it?" I turned back – she was gone.

The amphitheater-style classroom for Chemistry 101 was packed with freshmen, mostly men. I found a seat in the middle. A chubby young professor walked to the podium and glanced at his watch in a way that made it clear that he didn't want to be there. "The University of Washington accepts 30,000 freshmen. It's our job to flunk 20,000 of you the first year." This set the class on edge, shifting in their seats. For most of them, flunking meant they'd be drafted and sent to Vietnam.

"Shit," said a tall, gangly boy in the row in front of me. He had rough hands, a rumpled shirt, and a crew cut. He smelled like cornflakes. I couldn't see his face, but I imagined it with freckles.

"What do you have to worry about, Greg Engel," said the red-headed boy next to him. "You're the smartest guy in this class." The lights went down, the overhead projector threw chemical formulas on an overhead screen, and the professor mumbled his way through a lecture on valence electrons.

I forgot about the smart boy in chemistry class until two years later when I sat down next to him in an advanced marine botany lab. I had just cut my hair into a short, boyish style and bought a pair of black horned rim reading glasses that I wore with a necktie. I was scheduled for my medical school interview that afternoon and had my high school and university transcripts with me.

I caught Greg looking through them while I hung up my coat. "Very good," he said when I sat down on my lab stool, which he had moved next to his. "You'll make a good lab partner. I want to ace this class."

Greg proposed a year later on a tugboat in the San Juan Islands. We were collecting echinoderms for the marine zoology lab in Friday Harbor. We'd both been accepted to medical school and were known to our friends as the dynamic duo. We worked well together, played well together, and Greg never asked me about my past. We only spoke about the future.

I was twenty-one when I married him and we made love for the first time. Everything about that experience was new to me. In the safety of his arms, I opened myself, folding him body and spirit into my universe, which expanded until it exploded. I had never felt such joy.

Chapter Forty-four

Solitude

In May of 1980, Mount St. Helens blew its top and shook Seattle. From our house in Laurelhurst, I had a clear view south to Lake Washington and Mount Rainier. One moment, Mount St. Helens had floated peacefully on the horizon, then kaboom…it exploded. I sat in my nursing chair on the balcony, rocking my sleeping baby. What should I do? My daughter was one month old, my son was two and a half. I was home alone with them, recovering from a difficult pregnancy and my second C-section.

Now, where Mount St. Helens used to be, a cloud of ash bloomed and billowed. Was it heading to Seattle? We'd been warned that, in case of an eruption, we should evacuate the city and drive east. My Oldsmobile station wagon was packed with food, water, and a full tank of gas. I had candles, face masks, and medical kits. From my hillside perch, I looked down on both floating bridges. No one was driving anywhere. Every vehicle had stopped. People were out of their cars, gawking at the volcano.

The television was on in the bedroom, showing live helicopter footage of mudslides flooding the Tootle River. Where was that? I tried to call Greg. I wanted him to come home, fold me into his arms, and tell me we'd be all right – but he was an orthopedic surgery resident at Harborview Hospital assigned to ER trauma duty. We were both doctors in training. I would have been in the Radiology Department, but I was taking maternity leave. The phone was useless. The exchanges were overloaded. There was no chance of reaching anyone.

The neighbors were out on their front lawns, pointing at the ash cloud and talking excitedly. Dr. Skip Lindstrom, a geologist at the university, called up to me to say that the ash cloud was heading toward eastern Washington. For now, it was best to stay put. He'd help me if we needed to evacuate, assuring me that my babies and I wouldn't be left behind.

I brushed my fingers over the pale down of my daughter's cheek, feeling her warmth. She stirred when I kissed her tiny fingers. Her eyes wandered and locked on mine. She gurgled and squeaked, legs kicking, arms flying. I smiled, but felt the prick of fear. It rippled through me and flowed into a hot stream of terror much deeper than the volcano. I'd felt it at her birth when I first looked into her face – a tiny mirror of my own.

I knew that I had to protect her from more than exploding mountains, but from what? Where did this irrational fear come from? Was it childhood? I had no memories of my early years. Was I ever a baby? For all I knew, my life had begun the day I started at the University of Washington and that was fourteen years ago.

I had plunged into college life at a gallop, in a flurry of friends, work, study, and blustery weather. Within a few weeks I had a job typing autopsies in the basement of the University Hospital. It was a job that no one else wanted and for good reason. The backlog of blood-spattered autopsy notes had been stacked for years in foul-smelling piles several feet high. Nobody minded that I was only seventeen as long as I was willing to clean up the mess.

I didn't mind either. It gave me a chance to learn medical terminology – good training for the pre-med student that I wanted to be. I used my art skills to turn the dreadful sketches made by the pathologists into decent illustrations and taught myself some anatomy. After I worked my way through the basement, I was moved upstairs into the steno pool where I did piece-work. That gave me a chance to meet real doctors and learn who was important at the medical school. The University of Washington was the only school that I'd be able to afford on my own. Fortunately, it was one of the best.

I knew they only admitted three women to their classes of one hundred students every year. I was sure that most of those applying had family connections or important recommendations. I had none of those – just my brains and determination. I set to work meeting the professors and making the connections I needed.

On weekends, I sang in a group called Shotsie and Godiva at the Northlake Tavern. Greg would join me there for free pizza. Afterwards, he'd drive me home and we'd park by the lake to steam up the windows of his Pontiac Firebird.

I could remember every motion-packed minute of college as I worked my way toward a bachelor's degree in biology. Then followed the busy years of medical school, my marriage, internship, residency, and now a house with two children. I was a modern success story, a role model for women who wanted both careers and families. When people asked about my early years, I made something up. Fortunately, Greg rarely asked. I didn't need those memories to live a good life and be a whole person – at least not until the birth of my daughter.

Now, I was afraid to sleep, terrified that I would close my eyes and she'd be snatched away and taken to a terrible place where men in purple robes would hurt her. The thought of a bloody cross carved into her tiny forehead made me crazy. I needed total vigilance to protect her – but why?

I tried to explain my fears to Greg. I needed him to help me stand vigil, but he was seldom home. When he was, he'd fall asleep dictating patient charts. When I finally succumbed to exhausted slumber, I was whisked away on a psychedelic train painted with peace symbols and flashing neon. Rock music rattled the windows. Hippies with wild hair fornicated on the bright, oversized floor cushions strewn with flowers. They climaxed as one, the door opened, and they jumped to their deaths, trying to pull me with them. I'd jolt awake, shivering – my sheets soaked with sweat. If I slept at all, the dream began again.

Now I watched the ash cloud that had once been a mountaintop rise miles into the sky and stream eastward, aware that a lake of magma also churned and burned in my personal asthenosphere. Soon, KING 5 News announced that Seattle was safe – but day had turned to night across the mountains in Yakima and ash was falling like snow on Wenatchee.

I lifted the baby to my shoulder, her legs thrusting against my thighs. She tried to throw back her head, but I held it and kissed her neck, inhaling the milky scent of her breath. "Such a strong girl," I cooed, but my tears soaked her hair.

Since her birth, I'd become an open spigot of tears. My obstetrician had diagnosed post-partum depression and exchanged knowing looks with Greg. But I was a doctor, too and I knew there was more. I had symptoms of Post-Traumatic Stress Syndrome. I'd seen it in combat veterans from Vietnam. They often suffered traumatic amnesia, but they had been to war. What was my excuse?

Greg stayed at Harborview all week, treating emergency cases from east of the mountains. He said that I'd be okay and I should be happy because my parents were coming on Father's Day to see their new granddaughter. I didn't want them to come. Something dark had been awakened. It lurked beneath my veneer, threatening to erupt. If anyone held the key to my forgotten past, it was my parents. We never spoke about it when I saw them at Thanksgiving or Christmas. I never asked. Instead, I'd constructed a family that looked loving and real – that had been enough until now.

Days passed. Rain beat the windows and overflowed the drainpipes. Thunder rolled. The room darkened and I reached for the lamp. There was a brief flash and the fuse blew with a pop. I rocked my startled baby faster in the fading light. Visions blurred in the rain and rolled on the walls like bad movies that wouldn't shut off. The baby fussed. Did she sense the danger, too? I put her to my breast. The milk flowed and she settled into the warmth of my arms. As soon as both children were asleep, I sat between their beds and wrote a poem that I mailed to Father.

Thirty years of solitude,
All safely nestled in,
With ne'er so much a follitude,
Ne'er so much a sin.

Thirty years of solitude,
Each day to close the door,
And never to again allude,
To what had passed before.

But inside gears are turning,
And the spirit's burning bright,
And locked inside my learning,
Pounding questions split the night.

Till the night skies are on fire,
And my works come tumbling down,
And the peace that I desire,
Is never to be found –

Inside these walls of solitude,
This fortress that I keep –
With walls of stone and flesh and bone
Till someone finds the key,

And cares enough to find the lock
And force the rusty door,
To let a ray of sunlight in
To tease the dusty floor.

Father corrected the punctuation and sent it back to me without comment. My parents never came for Father's Day – or any other day. They bought an Airstream trailer and moved to Mexico. Greg wanted to know what I'd done to drive them away. I tried to explain that something was wrong with my family that went way beyond anything I might have just said or done. I showed him the poem, but he shrugged. It meant nothing to him.

I no longer slept at all. I stopped eating until my eyes grew huge in their sockets. My hair hung in stringy shreds. I was terrified of losing my mind and becoming a danger to my children. I would kill myself before I let that happen. I certainly knew how to do it. Doctor colleagues had shot, hung, overdosed, and drowned themselves.

I made an appointment to see Dr. Furedy, the only psychiatrist I'd known since medical school who I believed was smart enough to help me. I called and said it was urgent. The following day, I entered his consulting room with my baby asleep in her carrier. I put her on the floor and sat on the edge of my chair. I didn't wait for him to speak, but asked, "Am I crazy?" If he said yes, the Freedom Train would fly away tonight with me on it. This time I'd jump out. I'd do it to save my children.

Dr. Furedy looked me over as if sensing how important his answer would be. "I've known you for a long time," he said. "You were first in your class at medical school, you've excelled in your internship and residency, you've written cutting edge scientific papers, you have two children, and I've seen the building site for your waterfront mansion on Mercer Island. You're exhausted, overworked, have trouble defining your own limits, and are clearly deeply troubled, but I can say for certain that there's nothing wrong with your mind. You're not crazy."

I fell back in my chair, sobbing. The weight of the world was lifted from my chest and I could breathe again. He waited, watching me cry my way through a box of Kleenex. I stopped when my baby stirred to rock her back to sleep. Watching her scrunched-up little face relax, I longed to lie down beside her, suddenly too sleepy to keep my eyes open.

Dr. Furedy cleared his throat. "You need to get some rest. I recommend we start therapy three times a week. Whatever is troubling you may be buried deep in your past," he said. "Retrieving memories can be very hard work. It can take years. Are you ready to start?" I gave him a weary nod. "Now, tell me about your childhood. What is your earliest memory of your mother?"

I shrugged, drawing a blank. Like the rest of it, Mother was missing.

CHAPTER FORTY-FIVE

RUSSIA

January 1990: Moscow felt oddly familiar from the moment I arrived. The Berlin Wall had just come down, the Iron Curtain had fallen, and the world was celebrating the end of the Cold War. Russia was now our friend.

I'd been recovering from a difficult divorce when I was invited to Moscow as a radiologist and prenatal ultrasound specialist for the Soviet/American Citizens' Summit. The last-minute invitation had seemed like chance until the Aeroflot charter landed at Sheremetyevo Airport and our group of Americans was escorted into the city. I'd never been to Russia, but it looked familiar. I'd never studied the language, but I could read the street signs in Cyrillic. Russian words and phrases kept popping out of my mouth.

I surprised our KGB minders by commenting on how the city center had changed since the construction of the Hotel Rossiya next to the Kremlin. I pointed out where ancient churches along the embankment of the Moscow River had been torn down. I couldn't explain where my knowledge was coming from, but part of me seemed to belong to this strange, foreign place. I was drawing attention from the KGB and needed to stop talking.

Our first stop was snow-covered Red Square. The moment my feet touched the cobblestones, I heard the clicking of a wheel within a wheel. I knew this was a memory and tried to ignore it, blaming jetlag. I walked quietly with the group until the Kremlin clock tower chimed and I heard a whisper from the past, "Run!" I froze in a crouch, my heart racing. I spun in place, hunting for the gunmen who were coming to kill me.

People were staring – I had to collect myself. I claimed to have a headache and returned to the bus while the group walked across the square to visit Lenin's tomb. I curled up on the seat, pressed my forehead against the frosted window glass, and searched my mind for answers.

For years, I'd been working on recovering memories, utilizing many techniques to re-awaken my past while continuing my medical career and raising children. I did psychoanalysis three days a week. When I had more time, I added family therapy. I wrote reams of disturbing poetry and flow-of-consciousness journals, and filled sketchbooks with drawings.

I spent time with my brother, an accomplished artist, welder, and painter. He had an art studio in Pioneer Square where he painted frightening images from the past. He had chosen not to have children and decided that he didn't share my urgent need to remember. He married and moved on. I couldn't stop.

I was unable to predict when memories would awaken. At any moment a smell, an image, or a sound could open a pathway into a snippet of horror that made no sense at all. I knew enough to understand why my parents wouldn't return to the United States. I could send them to prison. As long as they stayed in Mexico, I didn't have to make that decision.

I chose not to pursue them because I didn't want my life to be embroiled in vengeance. I wanted to move on like my brother and heal my marriage, but it eventually broke anyway. Greg was happy with his life as a successful surgeon while mine was crumbling into sand. The constant push/pull between wanting to forget and needing to remember had become the conflict that defined me. Greg found solace in other places and we separated. When I arrived in Moscow, my memory was like Swiss cheese. I had constructed elements of a solid geographical framework, but my childhood was still mostly holes.

I dozed, waking up when the other delegates re-boarded the bus. We continued our tour into parts of Moscow that had been closed to foreigners for seventy years. Driving along the Moscow River, I recognized Taganskaya Square. I heard the clicking of the wheel again and another remembered voice said, "You've made it! Good work." Through the window, I saw a familiar building topped with a red neon sign that said, "ROS-TELEKOM." I asked my KGB host about it.

"That was Central Communications Directorate of KGB. All calls from USSR were routed through a secret underground center for monitoring. That closed in 1963. Now it's ordinary telephone exchange."

With a strange, map-like overlay on my vision, I seemed to be looking through the earth into a labyrinth of tunnels. "Are there tunnels under here?"

"Of course," he smiled, flashing gold teeth. "We have bomb shelters for hundreds of kilometers under Moscow. Unfortunately, they are good for one kiloton atomic bomb only. They were obsolete by 1970s."

The sun was setting when we drove back to the Hotel Cosmos. Moscow looked gray and battered in the twilight. Most of the streetlamps were dark. Light bulbs draped in festive strings along the buildings and bridges were nearly all broken. Shop windows displayed faded drawings of fruit and vegetables instead of real food. Shabbily dressed Muscovites waited in long lines outside each shop, stomping their feet against the –20° cold. The city looked defeated. Even so, I felt like I'd come home.

The following day, I became the first Western doctor to visit a Russian birth house. The Russian doctors who came to escort me from the hotel were familiar with my work on prenatal ultrasound. They'd read my scientific papers and wanted me to demonstrate my techniques of fetal diagnosis. I was loaded into a black Volga and driven to their most modern birth house – a shabby, five-story concrete building with rust stains streaking the exterior walls. We parked in front of a bright blue wooden door that the chief obstetrician opened with a latch key. I was ushered into stifling heat in a dim hallway with peeling wallpaper, water-stained walls, worn linoleum, and plates of chicken bones on the floor. "What are those doing here?" I asked.

"Feeds the cats," said my guide and translator, Dr. Yuri Puchkov. "Cats keep away rats."

We entered another hall where an elderly lady in a white coat and a tall hat that looked like a baker's sat at a wooden desk. "Is this the main entrance?" I asked. "Where are your wheelchairs and stretchers?"

"Russian women are strong," the obstetrician explained. I understood that a woman in labor was expected to walk into the facility on her own two feet. There, she was stripped and hosed down. Then her pubis was shaved and painted with gentian violet antiseptic.

I was shown into a pre-labor room where pregnant women in robes and slippers sat on chairs or paced the room. Some moaned, but most were eerily silent. "Why are they so quiet?" I asked.

"Shame," said the obstetrician.

"They don't want to make nurses angry," Yuri added. "Bad politics."

The birth house had no elevators. We had to climb up four flights of stairs to reach the labor rooms. We passed women in gowns, making their way slowly and painfully up the worn, uneven steps. "The top floor is best for sanitation," Yuri explained.

In the labor room, a dozen women lay on stretchers. Several turned to stare at us with terrified eyes, their faces contorted in pain. Some moaned and some wept. The nurses ignored them all. They didn't seem to be following triage protocols as to which woman should be taken to the delivery, based on stage of labor. Again Yuri explained: "Everyone is equal here. It is first come, first served."

"What do you do if a child is crowning?" I asked with growing concern. "That woman should be delivered first."

Yuri consulted with the nurses. "They tie her legs together to slow the labor."

"What if the woman who's next in line isn't ready to deliver?"

"They will demonstrate," said Yuri. I watched in horror as a nurse climbed up on a table and pushed down on a woman's abdomen with her foot. The woman screamed in agony.

"That's terrible," I said. "And it's dangerous."

The woman continued to wail. A second nursed rolled her eyes and rubbed at the base of the noise maker's nose until she quieted.

"That's cruel!" I exclaimed. "It's such a painful thing to do."

"The nasal spine is the only thing that hurts worse than labor. It keeps them quiet," said Yuri.

"What about anesthesia? Where are the drugs?" I asked. Yuri shrugged and shook his head. The woman started to cry again and the nurses screamed at her. "What are they saying?"

"They say, 'This is your fault. You're the one who had sex, not me. Shut up.'"

I was stunned. This was birth by terror – and it didn't end in the labor room. Yuri helped me don a heavy, blood-spattered rubber apron. We followed a stretcher into a delivery room, where doctors were delivering babies on three tables at a time.

The overheated room reeked of iodine, and the stench of blood and afterbirth was worse than anything I had experienced in my years of medical practice. Suddenly another memory hovered on the edge of my senses – the cloying stink of clotted blood accompanied by the smell of tidal flats and open sewage. I felt dizzy. I thought I might vomit. The heat made it worse. Yuri sensed my distress and helped me out of the filthy apron. "Follow me, please," he said, guiding me into a dark corridor.

I leaned against the wall and my eyes adjusted to the dim light. On one side of the hall, the mothers who had just delivered lay on stretchers, unattended. Their naked infants were lined up in basinets on the other side. Both were still battered and bloody from birth. A tabby cat walked down the aisle between them. I'd had enough. "What the hell is this?" I exclaimed. "This is terrible! That woman's vagina is torn. She needs a repair to stop the bleeding. This baby needs to be cleaned and warmed up immediately. Get that damn cat out of here!"

"Please, please," Yuri pleaded. "You'll make the doctors angry." Yuri explained that there would be no vaginal repairs for the mothers and no resuscitation of the infants until two hours had passed. "It is a time of reflection." I could see that one of the infants was in trouble. The edge of her blanket had fallen over her face, blocking her nose. She wasn't moving. I reached out to pull it off. "Stop," said Yuri, holding my arm. "This is in God's hands."

"Baloney," I said, shaking him off. I scooped up the tiny baby and wiped her face and nose with a tissue from my pocket. Her skin felt cold and her lips were dusky blue.

I wrapped her in my soft cashmere scarf and bounced her in my arms, suddenly recalling another little body that I had wrapped in butcher paper and carried across a wetland marsh. That one had been dead. Anger heated my veins. I wasn't going to lose this one. "Come on, little girl," I said, patting and rubbing her back with her head tilted forward. "You can make it. You can grow up and be beautiful. Come on!"

The infant jerked and sputtered. She gave a hearty cough and spat out a plug of mucus. Her lips turned pink, her mouth formed a perfect O, and she bellowed like an opera star. "That's my girl. That's my little angel."

The mother was weeping across the hall. "*Moi ribionik… maya doichka…*" She extended her arms.

"She's asking for her daughter," said Yuri. I placed the newborn on her chest.

"*Kak ona zavoot?*" she asked, kissing her daughter's cheek.

"She wants you to name her," said Yuri, wiping away tears.

"Conchita," I said. A lump ached in my throat. I had loved someone by that name – I must have.

"Chita…" said the mother. "*Krasivaya Chita.*"

"No… beau-ti-ful *Con*-chita," said Yuri.

"Boo-ti-ful Chita," the mother beamed.

"Chita it is," I said.

The tour moved on to the ultrasound laboratory, where I demonstrated our procedures on their aged equipment. On the way back out, I pushed open the door to the corridor where the mothers and babies had been left alone. Something had changed – every baby was now with its mother. "This looks more like God's will to me," I smiled. The nurses had thought so, too. They had moved them all.

At that moment, I understood the opportunity that was being offered to me. I saw how simple it would be to change Soviet childbirth practices by introducing gentler, kinder techniques that made both patients and staff feel better. In addition, we could reduce infant morbidity by teaching basic sterile techniques to staff, childbirth education to mothers and promoting prenatal care. I realized that the Russian doctors had brought me there to do exactly what I'd done. By moving the baby, I gave them permission to change things – to provide the compassionate care that was already in their hearts to give.

I could think of nothing else when I returned to Seattle. I couldn't ignore this opportunity to prevent the death and suffering of thousands of women and children. Within a year, I shocked my colleagues and friends by selling my medical practice and using the funds to start a nonprofit, MiraMed Institute – Mira for peace and Med for medicine – to advocate for birthing reform in the Soviet Union.

I had found my calling in that sad, strange country that felt like home.

Chapter Forty-six

The Lost Girls

American universities donated time, staff, and materials. MiraMed made rapid and positive strides by sponsoring training exchanges between professionals in both countries. Companies wanting to enter the Russian markets donated medical equipment and supplies for our new birthing center in Moscow. Russian media ran exposés on the terrible conditions of birth houses throughout the USSR, which led to a public outcry for reform. But we had barely gotten started when the USSR collapsed and the counterrevolution of 1993 plunged Russia deeper into economic chaos. Children were being abandoned to orphanages in growing numbers, where they were dying for lack of food, clothing, and medical care. Western relief was no longer getting through Customs because of the massive theft. We had to find another way.

I organized a program called, "Travel with a Cause." American tourists brought tons of clothing, medicine, and school supplies in their suitcases to help twenty-three rural orphanages survive the worst of the crisis. Summers, we sponsored groups of volunteers to teach in the orphanages, instructing the children in English and life skills.

In December 1996, I received an urgent fax from Svir Stroi orphanage, a large institution with 165 children a few miles from the Finnish border. They were desperate for winter coats and boots. Seattle churches and Soroptimist Clubs gathered supplies. We made sure every child had a coat, hat, sweater, boots, and school supplies. Their names were pinned to the jackets and candy hearts were placed in each pocket. Boeing carried me and 47 large boxes to St. Petersburg on a new 737 that was being delivered to Aeroflot Russian Airlines. After three tense days shepherding the shipment through Customs, I was met by Nina, the orphanage director, and Valeri, an ex-prizefighter turned bus driver, for the harrowing drive northeast on the frozen Murmansk Highway.

When the bus jolted to a stop in Svir Stroi eight hours later, everything was sorted, sized, and distributed to the children before they left for school. When the children were gone, I walked through the halls, looking into empty dormitory rooms lined with rows of neatly made beds and into the storeroom to check the remaining provisions. To my surprise, fifteen coats hung there untouched – all for teenaged girls.

I'd seen those girls every summer since they were small. I'd brought photos and a videotape that I'd made of them doing a musical play the previous summer. Where were they? No one on the staff would tell me. They simply put their heads down and turned away when I asked. I waited until the other children returned from school. Over tea and cookies, they told me that a bus had come from Finland and taken the girls on a picnic.

"In February?"

"They went last summer."

When I finally cornered the orphanage director, she burst into tears and tried to walk away, but I wouldn't let her go. "Have you called the police?"

"The police?" she spat. "The police do nothing."

Horrified, I started talking to children and staff in other orphanages near the border. I learned that the same buses returned summer after summer to take away teenaged girls. No one ever returned. Police in the northern border towns told me that girls were always trying to cross into Finland or Norway to be prostitutes.

I didn't believe them. The girls that I knew dreamed of careers, marriage, families. At each orphanage, I collected Xeroxes of the missing girls' passport photos until I had a dossier with dozens of girls. I followed the trail further north where I began working with the Women's Congress in Murmansk. We discovered that buses with Russian girls as young as twelve were crossing the Finnish border as mobile brothels. The girls were never allowed to leave the bus. Men would pay to board and rape them. Then the brothel rolled into the next town and over the next border toward northern Norway.

From Murmansk, I took a bus across the Norwegian border to Kierkenes, where I met with police and Interpol. A Norwegian immigration officer told me, "We find the bodies of Russian girls around here all the time. We call them Natashas. If no one claims them, they are assumed to be Russian prostitutes and buried in unmarked graves." He showed me a drawer full of Polaroid head shots of Natashas, all of them very young.

I didn't recognize any of the battered faces. No one I spoke with in Norway knew anything about those poor girls – nor did they seem to care. But I cared. Violent crimes were being committed against children, and those who should be protecting them were either indifferent to their suffering or fearful of the organized crime groups running the cross-border trafficking.

I wasn't afraid – I was furious! The missing girls of Svir Stroi had awakened an ancient rage in me – undefined, but linked to the abyss of my forgotten past. Those girls might be helpless, but I wasn't.

I returned to Seattle and within a year, I had a grant from the United Nations Violence Against Women Trust Fund. The following summer, I organized a team to investigate the extent of child trafficking in northwestern Russia. We found evidence of abducted Russian children working in bars as far away as Tromsø, Norway. From there, they were sold by well-organized rings of human traffickers to brothels in every major city of Europe.

The trade was huge, generating billions in profits and unimaginable misery and suffering. In 1999, I delivered our findings at the United Nations in Vienna and at the Vatican in Rome. Within five years, I had set up and was operating an underground railroad to rescue children throughout the former Soviet Union.

We were funded by the Trafficking in Persons Office of the US State Department, the International Organization of Migration, Save the Children, Global Ministries, Starr Foundation, and World Childhood Foundation. The operation partnered with Russian federal and regional police, prosecutors, and the ministries of health, education, and interior. We coordinated thousands of rescues, ran shelters in several regions, and did police training throughout Russia and Central Asia. We called our underground railroad the Angel Coalition.

I never found my missing girls from Svir Stroi. I kept them alive by watching the video I'd taken the summer when they had danced and crowned me with a wreath of flowers. Those were the first of my Russian lost girls that I carried with me in my black canvas satchel. There they laughed and sang with the other little stars and angels in a half-forgotten painted sky.

CHAPTER FORTY-SEVEN

THE FUSION

San Diego, May 2012: I'm running hard, breathing hard. My heart pounds to the rhythm of my shoes striking pavement. Tendrils of fog drift over the path along San Diego Harbor.

I've returned to Southern California for the first time in fifty years and I'm out for an early morning jog. Cops run in front of me, cops run behind me. They lap me for the second or third time with a salute and, "Passing on the left, ma'am." The only cops I can outrun anymore are the vice squad. I see their Hawaiian shirts and ponytails at the breakfast buffet when I jog past the hotel. The ones who are passing me on all sides are mostly ex-Marines and Special Forces. These are tough guys, wiry and lean. They are the good guys in the fight against child trafficking. I've worked with these officers in places like Moscow, Kazakhstan, Morocco, and Dubai.

We've come to the Mexican border for a summit on cross-border security and child trafficking. Some of the best of law enforcement from Interpol, Europol, and the intelligence services of many countries are here. I've been invited to present my ten years of work with the Angel Coalition in Moscow and to lead a seminar on child survival.

Sadly, my work in Russia has ended. A few months ago, organized crime came down on our group and I had to flee the country. We had convinced the Russian Federal Bureau of Detectives to raid the child brothels along Moscow's notorious Yaroslavl Road. A Russian detective was shot and my protégé was killed and stuffed into the trunk of her car. Russian Military Intelligence warned me that it was time for me to go home to America.

Now I'm jogging through the mists of Southern California on what promises to be another perfect day. My usual speech – the one I've given at law enforcement conferences all over the world – plays in my mind, but it isn't resonating. There is interference, an intrusion in my consciousness.

My attention veers south across the harbor toward Imperial Beach. It's just a few miles from here, but half a century away in the timeline of my life. In spite of the work I've done to recover memory, most of my childhood is still missing. I've remembered where I went to school and that we moved all the time, but home life before Canada is pretty much a blank.

I have long accepted my partial amnesia, but a growing sense of loss haunts me since my return to America. I have something to share with my colleagues about child survival that runs much deeper than my work with Russian children. It has to do with what happened to me as a child. A desire for the truth is burning a hole in my heart. I know this feeling and that the truth won't stay buried much longer. The key to finding it is here in California. I smell it in the briny air.

My colleagues aren't helping. I told a San Diego cop friend that I'd lived at the Imperial Beach Garden Apartments. He looked me over and snorted, "Bullshit! Like hell you did!" I could only shrug – stung by his disbelief, but at the same time relieved that he couldn't connect me to the drug running and brothels that are still there.

Last night, I looked up the IB Apartments, Caspian Way, and the wetlands on Google Earth and confirmed my sense of the place. As I jog, I draw a mental panorama. I see it in black and white, sketched in pencil. I add details – IB Boulevard, the Little League Park, Mar Vista High School, and IB Elementary. It's accurate, but it's much too clean. Where is the dirt and the noise? There must have been children – certainly I had friends.

I sketch in some ten-year-olds with blank ovals for faces. What did they look like? I sketch an old bike with balloon tires. The name Blue Balloon comes to mind, but it quickly vanishes, swept into darkness by a river of muck. Is this a memory?

The fog thins – grey velveteen silhouettes of anchored naval vessels loom, but that's not what I'm looking for. I stare deeper into the drifting haze and command the mist to release the memories of my childhood friends. I know they're here. I left them behind where tidewaters wash into wetlands. I strain to hear their laughter. Surely this fog retains a memory of our games. But the only sounds are the scuffing footfalls of the other runners, their heavy breathing, and my own panting.

A breeze ripples the surface of the harbor, raising the smell of brackish water with a hint of gasoline. It triggers a jumbled knot of memories. A squadron of bicycles breaks free and Highland warriors tumble out of the mist, waving cardboard swords and shouting Gaelic curses. Excitable, redheaded Patrick pedals by with a whoop, arms in the air. Glamour girl Linda rides along in her petticoats and poodle skirt. Albert the scientist carries an old radio on his handlebars. Gary and Rock fire machine guns from their Spitfires.

Seeing their faces raises a guilty ache in my chest. I never said goodbye. I don't know what happened to them. They race by me and vanish. I wait for one more – a little girl in a kilt and aluminum pie-plate armor. She is my link to the year that childhood ended and my spirit was tempered into steel. She is the key to my missing past – but she remains a wraith.

I'm a hard-breathing, sweaty puddle by the time I finish my run and head into the hotel for a shower. I make it to the conference room in time to grab the last bagel, entering just ahead of an armed escort wearing black suits stretched over Kevlar vests. These are bodyguards for the governor of Baja California.

They lead him to the podium, then turn to glare at the crowd. They are packing serious firepower because the danger here is real. The governor has taken a courageous stance against human traffickers in Tijuana. The lights dim and he shows slides of the Zona Norte, where young boys and girls line the streets, selling their bodies while pimps hover in shadows. He focuses on trafficking in children. He has come to share what the government of Baja is doing to stop the rape of children in mobile brothels that operate in the wetlands. Guns and drugs are an unspoken reality that he doesn't need to mention to this group.

My mind wanders to a conversation I had with a Homeland Security agent working as an observer at the border. When I told him that I'd lived as a child in the IB Apartments, he said, "It's amazing that you never got hurt." I *did* get hurt. But I reinvented myself when I got away. A journalist asked me recently what my greatest fear was and I blurted, "I'm afraid that I'll wake up one morning and still be ten years old."

The governor's speech is followed by presentations of law enforcement officials from Mexico and Central America. One terrible story follows another. Hopelessness spreads through the room. The police may be tough on the outside, but I know that they feel the pain of this human tragedy more than most people because they confront it every day.

I want to stand up and shout, "Hey guys, it's not hopeless. I made it. Look at me." That's the speech I want to make. But then what do I say? I close my eyes and try to remember. I'm a child again, running through a garden of pampas grass that shimmers in the shadow of a church steeple. A hot wind stinks of the wetland sewer. I run up stone steps into a chapel with high wooden beams that arch like the inverted ribs of a ship. I've come to see God. I've come to tell Him the truth and save myself.

Another layer of memory intrudes. A book opens. A cartoon park with cerulean sky, yellow daisies, and chartreuse grass pops up. Cartoon bluebirds fly over a rainbow. A jukebox lights up and starts to play:

Boom, boom, yeah, yeah, yeah.
Boom, boom, yeah, yeah, yeah.

Am I losing my mind? Red lights flash. A train is coming. I'm on the Wild Toad Ride at Disneyland. I shiver. My clothes are wet from rain. A man's hand slides up my skirt.

The lights come back on in the conference room. I blink and half a century dissolves in a cloud of silver flakes. The security detail hurries the governor out of the room. While we wait in our seats, the voice of logic intercedes in my brain: "Why can't you just leave the past behind you? Why risk your professional credibility by sharing something that you barely remember?"

These colleagues know me only as the accomplished woman that I've become. I'm safe in this persona. This is how my grown-up son and daughter know me. They've made it clear many times that they don't want to learn any more about me than this. But I know that the past never leaves us. It impacts a family through generations. Knowing is the only way for them to break free of this curse from distant history.

My breathing quickens and my cheeks flush. I'm at one of those critical folds in time when the past threatens to rise up and drown me. I may not remember it, but it affects every decision I make. I've taught many others to be proud that they are survivors of human trafficking, yet I've never admitted that I was a victim, too.

When the men with guns are gone, the rest of us stand up and stretch. We wander outside into the sunshine while the hotel staff sets up for lunch. The fog has burned away and I stroll to the harbor. The day is redolent with familiar smells and I strain to pick up a scent or sensation that I can follow to another time. I hear my name. I'm being invited to join a prosecutor from Bogota and some federales at a café table. Pretty soon, we're drinking Mexican beer and telling stories. Our laughter refreshes my mind like an aperitif between courses. I need to stay sharp in case anything from my past rises to the surface again. A memory that doesn't want to be found can morph and vanish in a flash. I mean to catch it this time – grab it by its slippery tail and reel it in.

We are joined by a psychiatrist and some social workers from Costa Rica. Soon, we're talking about the treatment of trafficked children – how to mend them physically and psychologically. It is a fortuitous choice of topic, since walled-off memories like my own are the traumatized child's first and best line of defense. We all agree that they can also prove a serious stumbling block to psychological healing in the adult.

I talk about Russian psychologists and their use of sandbox therapy in our Moscow shelters. They provide children with boxes of sand and dozens of colorful little toys representing the objects of ordinary life. The children are left alone to play with the toys. Experienced therapists can discern the nature of a child's trauma and much about the dynamics of their environment by observing the choice of toys and how they are arranged.

The others at the table start speaking Spanish, so I just nod and smile. I imagine that I'm sitting in front of an empty sandbox. On each side are shelves stacked with little plastic toys. How should I start my tableau for Imperial Beach? What about Christmas, 1959? I'd start with a Christmas tree, not a whole one, but a piece of one – a wooden pole and a cardboard box filled with plastic branches.

A bath was involved at some point, so I add a bathtub. Then I put in a little girl and her parents and, somewhere nearby, a black van with the motor running. Next, I add…what? The memories are still boxed up tight. Which one contains the rest of Christmas? Sounds, smells, music… where is my way in?

I surround my little girl character with boxes. I pile a mountain of them between the child and her parents as I search for any little crack in time that I can use to break through, but I cannot grab hold of the story. The characters in my memory are as stiff and motionless as the little plastic figurines. I know that the real scenario was more ominous. I take a deep breath and let it go with a long, slow exhalation. I see more silver flakes. This isn't working – or is it? I remind myself to be patient.

Wendy, a psychiatrist friend from Seattle, is eyeing me. She and I have worked on a number of child trafficking cases. She has been to Moscow to train with our therapists. "Are you mentally preparing for your talk tomorrow?" she asks.

"I'm thinking about doing something different this time," I say. She is silent. It's a psychiatrist's technique to wait until I blurt out what is on my mind. "I want to share that I am a survivor of child trafficking myself."

"I didn't know that," she says. "I'm sorry. How did that happen?"

"My family was involved with some kind of pedophile ring in Imperial Beach and other places." I feel light-headed. I want to be wrong. I'd rather be crazy than right. "I don't remember very much."

"Is that why you came to San Diego?"

"I'm certain that the key to my past is here – or rather over there," I nod toward the harbor. "I haven't been near Imperial Beach in fifty years. Everything I see or smell starts triggering memories of the place that don't quite materialize."

"People like you who are crazy dedicated to a field like child trafficking are likely to have suffered some form of abuse. As you know, the best therapists can be the ones who need the most therapy."

A lump swells in my throat. I sip my beer. "It's important for me to share my story of survival. But I need to know the whole story, and I don't yet." I don't mention that I've been to Washington DC and reviewed hundreds of pages of Congressional testimony on the CIA mind-control programs conducted on children in the 1950s and '60s. My symptoms fit the descriptions of those subjects, including extreme memory loss. My family fits the profile with my uncle high up in the NSA, and my family's connections to OSS, Shriners and Templars, but I have no proof. I grow impatient with Wendy's practiced silence and start to bargain, "Maybe I don't have to remember the worst parts. How much do I really need to know, anyway?"

"If you're determined to tell the truth about yourself in a public way, you better have a firm grip on what that truth is. You won't help yourself or anyone else by going off half-baked. You'll get blindsided." She thinks for a while and adds, "It would be a real gift to therapists to hear what you have to say. You know very well that not many victims survive intact, let alone have success in life like you have."

"On the flip side, why should I risk capsizing my own boat? Why not just keep telling other peoples' stories?"

"You could do that, but you won't. You've got the skills to process the past and tell your own story. You of all people know how powerful that is."

"Maybe I'm not strong enough. Maybe remembering will drive me insane."

"Oh, stop it," she snorts. "You've developed some amazing tools along the way. How about sharing them to help others? Tell me in one word – what was the key to your survival?"

"Fantasy," I say. "I created complex worlds that were more real to me than reality. By the time I was ten, I was drawing other children into my fantasies. We were able to help each other through the worst by escaping into worlds of our own. I see the same dynamic in orphanages and shelters in Russia. I always respect the importance of fantasy as a survival tool and believe that children should be encouraged to retreat into their imaginations as much as they need to. What else can they do when life becomes unbearable?"

"The deeper you're willing to dig into your own trauma, the greater the value to the professionals you share it with. You know that. But you have to be ready to share, and from what you're saying, you're not. I'm curious – why choose now?"

"I'm getting older. My work in Russia is finished. It seems like now or never."

"What's holding you back then?"

"I'm afraid that people will see me differently, like I'm still a victim, a child prostitute." I shudder, suddenly remembering Father's words: "Damaged goods." I can't voice them.

"Nothing is going to change who you were then, or who you've become. And by the way, you aren't a kid anymore. People see you for who you are today. I think that, in terms of credibility, the risk you run is that people won't believe you."

I tell her about my cop friend saying, "Bullshit."

"The psychologists and social workers in the group won't be quite so surprised. You have a reputation as a fanatic. No one gives up the cushy American life and sacrifices everything the way you did without serious motivation – usually traumatic. But your colleagues in law enforcement tend to think in black and white. They have to for their sanity." She pauses, then asks, "How much of your story do you plan to reveal? Have you decided?"

"I'm not sure. There's still too much that I can't remember – like most of it before age ten. There were a lot of drugs involved." I fight back tears. "I cry whenever I try to talk about it. I don't even know why."

"That's what I mean about getting blindsided." She looks concerned. "These are only memories. They can't hurt you anymore, but the demons that drive them can. Powerful repressed memories like the ones you carry have the potential to cause all kinds of mayhem for you and for everyone around you."

The truth of what she says hits me hard. I've risked my life and the lives of those close to me many times, yet the pivotal events that motivate me were always inaccessible. Those forces have driven me to the edge of my physical and mental limits. "What starts coming to me is so crazy that I'm afraid I'm losing my mind."

"Let it come, no matter how crazy. You were just a kid. You're dealing with kid memories from long ago. Now you can look at them as an adult."

"I don't want them to be true."

She pats my arm. "They are what they are."

After lunch, Wendy and I sit on a panel together and, later, we participate in a victim assistance session where I present my work on empowering trafficking survivors. The afternoon requires my full attention. I concentrate on other people's stories and work with them to find solutions to clinical problems. My past recedes. I'm a consummate professional until I look at the other people in the room and they have morphed into fifth graders. Maybe we should take a recess, run around outside, and play some kickball.

The session drones on and I struggle to stay awake. I look at the conference program entitled, "Planes, Trains, Trucks, Boats & Automobiles" – all the ways that trafficked children are transported. There is a colorful picture of a train on the front cover. How old is that train, I wonder – 1950s maybe?

I suddenly remember arriving in San Diego fifty years ago on a train that looked very much like that one. I stare at the engine and imagine it rolling down the track, off the page, and across the table in a cloud of steam. I smell diesel. I hear the roar of the engine and the pounding rattle of wheels on iron rails.

The train picks up speed. My fantasy fills the room with smoke and fury. The locomotive races across the Great Plains. Packards and Studebakers wait on a country road behind wooden barriers. Stoplights flash red and a klaxon warns of danger as the train roars past.

Lights illuminate the windows and I see people inside. I see myself, working my way up the crowded aisle, pushing past men in rumpled suits and brown fedoras, conductors punching tickets, black ladies with funny hats holding black babies. I'm looking for someone special. A French sailor with a pompom on his hat winks at me. "C'est la vie," I say, winking back.

He nods toward the window seat across the aisle. A little girl with a crooked smile and upturned nose sits there. She wears a kilt, white blouse, and tidy penny loafers. Her hair is a blue-black, shiny pageboy like Prince Valiant's. She pats the seat next to her, inviting me to sit. She looks friendly, but I'm wary. "Is this the Freedom Train?" I ask.

"Don't be stupid," she chuckles. "It's the Atchison, Topeka & Santa Fe. Don't you remember?"

I do remember. "You're Sparky!" I gasp. "You're me at ten. You're the key to my childhood."

"Very good," she smiles, crinkling the spray of freckles across her nose.

"I thought you went to Scotland." I choke back tears. "I thought you left me."

"That's pretty tough to do when I am you," she winks. A yellow bi-plane buzzes past the window and flies circles in the sky. Two young pilots wave from the cockpit, one blonde and one with black hair like mine.

"Paulie's plane." I smile and wave back. "There's Nicky. How could I forget?"

"You didn't. We've been with you all along. The memories are coming back now because you're ready for them." She holds up her hands, fingers splayed. I hold up my hands to mirror hers, then draw back, anticipating the harsh grating of mismatched gears. But she persists. "Don't be afraid. Touch me."

My fingertips approach hers again. This time we do touch, and the fusion of past and present is soft and kind like the purr of two engines coming into synchrony. My inner and outer spheres meld into one whole person that stretches across time and my life unrolls in chronological sequence for the first time. I am infused with joy. "Do you remember the book?" she asks.

"*The Miracle Sword of the Clan MacGregor?*" I am startled at the memory of that frayed remnant of a volume that I'd found in Mema's hatbox. "Mother threw it away. Do you have it?"

"Not that book – this one." She hands me a little white book. I run my hand across the synthetic leather, reading the embossed gold script: St. James Lutheran Church of Imperial Beach. It was the Bible Pastor John gave me. I remember the kindness of Mrs. Pendrake, Pastor John, and Mrs. Pastor John. "Have you read it?" she asks.

I open it to *Genesis,* but the cross on my forehead burns. I smell cinnamon and pine. A yule log cracks, spewing sparks onto a stone hearth. I slam the book shut and toss it back to her. "The words are too complicated. They spin on the page. I can't read them."

"Don't worry," she says. "It's just a spell from your Sex Magick days. We'll break it and read together."

I recall the wheel spinning within in a wheel, the symbols and incantations… *there is no good… there is no evil… there is no God… only the Prince of the Air.* I struggle to hold back tears. "I can only give comfort, not take it," I say.

"Nonsense," she says, cocking her head: "Don't you remember what Pastor John said?"

The boundary of time dissolves and I am a child running up stone steps into the chapel of St. James. It is cool inside and smells of new wood. Mrs. Pastor John offers me a plate of warm oatmeal raisin cookies. "He said that God's grace is a gift. We don't have to earn it." I hesitate: "Do you believe that?"

"Of course. We're here, aren't we?" She smiles. "Now, do you remember your promise to me?"

"I promised to tell my story and make it beautiful. But I still don't know what it is."

"Start writing and you'll remember."

"I've tried, but it's always too crazy," I shake my head. "It's an ugly story. I don't know what it means."

"Write the truth." She squeezes my hands. "You survived and that's a beautiful thing. You have grown children – a lawyer and a teacher. You have grandchildren who live normal lives. You must be very proud of them."

"I don't think my children are ready to hear my story. They may never be."

"Then write it for the boys and girls you saved in Russia," she smiles.

"Where do I begin?"

"Start there." She points out the window. We are in Seattle. I see clouds thicken above tall evergreens. Fog coats Lake Washington. A little girl gallops and whinnies along the beach, her breath steaming in the cold.

"I remember this," I exclaim. "It's 1955. There's Seward Park. That's me at six years old. This is the day that I lost Daddy."